The Darkroom

THE DARKROOM

Case Files of a Scotland Yard
Forensic Photographer

A.J. Hewitt

SEVEN DIALS

First published in Great Britain in 2024 by Seven Dials,
an imprint of The Orion Publishing Group Ltd
Carmelite House, 50 Victoria Embankment
London EC4Y 0DZ

An Hachette UK Company

1 3 5 7 9 10 8 6 4 2

A CIP catalogue record for this book is
available from the British Library.

ISBN (Paperback) 978 1 8418 8485 1
ISBN (eBook) 978 1 8418 8486 8
ISBN (Audio) 978 1 8418 8487 5

Typeset by Born Group
Printed and bound in Great Britain by Clays Ltd, Elcograf S.p.A.

MIX
Paper from
responsible sources
FSC® C104740

www.orionbooks.co.uk

To my mother, who assures me that life's too short for dull stories and serious faces. Thank you for filling my life with love and laughter. This book is a reflection of the resilience your quiet strength has nurtured in me.

To all forensic photographers, the silent witnesses whose photographs speak louder than words. Your work, though rarely in the spotlight, has a profound impact on the lives you touch. May these pages stand as a token of appreciation for your essential work and your unwavering pursuit of justice for the voiceless victims of crime.

To be a photographer is to willingly enter the world of the lonely . . . The person with the camera is not hiding but receding. She is willfully removing herself from the slipstream of life; she is making herself into a constant witness, someone who lives to see the lives of others, not to be seen herself . . . The photographer moves through the world, our world, hoping for anonymity, hoping she is able to humble herself enough to see and record what the rest of us are too present to our own selves to ever see. To practice this art requires first a commitment to self erasure . . . The lens may distance the photographer from the rest of humanity, but with that distance comes an enhanced ability to see what is overlooked and underloved . . . Photographers are both absent and present: we don't think of them, and yet at the same time, we are seeing through them. They are possessing us and yet they are allowing us the gift of not thinking ourselves possessed at all. In the microsecond it takes for the shutter to blink, some communion has been found . . . an unseen life has become a seen one . . . attention has been paid, an act of witness has been accomplished . . . *Click*: I see you. *Click*: I see you. *Click*: I see you. You are not alone.

Hanya Yanagihara

Author's Note

In this book I share my experiences as a Police Forensic Photographer (Senior Photographic Officer) with New Scotland Yard.

I have taken great care to protect the privacy of all individuals featured in this book. I have changed the names, locations, ages, nationalities and timelines, apart from cases that were so well documented in the news media that they were impossible to disguise. I have also omitted other potentially identifying details of individuals and organisations to protect privacy, while still presenting an accurate portrayal of events.

It's important to note that the depictions of suffering presented in this book are factual and, in most cases, a matter of public record. While some cases are harrowing, my intention was never to cause any distress to the families or friends of the victims mentioned. Rather, I aimed to present the cases with sensitivity, respect and empathy, while recognising the privacy and well-being of those who have suffered loss.

It is my sincere hope that this book lifts the veil on a world that until now has remained hidden from public view, and that it sheds light on important issues and events, while also acknowledging the human cost of acts of violence and tragedy.

Thank you for taking the time to read my book.

Contents

Introduction

On the day a man murdered Stephanie Warren with an 18-inch machete, children played happily in the street outside her home. Dogs barked and boys on bicycles zoomed about. The street was alive with the high-pitched squeals of children's laughter. Warm autumn sunlight bathed the street of red-bricked houses. I soon spotted the tell-tale blue-and-white crime scene tape, draped around trees, and looped around the mirror of a police car. It cordoned off a small house, second from the end of a row of twelve council houses. They felt oddly out of place among their more imposing Victorian neighbours. A fresh-faced police officer, standing guard at the crime scene cordon, studied me as I approached.

'*You're* the photographer?' he asked.

'Yes. I am,' I answered wearily. I knew that look, familiar from the thousands of crime scenes I'd attended over the years. They never expected the crime scene photographer to be *a woman*.

'Chris, the lab sergeant, is waiting for you inside,' he said, while I showed him my police ID and signed the crime scene log sheet on his clipboard.

I ducked under the cordon tape and headed towards the house. When I reached the front gate, I noticed a beautiful little girl, about six years old. Perched on top of the gate of the house next door, she looked at me, then at my camera gear. Her eyes bright with curiosity, she asked in a small voice, 'Are you going to take some-one's photo?'

Her innocent question derailed me. Sadness gripped my throat. Her inquisitive brown eyes broke my heart, because I knew the truth. I knew the horror that awaited me.

'Something like that,' I said as I smiled sadly at her.

'What's the worst thing you ever saw?' people invariably ask me when they find out I'd spent almost a decade as a police photographer for New Scotland Yard.

It is a hard question to answer.

Over the years, I photographed people who were shot, stabbed, decapitated, dismembered, mutilated, axed, blown to pieces, crushed, drowned, hanged, strangled, burnt and mangled in car wrecks. I witnessed and photographed almost every manner of injury and death imaginable. I saw and photographed things that other people will never see. My job was to never look away.

I never cried at a crime scene. I never vomited at a crime scene, despite the sights, the smells and the horrors I photographed. It didn't mean I was cold or unemotional. It didn't mean I wasn't shocked and horrified by what I saw. It didn't mean I didn't care. I was there to do a job. With purpose and determination; without fear or favour. I was not there as a voyeur. Through my photographs, I was there to speak for the dead.

Police photographer is not a role most people think about. TV crime shows and movies often depict the police photographer as a silent figure, clad from head to toe in white crime-scene garb. On screen for no more than a few seconds, and largely ignored by detectives. The police photographer is almost an afterthought at the scene. Out of focus in the background. Standing over a dead body, they shoot photographs, flashes firing indiscriminately, while detectives lift evidence with a pen, or a handkerchief. CSIs (Crime Scene Investigators) in protective clothing crowd the scene. Detectives, not wearing any protective clothing, crowd the scene. It's noisy and chaotic. Police cruiser lights flash. It makes interesting television viewing. But, it's not like that in reality. A real crime scene (indoors) is a silent and still environment. Initially, there are one or two detectives, and no gangs of CSIs. The only sounds, the heavy clunking of my camera shutter; the explosive bursts of my flashguns; and the high-pitched whine as they recharge.

In real life, forensic photography is an integral part of every *thorough* criminal investigation. The police photographer plays a pivotal role in the documentation, investigation and conviction of crimes. Crime scene photographs are invaluable. They tell the story of what happened at the scene. They show a true and accurate representation of the scene. They provide detectives and other investigators with a permanent record of how and where the crime was committed. Photographs of shoemarks, bullet casings, blood spatter patterns, bloodstained fingermarks, weapons and the decedent's body, which is a rich source of evidence, all play an integral role in an investigation.

The crime scene photographer is, or *should be*, *one of the first and only people* allowed into a crime scene. It's critical that the photographer arrives on scene as quickly as possible. Time is of the essence in every murder investigation, as much of the evidence is fragile and transitory. The work of the lab sergeant, the scenes of crime officer (SOCO), fingerprint officers and other forensic specialists cannot begin until the photographer has taken the initial photographs. Keeping the scene as pristine and free of contamination as possible, until the photographer documents every inch of the scene and all the evidence, is essential. Photographs aid in scene reconstruction, crime scene and cold case analysis and much more. When the case goes to court, the photographs provide the judge and jury with a visual record of what the scene was like at the time the crime was committed. Judges have the final say as to whether the crime scene photographs are shown or withheld from the jury.

Nobody should search the scene, touch anything, disturb, remove, or examine anything before it's photographed in meticulous detail. Primarily, first responders must protect the scene from contamination or damage to evidence. Numerous poorly managed crime scenes come to mind, infamous cases in the United States, India, Canada, Australia, Italy and Portugal, to name just a few, where police officers and others failed to follow standard crime scene procedures in the first critical hours after a murder, which caused the investigations to fall apart. Perpetrators were never brought to justice, or courts wrongfully convicted individuals. These issues must never be far from the mind of any police officer or police photographer when they arrive at a crime scene.

Once the initial photography has taken place, the work of the forensics team begins. The photographer works collaboratively to meet their needs, such as documenting blood spatter patterns, fingermarks before they're lifted, or shoemarks before they're cast and recovered. Photography of these critical items of evidence is undertaken in case the lifting or casting process destroys the prints or the shoemarks, which can happen on occasions.

Scenes are tightly controlled, *or should be*, even for police officers who sometimes request permission to pass the cordon and enter the scene out of professional curiosity. At my scenes, if they did not have a vital role to play, we refused them entry, no matter their rank. Analysts and detectives, not permitted to enter the scene, scrutinise the photographs during an investigation. Detectives use crime scene and post-mortem photographs during suspect interrogations, with witnesses and in court.

I never had the luxury of a do-over, a reshoot, at any of my crime scenes. I could not allow the pressure, my emotions, the smells, or the sights to distract me. I knew grieving family were waiting to find out what happened to their daughter, son, their baby, their loved ones, so there was an incredible amount of pressure on me to work smartly but thoroughly. I could not afford to miss anything at a scene. I could not afford to make mistakes. My shots had to be perfect first time, every time.

Whether it's a terrorist bomb in London's financial district, a multiple murder scene, a boating accident on the River Thames, a plane crash, or a train derailment, a police photographer will photograph the horrifying carnage of all these incidents, and other major crimes. When the photographs are taken, and the blood and gore are hosed down by the fire service. When the crowd dissipates, only the fragments of crime scene tape, hastily ripped from lamp posts, remain. Soon after someone's life is extinguished, all signs of their violent death vanish. For the police photographer, the crimes, the victims and the locations are not forgotten. They're seared into the photographer's brain. Ask any police photographer the world over and they'll take you on a tour of their city, murder scene by murder scene, fatal accident by fatal accident.

Although I now live far from London, every time I return to the city, a smell, a sight, or the sound of a siren is often enough to trigger a memory in the city of ghosts. That's the hotel where I photographed the man who jumped from the twentieth floor. That's the forest where I photographed the man who drowned himself in a lake deep in the woods. That's the park where I photographed a woman's naked dumped body. That's the street where I photographed a huge bomb explosion. That's the bank where I photographed the teller shot by a teenager with a sawn-off shotgun. You can take the photographer out of the job, but you can *never* take the job out of the photographer. Over the years, I came to realise I had inhabited two different worlds. Two different Londons. A world where most people reside, safe and protected from the violence and inhumanity of the city, sleeping soundly while I worked. The other, a world of misery and grimness, where the raw immediate aftermath of violent death was a daily occurrence for me. Mine was a world most could not comprehend.

'I've got a murder for you,' was a familiar phrase I heard day and night from Charles, one of the photographic duty officers. My phone would ring in the dead of night and the familiar voice would summon me to all manner of murder scenes in a matter-of-fact way. Murder and mayhem kept him awake, when most of the city slept. When all hell let loose in the blackness of the night on London's streets, he fielded the harrowing non-stop phone calls and allocated the crime scene team to assorted horrors. Although a gruff man on the surface, he had a sharp wit and a willingness to make fun of the photographers at every opportunity. In fairness, he took as good as he gave, he cared about us. He *had our backs,* no matter the hour of the day or night. He'd served his time as a crime scene photographer on the streets of London. He knew the dangers and the challenges we faced. He'd seen horrific sights. He'd photographed the horrors people inflicted upon one another. He understood.

It's impossible not to be changed by witnessing and photographing so much brutality and death. Most people are lucky enough to have very little experience of violent death. They can go about their lives believing that human beings are essentially decent, like them. But I didn't have that luxury. I was reminded, day after day, night after night, that there were people out there capable of terrifying acts of horrific violence and cruelty. It made me realise how precarious and precious life is. A life ends in a split second . . .

Time and distance haven't changed the fact that Scotland Yard comes calling when they catch a killer for one of my old murder cases and they need my testimony in court. Inevitably they summon me back to a life I've chosen to leave behind. Back to the city of the dead. John Irving once said in his book *A Prayer for Owen Meany*:

> Your memory is a monster; you forget – it doesn't. It simply files things away. It keeps things for you, or hides things from you – and summons them to your recall with a will of its own. You think you have a memory; but it has you.

The little girl on the gate had gone when I came out of the scene. By the time the lab sergeant and I had finished our work, Stephanie's ex-partner, and the father of their child, had already surrendered to police. A wave of anger washed over me when I heard this. 'I want to see the bastard who did this,' I said to Chris, who raised his eyebrows. I knew it wasn't possible to see Stephanie's killer, but the urge was overwhelming. Chris nodded his head in understanding and we left it at that.

I sat in my van to write my scene notes and statement for court, while it was fresh in my mind. It wasn't long before my police radio crackled into life and Charles sent me to my next murder, a male victim stabbed forty-eight times, by another man, in a frenzied attack, and then set on fire.

'I'll be there as soon as I can,' I reassured Charles. 'I need to go home and eat first.'

Driving home in a daze, Stephanie's violent death scene came to me in flashes: the abandoned breakfast for two set on the table, the large bloody handprints on the staircase walls; the sun coming in through the pink bedroom curtains; Stephanie's mutilated body; blood splashed in lines across the ceiling; blood dripping down the wardrobe mirrors and splashed on a photograph of a smiling little girl in a school uniform; Stephanie lying in the foetal position at the end of the bed; the unfathomable violation of her arms, legs and skull from the heavy machete blade. I thought of the rage-filled blows he rained down on Stephanie. How he had not just killed her, he'd tried to obliterate her. Destroy her completely. How it did not surprise me anymore. The continued onslaught of horrific overkill violence by men against women and girls.

During police interviews, Stephanie's ex-partner admitted to killing her. He said they'd been in a relationship, on and off, for over a decade. Stephanie had met him when she was in her early teens. At seventeen she'd given birth to their daughter. Two years before he killed her, he'd gone to prison for bursting into her home with a bottle of acid and a machete. Their turbulent relationship had deteriorated when he'd become convinced his brother was *the real father* of Stephanie's daughter. After his release from prison, they started living together again but had later separated. Although they hadn't been in a relationship for a long time, he became enraged after his young daughter innocently remarked that she'd seen mummy kissing another man. He flew into a jealous rage. He told detectives he'd used both hands to strike Stephanie with the machete, at least ten times, while their six-year-old daughter cowered nearby. By his own admission, jealousy was his motive for killing Stephanie.

I learned from detectives some time later, that a jury at the Old Bailey found him guilty of Stephanie's killing and the court sentenced him to eight years in prison. In the UK justice system, he would have been eligible for parole in four years, with good behaviour. I couldn't believe that a man with such a long documented violent history, who'd committed such a brutal killing in front of their daughter, received such a lenient sentence. Why hadn't social services, the police or the criminal justice system stopped him *before* his violence escalated to Stephanie's gruesome death? It appalled and angered me. It enraged the police officers in the case. Sadly, all these years later, not much has improved regarding the sentencing or monitoring of dangerous men in these types of domestic violence, femicide and homicide cases.

I don't remember that journey home at all. I drove home on autopilot. Shock had set in but I hadn't recognised it at the time. I'd become so accustomed to seeing and photographing horror after horror and moving on to the next murder scene. I just kept going.

Dead people, they are with me day and night. They have been with me for decades. They come to me in a silent procession. They have passed through my life many times. I have passed through their deaths but once. It is a unique bond; one most will never grasp. A rich and inviolable legacy. Somehow, they live on in death, inside my head. They are not forgotten. Years have passed, but the myriad images still come easily. I close my eyes and the memories dance before me in a pantomime of vivid and gory colour. Who could forget?

Who could forget those sparkling bright blue eyes, in a handsome tanned face, looking back at me through my camera lens? Eyes meeting for the first time in death. The mortuary is no place for introductions.

Who could forget the nineteen-year-old woman, stabbed forty-eight times by her boyfriend's mate because she rejected his sexual advances?

Who could forget the reedy little woman in a buttoned beige camel coat and floral headscarf who took her own life in the dank chilly waters of a filthy London canal?

London is where our paths crossed. They were rich and poor. Every creed and colour. They were cab drivers, bankers, builders, housewives, fashion models and factory workers. They were drug dealers, addicts, pimps, prostitutes, paedophiles and murderers. They were babies, children, teenagers, students, the homeless, the unemployed and the elderly. Beloved or reviled, they were all loved by someone, once.

In their final moments, some gave up on life. They jumped or hanged or drowned or shot themselves in desperation. Others begged for their lives and pleaded with their killers. They fought courageously and it showed. Man's inhumanity to man etched on their faces, each a death mask frozen in time, captured in my photographs. This was my London, through my lens.

My London was a savage place. A grim and hidden London. A subterranean world of darkness, violence and death. It was the shock of a telephone ringing in the dead of night. Find the flashing blue lights and you know you're there. My London was menacing grey concrete tower blocks, infested with cockroaches and crime. Filled with angry, frightened, forgotten people, scurrying home to their prisons in the sky. It was grubby flats that reeked of stale food, fags, booze, old age and desperation. It was violent teenage drug dealers shamelessly plying their trade in dingy urine-soaked concrete stairwells of depressing East End tenements.

My London was wailing police sirens and blue-and-white crime scene tape. It was the dead of night in treacherous no-go areas. The crackling of police radios and world-weary, exhausted detectives. It was body bags, mortuaries, pathologists and green rubber aprons. It was post-mortems, stainless steel slabs and surgical instruments. It was the sickening stench of decomposition and disinfectant. It was pale men in black suits driving the dead in unmarked vans.

This was my London. Through my lens. Who could forget? Not me.

* * *

Tears run down my face and splash onto the balled-up wet tissue in my hands, while I speak about Stephanie's horrific machete death scene. Sarah, my therapist, a tall Texan, with jet black hair in a pixie cut and intelligent, lively brown eyes sits opposite me in jeans and a crisp white linen shirt. I sit in her office many years after I've stopped photographing crime scenes. Sarah is an experienced therapist with a background in helping torture victims and trauma survivors. Her calm and soothing voice and relaxed demeanour provide me with a safe and supportive environment in which to explore the feelings and express my thoughts about my police photography work that I'd never had an opportunity to process or speak about before.

'Why am I crying now for things that happened years ago?' I ask her.

'Crying is cathartic,' she says, calmly. 'It's a kind of safety valve. It provides an emotional release of tension when the pressure inside you becomes too great.' I pull two tissues from the box, wipe my nose and listen as my tears continue to fall. 'It allows you to release the sadness and the feelings that have been causing you pain,' she continues.

I'd never consciously attempted to forget or gloss over my exposure to the horrific incidents I'd photographed in my police work. But clearly those unexamined wounds had impacted me in ways I'd not even recognised.

'This is probably the first time you've given yourself the opportunity to process all of the death, violence and tragedy you witnessed as a police photographer,' Sarah says, in that soothing therapist's tone.

'Yes, that's probably true,' I reply, as I consider her statement. 'When I started to write about what I'd seen over the years, I found it cathartic. When the words began to flow, the tears began to fall; sadness that I'd never expressed,' I say.

I reach across to the box of tissues on the coffee table and hold it on my lap. I wipe my eyes as I try to reply through my tears.

'Tell me more about that,' she says, encouraging me to continue.

'As I wrote about my police work, I cried for all the dead people I'd photographed over the years. I was right back there at those scenes again. I cried for all the families who'd lost their loved ones. I cried for myself,' I continue.

My return to London to testify at the Old Bailey in one of my old murder cases had unsettled me in a way I couldn't quite fathom. It stirred up deeply buried emotions and unresolved pain I knew I needed to explore and understand.

When I left Sarah's office, I felt exhausted and yet relieved, lighter somehow. After all these years, with her expertise and support, I had finally begun to reach down into a deep well of sadness and pain. I had *no idea* I'd been storing or suppressing unprocessed trauma from the tragic incidents I'd witnessed and photographed over the years. The constant exposure to murder, suicide, domestic violence, femicide, child abuse and horrific accidents had gone unremarked by Specialist Operations (SO3) managers and colleagues. We had become inured to it. And in me, it had gone unexamined until my return to London had opened my own Pandora's box.

I will carry this load forever. I will carry the grief of the families who lost loved ones to violent deaths I photographed. I will carry the nightmarish stories of the traumatised victims, who lived to tell me the graphic tales of their brutal rapes, assaults and near-death experiences. I will carry the scenes my colleagues photographed and shared to manage their distress. I will carry the images of the remorseless killers, eyes defiant despite their guilt.

I will carry the faces of the dead. The smiling, hopeful faces I saw in the newspapers after their murders, and the faces I photographed at their murder scenes – battered and bloodstained. Their staring eyes, wide with terror. They could not speak for themselves. That was my job. As W.H. Auden once wrote in an article for *Harper's Magazine*, 'Murder is unique in that it abolishes the party it injures, so society must take the place of the victim, and on his [or her] behalf demand atonement.'

1

The Gory Box

An elderly woman lay at the bottom of a steep carpeted staircase. Her killer had savagely woven wooden chair-back spindles through her torso, thighs and arms, in a bizarre post-mortem ritual.

The duty officer Charles, an avuncular man in a grey cardigan with a shock of silver hair and glasses, had taken a stack of colour 10x8 photographs and spread them out on the table before us. The 'Gory Box' overflowed with pin-sharp crime scene photographs; a catalogue of carnage. A mischievous grin flashed across his face. 'Well,' Charles announced, 'if you're going to be police photographers, you'll want to look at the photographs your colleagues have taken over the years.'

My three new colleagues had expressed an eagerness to look at the photographs. Not me. Panic-stricken, a growing sense of dread washed over me.

Grisly images of post-mortems, murders, fatal accidents and suicides splayed out before us. Mangled bodies; pale mottled flesh; bloated cadavers; gaping knife wounds; and pink brain matter – all of it there in front of us. It was beyond horrifying. Shocked, I recoiled instinctively.

My heart raced. Faster and faster. Drumming louder and louder in my ears. The room began to swim. Voices grew distant and distorted.

'Charles,' I called out, 'I'm going to faint.'

His grin turned to concern. He leapt to his feet and shouted, 'Quick, fetch her a chair.' I lost consciousness, and hands guided me into a chair. 'Take a deep breath. Put your head between your legs. You'll be fine,' Charles said, matter-of-factly. The others carried on talking like nothing had happened. Nobody made a fuss. Disoriented and too woozy to feel mortified, I followed his instructions and began to recover.

When I raised my head, the muffled sounds of the Duty Office in the Photographic Branch at New Scotland Yard became crisp and clear again. Phones rang incessantly. Charles and Dean, two ex-military men, screened hundreds of calls, day and night, from police officers who required a photographer. They sat in a glass cubicle in the middle of a vast rectangular open-plan office. In front of them, a large whiteboard, covered in neat rows of photographers' names in red, black and green marker pen, adorned the wall. A collection of phones sat on their paper-strewn desks.

Charles quickly removed the offending photographs, and returned them to the Gory Box, a heavy brown cardboard box, which had been suspiciously nearby. The cruel initiation came to an end as quickly as it had begun.

Rain splashed off my black polished shoes and the wind whipped around my legs as I walked from St James's Park Tube station to New Scotland Yard. Dressed in black from head to toe, wearing tailored trousers and a turtleneck, with my long, dark brown hair in a ponytail, I hurried across Victoria Street as cars splashed past me on the rain-soaked streets. Filled with a mixture of pride and excitement, and feeling a little nervous, I couldn't wait to start my first day as a police photographer (Photographic Officer) in one of the largest, oldest and most famous police services in the world.

New Scotland Yard, the headquarters of the London Metropolitan Police Service (MPS), stood before me, a silver monolith on a triangular island of concrete in the heart of Westminster. Its mirrored windows reflected a grey London sky. Dwarfing the nearby buildings at the confluence of The Broadway and Victoria Street, the nineteen-storey beacon of law and order loomed large. In front of me, the iconic New Scotland Yard sign revolved in silent deliberation of its newest young recruit. It was a cold, wet April morning and I had just turned twenty-four.

Pushing through the revolving glass doors, I found myself in a grand marble foyer. An imposing colourful Metropolitan Police crest adorned a large wooden plaque that overlooked the lobby. Adjacent to the entrance I noticed a chest-high rectangular white marble monument. On top of the plinth rested two glass cases. On the left, a small golden eternal flame rippled upwards from an opening in the marble, a tribute to fallen officers and staff. On the right, a leather-bound red tome lay open – the book of the dead – displaying lists of names on yellowing parchment. A gold-leaf inscription carved into the marble pedestal read 'To the memory of those members of the

Metropolitan Police Force and of the civil staffs who lost their lives on active service or by enemy action.' Somehow calmed and yet saddened by the sombre words, I stood reading the names of those who had sacrificed their lives in the service of their city. The sound of footsteps approaching disturbed my reverie. A woman from HR had come to retrieve us. Along with three other new recruits, David, Noah and Carolyn, my eventful first day began. Various people from different departments spoke with us throughout the morning. Each addressed us on different matters pertaining to our employment. We filled in tons of forms and received stacks of paperwork. But much of the morning passed by in a blur, despite my best efforts to concentrate.

At lunchtime, in the busy canteen, we found ourselves in a sea of dark navy uniforms. Men in suits and ties of all shades stretched out before us. The din of deep male voices rose above the echoing clatter of knives and forks as diners relaxed and chatted together. I'd never been in a room with so many police officers before. It was unsettling at first, although I wasn't sure why. Then, it suddenly struck me. *Where were all the women?*

After lunch, we continued up to the photographic branch on the fifteenth floor. Specialist Operations (SO3) was home to a team of eighty-six photographers and thirteen administrative staff. Michael, one of the four chief photographers, shepherded us from office to office to meet our colleagues. A tall gentleman in a black suit and tie, his pale complexion and black slicked back hair reminded me of a silent era movie star. A gracious man, not far from retirement, he introduced us to a motley group of

men who welcomed us. Some jokingly asked if we realised what we were letting ourselves in for. We followed
him from office to office, and I wondered if Carolyn and
I were the only two women in the entire photographic
branch. We hadn't yet seen another female photographer
on our tour. Michael told us that the team of twenty-four
scenes of crime photographers worked off-site. They were
based at police stations across the London Metropolitan
Police district, which covered an area of over 600 square
miles. On that day, most of the scenes of crime team were
active around the city. Only a handful were at Scotland
Yard sorting their negatives and putting together their
scene photographs from the previous week's crimes.
The in-house photographers who undertook fingerprint
photography, film processing and printing, and other
specialist photographic tasks, toiled in offices nearby.
The telltale smell of film processing chemicals wafted out
from under the doors. Smiling until our cheeks ached,
names and faces blurred together after a dozen introductions. I knew I wouldn't remember the name of a single
person by the next day. With the afternoon almost at
an end, and a throbbing headache, I couldn't wait to go
home. Our first day had been a whirlwind of questions,
instructions, paperwork and introductions. And then
came . . . the Gory Box.

My fainting episode brought our first day at Scotland
Yard to an abrupt end. Charles sent us home and wished
us a good evening. We fled the building as fast as our
feet would take us. I took the train with Noah, one of
my new colleagues who lived not far from me. After a
brief exchange, we sat side-by-side in the tube carriage,

silent and shell-shocked, comforted by the pitching and rolling rhythm of the train as we headed home.

That night, still in a state of deep shock after the Gory Box incident, sleep eluded me. Every time I closed my eyes, horrific scenes flashed before me in vivid colour. Disturbed by the images, I couldn't shake it off. *How could people do such despicable things to one another?* I lay awake staring at the ceiling while the hours ticked past. *How could my new colleagues be so cruel to show us such horrendous images on our first day?*

After several hours, exhaustion took over and I drifted into a fitful sleep. Wrecked and anxious by the next morning, I'd no idea how I'd face day two at Scotland Yard. *What have I let myself in for? How will I cope? Had I made a terrible mistake?* When I'd answered an advert, in the *British Journal of Photography*, for a Photographic Officer job at Scotland Yard, I never imagined a young woman might be an unlikely candidate for such a job. Not for an instant did it occur to me that this might be a man's world. I never considered police photography as a *man's job* that I couldn't do. I'd loved photography for as long as I could remember. I had my mother to thank for that.

My mother tells me the story of my birth every year: The wail of sirens shattered the stillness of a cold February morning as the ambulance raced through the dark silent streets of London. Insistent in their rhythm, nee-naw, move-move. Blue lights flashed. Their reflections bounced off the sleeping shop front windows. The ambulance driver, frantic and alone.

Smithfield Meat Market teemed with white-coated merchants of death on that Monday morning. The air heavy with the clawing scent of blood and butchered carcasses. Suddenly, a screech of brakes as the rig shuddered to a halt. The driver jumped from the cab. Muffled male voices, the loudest the ambulance driver's as he screamed at those blocking his path, 'Get out of my way.'

Almost there. The ambulance pushed through the crowded market, slowly. The shriek of sirens bounced off the steel rib cage of the market's skeleton like ricocheting bullets. Finally, St Bartholomew's Hospital came into view. Relieved, he handed over a heavily pregnant woman to the waiting hospital staff. The lights and sirens, the blues and twos, a suitable escort for his precious cargo, a baby girl. I share a birthday with my mother, and not a year goes by when she doesn't remind me of my birth story and the terrifying ambulance ride she endured, on her birthday, at the hands of a kind but frantic ambulance driver. Thinking about it now, the wail of sirens, the blue lights and the smell of blood in the air – perhaps it was a fitting way for a future crime scene photographer to come into the world?

An inquisitive child, I drove my mother crazy with my questions: Why this, why that, why the other. What's outside the earth? What's outside space? What's outside the universe? When the questions became too frustrating, she'd send me out to play. There I found a willing audience. As the only child on our street who could read before I started school, the neighbourhood kids flocked to me with their colourful comic books. I read aloud to them in return for favours. Don't ask about the rabbit and the bitten finger.

On my first day of school, I sat in the front row of the classroom with my arms folded. When my mother came to pick me up, I asked her why all the other children in my class were crying. At four years old, I told her finger painting bored me. I wanted to read. They moved me up a class.

When I wasn't asking questions, I was observing those around me. I'd run to the door when guests arrived at our home. I'd study them from a safe distance, behind my mother's legs, and when I'd seen enough, I'd go back to my project. Always making something, growing something, dismantling something, climbing something, reading something, or trying to figure something out, I kept myself entertained. 'You were a precocious baby,' my mother said. It seems I'd figured out how to unclip the latch on my cot to escape its confines at seven months old; walking early; talking early; and reading by the time I was four years old. Quite the handful for my mother, no doubt.

Natural curiosity and a strong urge to dismantle everything, to see how things worked, meant my parents hid valuable items on high shelves in their bedroom. It didn't take long for me to figure out a way to get my hands on the most sought-after prize, my mother's Kodak Box Brownie camera. And so began my love affair with photography.

As a child, I hung around with my older sister and three boisterous boys who lived a few doors away. We all raced around the neighbourhood on our bikes, seeing who could ride the fastest. We made grass forts and staged mock battles in the summer sunshine. We climbed trees in the field at the end of our road, always competing to see who could climb the highest. We played football together and I played better than most of the boys. In summer, I collected specimens with a small yellow net and filled countless jam jars with all manner of tiny creatures. I studied them closely with my magnifying glass, marvelling at the sounds they made, or the dusting of powder that covered their gossamer wings. Never intentionally cruel, I released them back to where I found them, if they survived the glass jar ordeal intact, which some unfortunately did not.

I spent summers at the beaches close to my home. Beaches, filled with weird and wonderful things to discover, kept me occupied for hours. Each harboured its unique attractions for an insatiably curious child. On some beaches I collected shells, always searching for the unusual or brightly coloured miniature ones. On others, the pebbles fascinated me. Rubbed smooth by the tides, I collected them by the pocketful. On long sandy beaches, I marvelled at the turn of the tides and the ripple patterns left on the wet sand when the tide went out. Off I went with my bucket, my spade and my net. Before I headed for the rockpools, the only instruction my mother gave me was 'Don't let the tide cut you off. It comes in fast. And be careful on the rocks. I don't want you washed away by the waves.' I was an old soul, even as a child. I respected the power of the sea, even at that young age. A solitary child, although the second born of three siblings, I happily clambered over the sharp rocks by myself and explored the crevasses along the shoreline. I marvelled at the sounds of the sea and the power of the crashing waves, only returning to the family picnic when hunger pangs made my stomach growl.

As I got older, rules and routines irritated and bored me. Energetic and playful by nature, with a strong maverick streak, I was a risk-taker and a good problem-solver. I loved to tell stories. I loved to laugh, and make others laugh, and I read voraciously. My emotional sensitivity, talkative nature and high energy levels did not suit the 9–5 office job I took after leaving school. It didn't take long before I felt trapped and stifled. Watching others take the credit for my ideas annoyed me. I knew I needed to find a way out. Photography was my passion and my escape route. I felt alive and yet at peace with a camera in my hand. Even though both my parents were musical and artistic, and each had a natural talent for photography, they never considered that working as a photographer was a *proper job* for a young woman, but I knew it was what I loved, so I followed my heart and disregarded their concerns. I applied to art colleges to study photography and received several offers. I resigned from my job, told my parents after the fact, and off I went to begin my new life as a photographer.

My years at art college were some of the happiest times. Unlike many of the other students in my cohort, I was there because I wanted to fulfil my dream of becoming a photographer, and not because I was trying to please parents who'd plotted out a career path for me. Many of my classmates dropped out or failed to make the grade, and left the course before completion. I made the best of my time at art college. I worked hard and enjoyed every moment. The course leader warned us that succeeding as a professional photographer in a competitive and cut-throat business would be extremely challenging; that it was a tough career to gain entry to and succeed in. To drive home his point, our tutorial every week consisted of us lining up with our cache of black-and-white photographs we'd shot, processed and printed that week. He would review our work in the full glare of our fellow classmates. Next to his desk stood a large bin. If he didn't think our photographs made the grade, if they were poorly exposed, out of focus, poorly printed, or were creatively uninspiring, he threw them unceremoniously into the bin right in front of us. I didn't always agree with his assessment. I recovered my photographs from the bin in defiance of his opinion on several occasions, much to the surprise of my fellow students. Perhaps the fact that I was paying for my studies had something to do with my defiance, and my dedication. During my final year at art college, I started searching for photography jobs. When I saw an advert for a police Photographic Officer in the *British Journal of Photography*, I knew immediately it was the career for me. The job seemed fascinating. As an extrovert with a great sense of humour, comfortable with uncertainty, and with an insatiably curious mind, I thought the job was a good fit for my personality.

It was that same tutor who wrote in his reference for the police photographer job application that 'She is a mature, well motivated and highly likeable young woman with perception and intelligence of a high order, though with considerable reserves of common sense. If she can obtain a position compatible with her photographic interests, her employer will gain a motivated, intelligent employee who is able to mix and work with a great variety of individuals.'

With strong encouragement from that *tough love* tutor, I applied for the photographic officer job. As I was still studying, I received a reply showing interest and asking me to reapply once I'd completed my studies. I was disappointed, but I knew I wouldn't give up on my dream of becoming a police photographer. After I left college, I worked as an assistant to an impossibly tall press photographer, dashing about London with him, to various events, and struggling to stay on my feet in the paparazzi crush while he showed me the ropes. It didn't take long before I realised that a petite 5ft 4in woman was not well suited to a job that required me to battle in a scrum of burly, mostly male, photographers to capture the shots needed. I soon moved on to work as a photographer's assistant in a London studio that shot *Vogue* fashion spreads. The atmosphere was fun. My long workdays were filled with couture clothing, loud music, make-up artists, hairdressers and giggly 6ft-tall models who towered over me as they teetered about the studio on their high heels. They turned up at the studio wearing no make-up and cut-off shorts and t-shirts. I'd never have guessed they were the models. But they had incredible bone structures and beautiful eyes that came to life after the team accentuated their features for the photo shoot. When they stepped in front of the camera, the results were spectacular; they were almost unrecognisable as the same women who'd arrived at the studio hours before. My job was to set up the studio, arrange the lighting and backgrounds/props, load the cameras with film, keep the models happy, and to do whatever the photographer needed, to make each shoot a success.

New Scotland Yard's Specialist Operations Photographic Branch (SO3) was founded in 1901, to support the work of the Fingerprint Branch initially. That same year the Home Office authorised the purchase of film plates, chemicals and some equipment, as an experiment. During the experiment SO3 officers shot 162 photographs and made 100 prints. The following year they deemed the experiment a success and the Home Office granted approval to set up a permanent photographic branch. By 1937, police officers running the branch were producing 160,000 photographs per year and the workload grew exponentially over the years.

The Metropolitan Police Photographic Branch grew to become the largest single police photographic branch in the United Kingdom, providing photographic services in a wide range of areas that included surveillance, public order/demonstrations, studio photography, press photography and public relations, secure and confidential in-house processing and printing, scene of crime photography, and much more. A secret archive holds the photographic negatives of over a century of London's crime.

Between 1901 and the 1950s the photographic branch trained police officers to take photographs. However, in the late 1950s SO3 began employing civil police staff in photographer and apprentice photographer roles. Some joined at the tender age of sixteen. The protocol in those days was to train apprentice photographers on all jobs in the branch, while giving them an opportunity to study for photographic qualifications. They also learned from their colleagues, and from attending crime scenes with experienced photographers. By the time I joined the police, that system had changed. Scotland Yard employed only qualified and experienced photographers. Some came from a medical or military photography background, others from a commercial photography background, as I had. Going from paparazzi scrums on the streets of London and *Vogue* studio shoots to crime scene photography was quite the leap. But I knew I had what it took to become an accomplished police photographer. Now I had to prove it.

At the two interviews for the job, they asked me how I felt about seeing dead bodies, and if I minded getting dirty, or climbing over walls and fences, and whether I had a fear of heights. The climbing, the getting dirty and heights didn't bother me. I was a fearless child and happily climbed to the highest branches of the trees near my home, with my brother and the neighbourhood boys. But if you've never seen a dead body in your twenty-four years of life, how could you answer such a question. At an intellectual level, I knew I'd be seeing dead bodies. But somehow it doesn't register at a deeper level. You have no reference point to work from. Most people who've seen a family member die of old age, or illness, have no idea what a murder victim looks like by comparison, or what a decomposing body looks and smells like. And neither did I. It was beyond my comprehension. Although my answer obviously satisfied the three-person interview panel, because they offered me the job. Chosen from over 500 applicants, I was thrilled to secure one of only four jobs on offer. There was no way I was going to give up before I'd begun.

When I arrived at the duty office the day after the Gory Box incident, a group of photographers were standing together chatting and sorting out their assignments for the day. When they saw me, they cheered spontaneously, applauding and whistling. Charles turned towards me and shouted over the din, to no one in particular, 'Well lads, you have to hand it to her. She was brave enough to come back, after seeing the Gory Box. Good for her!' A small figure in the middle of a large crowd of men, I smiled while they cheered and clapped. They'd given it their best shot. But I prevailed.

A few months later, SO3 moved from Scotland Yard to a new state-of-the-art purpose-built Photographic Branch HQ.

Rain lashed against my windscreen as I drove to SO3 not long after dawn. My wipers struggled to clear the downpour. Thunder rumbled and trees bowed their heads against the gusting wind as traffic crawled through London's rain-soaked streets. Forty minutes later, I reached the gates of SO3, a two-storey, red-bricked building in a South London street that gave no clue to its identity. A three-metre-high, navy-blue security fence ringed the south perimeter of the building. The daunting anti-climb spikes atop the fence sent a clear message to any would-be trespassers, *Unauthorised access forbidden*. This was a place *so secret* it didn't have a name. A nondescript car park revealed no clues. No building signs divulged the mysterious world I inhabited.

The building, a labyrinth of beige corridors, housed thousands of square feet of specialist forensic police photography operations, processing and printing equipment, two photography studios, one large enough to fit a double-decker bus. It also housed a locked archive of crime scene photographs and negatives of some of London's most brutal and horrific crimes. And yet, the photographers who inhabited this anonymous location covered the walls in the bland corridors with large, framed colour photographs of the most spectacular sights, the beauty of nature, sunsets over the city, architectural and aerial shots of London landmarks, all stunning images. Ironically the photographers who shot these spectacular images of the city were the same people that recorded the horrors of the city.

My in-house training began in the album room. A workspace where photographers spent two days a week assessing and printing their negatives, collating prints and writing statements to accompany photographs submitted as evidence in court. When each photographer finished printing their photographs, they handed their prints and statements to album room staff who placed the 10x8 colour photographs into a set of comb-bound albums. The albums opened like a book so the photographs lay flat for use during interrogations with suspects and witnesses, and at court. With the volume of work the photographers produced, the album room staff remained busy, ensuring photographs reached forensic pathologists and detectives in a timely manner.

By assigning photographers to the album room first, it gave the new recruits an opportunity to see an enormous number of grisly images in a short period of time – an immersive and desensitising experience. So, by the time I attended my first crime scene with a body in situ, I'd seen thousands of images of the worst kind of horrors and carnage imaginable, and to some extent I'd become accustomed to the gore.

Looking at the images through a photographer's loupe gave me a sense of how the story of each crime scene unfolded and what shots to take and from what angles. I had an opportunity to speak with the photographers who shot the scenes and ask any technical questions that came to mind. All the newbies baulked at their assignment to the album room, but there was method in the management's madness.

After a humbling but enlightening stint in the album room and the administration office, where I fielded calls from gruff police officers requesting photographic albums for court, I moved into the fingerprint room. Finally, I got my hands on the cameras – 35mm, 645, 6x7 and 5x4 large-format cameras that we used to photograph fingerprints on objects from crime scenes brought to us after chemical treatment at the forensic science lab. The exhibits came in a constant stream – forged documents and cheques, weapons, bottles and other evidence dusty with powder. Each exhibit required careful lighting to make visible the fingermarks on their surfaces. It was painstaking work that required infinite patience and immense knowledge of photography, and some ingenuity, to light and photograph exhibits and fingermarks to the highest standards. Identifying a perpetrator proved a strong motivator when the volume of work felt overwhelming.

The fingerprint room had a labyrinth of black-walled tunnels between film processing rooms, an ideal location to lay traps for unsuspecting victims. In those darkrooms, we fed dozens of black-and-white films into the machines, every day, in complete darkness while using night vision goggles (think *Silence of the Lambs*) that allowed us to see what we were doing without fogging the film. The small processing rooms were pitch black, so an unsuspecting victim could walk out of the darkroom, minus their goggles, and into a sticky-tape trap, before their eyes had time to adjust to the light. The wide strips of tape would stick to their face and hair and they'd come flying out of the darkroom corridors like they were on fire, threatening blue murder on whoever did it. Removing tape from long hair was painful. It was easier for my mostly male colleagues who had short hair. But I must admit I was both a victim and a perpetrator of this hilarious prank. Laughter had tremendous therapeutic value for us, because we were dealing with an enormous volume of disturbing material day after day.

Expect the unexpected was my go-to phrase where my colleagues were concerned in the fingerprint room. I never knew what practical joke was coming my way next, or what kind of high jinks I might encounter on my darkroom adventures. On one occasion a particularly agile team member thought it would be fun to scare me in the darkroom while I fed films into the processor. He climbed up onto a ledge high above the machine and, while I fed my films into the processor, he jumped down from the ledge and almost gave me a heart attack. I hadn't heard him breathing, as the goggles make a high-pitched whining sound. I swore a blue streak at him as I dashed from the darkroom, heart pounding. My teammates laughed hysterically. They thought this was the most amusing prank anyone could pull. But never fear, I eventually took my revenge on the perpetrator, when he least expected it. One of the more smelly but harmless pranks I'd learned, involved hiding a small raw fish in the exhaust pipe of a colleague's van. When the vehicle's tail pipe heated up, the smell of fish permeated the victim's van, clothes, equipment, hair etc. The unsuspecting person rarely thought to look in the exhaust tailpipe. Watching the unfortunate target unloading all his equipment in the car park, to try to discover the origin of the foul smell gave the prankster a great sense of satisfaction and much amusement. Juvenile though it might sound, this inventive and harmless mischief fostered cooperation, bonding, collaboration and a strong team spirit. It provided us with a brief respite from the time we spent focusing on violent criminal cases. We all worked extremely hard and the work kept coming at a relentless pace, so we needed laughter and playfulness to break up the day and recharge our batteries.

Adjacent to the fingerprint room were the darkrooms and the C41 (colour film) processing room. We processed hundreds of thousands of rolls of 6x7, 645 and 35mm colour film through an industrial-sized C41 processing machine. We also processed thousands of rolls of black-and-white film, on an industrial scale. We printed our crime scene 10x8 prints on half a dozen commercial-sized printing machines that used giant rolls of photographic paper. We had several large darkrooms where we printed specialist work on traditional-style enlargers and used wet tray processing. Each photographer spent several months on rotation in the C41 processing room. That responsibility was enormous. Processing times and temperatures had to be spot on to produce consistently high-quality negatives and accurate results. Unlike black-and-white film processing, colour film processing is unforgiving. If the temperature of the chemistry was even slightly off, it could have destroyed the photographic evidence of hundreds of crime scene films processed on any given day. Although nobody's favourite rotation, the C41 processing job was a critical role in the photographic branch. This apprenticeship in the album room, the C41 processing, the fingerprint room and the darkrooms proved a vital training ground that instilled patience and scrupulous attention to detail in each of the photographers. Photographing a major scene, such as a murder, takes time, patience, focus, attention to detail and a high level of technical skills. It's often the tiniest of clues at a scene that help to crack a case. Every crime scene photograph is documentary evidence in and of itself. Photographs must be of the highest quality, well lit, in sharp focus, with sufficient depth of field and have no flash hotspots, deep shadows or other technical errors, which could cause confusion or mislead a judge and jury. If the photographs don't meet these high technical standards, they are inadmissible in court, which could cause a prosecution to fail.

Unlike TV crime dramas, the photography of a murder scene takes hours or days in some cases, with hundreds of photographs and video footage shot at each scene. The pressure on a crime scene photographer, from investigating detectives, the coroner's officer, the forensic pathologist and other forensic specialists at the scene is enormous. Each has a role to play in the investigation, but they must wait until the photographer finishes his or her work before they can begin theirs. Despite the pressure on the photographer, it's critical to shut this out, and not allow it to interfere with or hurry photography of the scene.

When a case goes to court, a photographer may need to testify to the veracity of the photographs taken and explain to the judge and jury the technical aspects of the scene photography. We all attended court as expert witnesses during our careers. Cross examination can be brutal. A poorly trained photographer, with limited crime scene experience, or scant technical skills and knowledge of the multitude of photographic techniques and equipment used in forensic photography, may be torn to shreds on the stand, weakening the prosecution's case.

Police use forensic photographs during interviews with witnesses and suspects. Sometimes suspects will confess when confronted with the crime scene photographs. This happened in one of my cases where a man stabbed his wife to death and tried to decapitate her with a kitchen knife. The killing took place in a small bedroom in their flat. My photographs disproved his version of events. He had claimed that his wife had kept the weapon under the bed and during the struggle he grabbed for it and killed her. However, there was no possibility of this being true, because the mattress and bed frame lay directly on the floor next to the decedent. There was no gap under the bed. My photographs showed this clearly. He could not have grabbed a knife during the killing as he had testified. Sometimes it's a small break like this that catches the suspect in a lie that causes the dominoes to fall and the suspect to confess.

After I passed my six months probation, I attended the police clothing store to *get kitted out*. When I arrived for a fitting for a jacket, rubber boots, boiler suit and other items issued to photographic officers, the man and woman at the uniform store stood and stared at me.

'Well, my lovely, I'm not sure we'll have anything to fit you. You're only a wee scrap,' said the woman, in a kindly voice. 'What size shoes do you take?' asked the man. He climbed the ladder to a shelf and took down a pair of steel-toed wellington boots. 'Here, try these on,' he said, handing me a giant pair of boots. 'They'll be too big,' I said. 'Maybe you can wear two pairs of socks to help them fit better,' he suggested. I pulled on the rubber boots and clomped around in them. They were loose. I knew they'd be a safety hazard. The store man tried to convince me otherwise, until I demonstrated how dangerous they would be at any scene. A ladder leaned against the racks of uniforms that hung high above our heads. I climbed the ladder and shook my right foot in his direction. The heavy boot flew off and almost hit him in the face. He jumped out of the way just in time. Reluctantly he said, 'Well then, I suppose we'll have to order you some custom-fitted boots.' 'I suppose you will,' I replied.

We worked our way through all the items I required and the same thing happened, over and over. Flabbergasted, I thought to myself this was an indication of how little they wanted women in the police service. They looked at me as if it were my fault – that I wasn't taller and a bigger build, despite the fact that I'm a 5ft 4in woman – the average height for a female in the UK. When I tried on the smallest size of navy blue police jacket, it was far too big. The sleeves were four inches too long. Their suggestion? Roll up the sleeves and it'll be fine. I couldn't have imagined them asking the same of a male police commander or uniformed officer on the beat. Working in a police photographer's role, my size didn't matter, there were no height requirements to join the job in my specialist role and they knew that. What should have been a fun visit to the police clothing warehouse turned into a disappointment. I came away with poorly fitted clothing, which could have been potentially dangerous at crime scenes and the promise of a custom pair of wellington boots. These issues with uniforms and equipment drove home the point that policing was a man's world which I had the audacity to enter, and I should be grateful for the cut-down, rolled-up-sleeve versions of the standard uniform jackets and footwear. The staff at the uniform store kept telling me there was nothing they could do about it, and that there was no money in the budget to purchase a fitted jacket for me. They were using small jackets designed for the male body shape. It doesn't look professional when you turn up to a crime scene, in the full glare of the waiting media, with your jacket sleeves rolled up on the outside and wearing an oversized pair of coveralls with hems rolled up.

But there was nothing more I could do. I had to make do with what I was given. The unwillingness of the MPS to accommodate the clothing and equipment needs of female employees sent a not-so-subtle message that policing was still a man's world. It was still a man's job.

I matured fast in those first eighteen months. I challenged myself personally and professionally. I knew I'd found a career I loved. Photography was not *just a job* to me; it was my passion. Exposed to a world I'd never imagined existed; I knew I'd found the right job. When I passed my six-month probation period, my confidence grew. Despite the handful of older male colleagues who felt that police photography was 'not a proper job for a woman' and made no secret of their views, most of my male colleagues welcomed the prospect of having more women in the department. Years later I discovered that some of my male colleagues had lobbied management to employ more women photographers. They were sensitive to the needs of female victims and survivors. They felt that having more women photographers in the branch was long overdue. They were not wrong.

After the weary fiasco at the police clothing store, I went to the in-house photography equipment store at SO3 with a long list of gear I required for my crime scene photography work. That experience was completely different, although the store keeper was no pushover, as I subsequently learned when making a case for additional or replacement items over the years. As a professional photographer, I was issued with equipment identical to that supplied to my male colleagues, as I'd expected. I received two Pentax 6x7 medium format cameras, three lenses, three Metz flashguns and a professional Manfrotto tripod, as well as additional items. In the photography equipment arena, I was treated the same as my male colleagues. Now, I was prepared to step out into the world as a crime scene photographer.

2

All the Lonely People

Elsie Cooper had been dead for 14 months by the time I photographed her. We found Elsie lying on a small sofa. A tiny birdlike creature, she was on her side, with her head on a cushion, palms pressed together under her cheek, like a sleeping child, facing a small television set a few feet in front of her. By now almost fully skeletonized, her hair had slipped from her skull. Covered in a layer of dust, her nightdress, slippers and blue quilted housecoat remained intact.

My heart had begun to race and I could hear the tightness in my vocal cords when I'd spoken to Ian, while we donned our personal protective equipment, outside the scene. Ian was an experienced senior photographic officer whose task was to oversee my first foray into crime scene work. This was the first suspicious death scene I'd attend, and the first dead person I'd see in real life.

The police officer on cordon duty had pointed us towards the open door of a Georgian house converted into bedsits. The run-down property stood on a busy street in Hackney, East London, next to a bus stop. Elsie lived in the bedsit facing the street on the ground floor.

I tried to remain calm while Ian and I walked into the dingy, dark hallway of the property, camera gear in hand. We stood in the doorway of Elsie's bedsit to discuss how I would handle the photography, under Ian's watchful gaze. The technical chat proved a welcome distraction. I could feel my breathing and heart rate slowing down. With my fear abated, my curiosity took over. 'Go on, take a closer look,' Ian said in a gentle voice.

I knelt in front of Elsie and marvelled at how nature had done a fine job of decomposing the little old lady's body. Most of her tissues and muscles had decayed, leaving behind a dry skeleton, her hair and clothing. By the time I arrived to photograph Elsie, I'd seen thousands of crime scene photographs of every type of death imaginable, but never a skeletonized human being.

'How did they not discover her before now? The smell must have been unbearable when she started to decompose,' I asked Ian, who remained standing in the doorway with his arms folded.

What I couldn't experience by looking at photographs in the album room were the smells a police photographer encounters at crime scenes. The smells are a gut punch at most scenes. When a person dies, their bowels and bladder release their contents shortly after death. Urine and faeces add another dimension to the ambient smells, like stale food, cigarette smoke, putrefaction, mould, sweat, dog pee, cat pee, vomit and blood.

I don't recall seeing CSIs or detectives on crime dramas scrunching up their noses at the bad smells, but I'd seen forensic pathologists do that. One always made faces when she progressed through the post-mortem, especially when she reached the bowels. She would say to me 'Stand back, I'm going to open the bowels now,' so I could avoid the smell. But it made no difference, six feet or six inches away, the smell was equally revolting. Horrible as they might be, smells at crime scenes (and at post-mortems) can provide you with a lot of valuable information. If you're sensitive to bad smells, then a police photographer career is not for you.

'Didn't she have anyone who cared about her, who loved her, who wondered what happened to her?' I asked Ian.

'You'll be amazed at how many of these you'll photograph over the years ahead,' he replied, in a resigned tone. My eyes stung with tears when I thought about Elsie's lonely death. *Was she frightened? Did she die in pain? Or did she slip away peacefully?* As if he could read my mind in the silence, Ian spoke, 'Let's get started. No sense dwelling on it too much. Letting it get into your head. We've got more jobs after this. So, best get a move on.'

As I photographed the scene, I could see a crowd of people through the grimy lace curtains, standing at the bus stop outside Elsie's window. Oblivious to the death scene mere feet from where they stood. I thought to myself, *so near and yet so far*.

When I finished photographing the scene, we stood talking with the officer on duty outside, while we removed our PPE. He said neighbours had noticed a foul smell for quite some time, but they'd ignored it, thinking it was the stench of rubbish bags in one of the flats. Eventually, after fourteen months, one of the residents called the police who forced entry to the property and found Elsie.

The Japanese have a word for dead people whose bodies lie undiscovered for months or sometimes years: *kodokushi* or 'lonely death'. There's a growing worldwide epidemic of loneliness and lonely deaths. People like Elsie, living lonely lives, in dreary flats and houses, offering scarcely a hint of their existence to the outside world until the stench of their decomposing bodies raises the alarm. With every lonely death I photographed, I discovered another human desperately in need of compassion, human contact and kindness. Over the years I photographed many hundreds of these lonely deaths.

* * *

Before I continue to share more of my case files, it makes sense to pause here to explain, at a very basic level, how a crime scene (specifically within the MPS district) is handled, from the moment a first responder arrives on scene after notification of a crime.

After the first responding police officer attends a murder scene and confirms life extinct, they cordon off the scene immediately, with between one and three cordons, depending on the type of scene and the location. A police officer, or several officers, protect the scene and keep a log of those entering and leaving, and each person's purpose at the scene. The senior investigating officer (SIO) attends the scene and the first responding officer briefs the SIO. A lab sergeant attends, and after the SIO has viewed the scene, wearing full protective clothing, he or she discusses the scene with the photographer and the lab sergeant, and leaves the scene in the hands of the experts, the lab sergeant, the forensic photographer, the forensic pathologist, the scenes of crime officer (SOCO) and the other forensic scientists. Contrary to what you might imagine, apart from the lab sergeant, the specialists attending, documenting, photographing and processing crime scenes are Scotland Yard civilian police staff. They are experts in their respective forensic fields; they are not police detectives. Although in their crime detection roles they are most certainly forensic detectives. These civil staff experts include forensic chemists (fire investigators), biologists, photographers, videographers, fingerprint officers, bomb disposal and ballistics experts, and so forth. Until about the early 1950s, police officers undertook these forensic tasks at crime scenes, but ultimately senior police management agreed, despite much resistance, that the attested powers of arrest were unnecessary for staff who gathered evidence, took photographs, lifted fingerprints or processed a crime scene. Their assessment proved entirely correct.

At no time does the SIO, lab sergeant or SOCO permit any non-essential personnel into the scene, because each person has the potential to damage or destroy vital evidence. If ambulance personnel and first responders left their boot prints all around the decedent in blood, it caused us challenges. Having their boots confiscated by the lab sergeant, for forensic examination to rule them out, made them mindful of not repeating that mistake at the next crime scene.

As an MPS crime scene photographer I worked autonomously. I handled technical problems and scene difficulties and challenges alone. I rarely required or sought advice from my team leader, although we kept in regular contact. If the scene was a large and complex one – a major disaster or terrorist incident – I assessed the situation and requested additional photographers to attend, if necessary. My level of responsibility was enormous, and a lot rested on my shoulders at every crime scene. Although all the scenes of crime photographers worked autonomously, police orders, practices and procedures governed our work. Having autonomy at scenes allowed me to consider the task requirements on a case-by-case basis; work collaboratively with detectives and forensic specialists; have the freedom to problem solve creatively on the fly; and access the necessary tools and resources to complete my photographic tasks to the highest standards.

By the time I attended murder scenes alone – 18 months after I joined SO3 – I made *all decisions* regarding the best method of photographing the scene, evidence, decedent, weapons, shoemarks, fingermarks, tyre tracks, bullet holes, blood spatter etc. Having spent six months at the forensic science laboratory working with the Serious Crimes Unit (Specialist Photographic Unit), and armed with significant forensics knowledge from my secondment, I enjoyed working alongside fire investigation experts (forensic chemists), ballistic experts, explosives officers, blood spatter experts and fingerprint experts. I learned a lot from these colleagues.

At scenes, I assessed the best method of documenting the scene and the sequence of shots. On occasion, the lab sergeant or forensic pathologist asked for specific shots and I obliged. Standard practice, when using film, meant I took two or more photographs of each subject/

object at differing apertures. The photographs were unrepeatable. One mistake, one poorly exposed photograph could exclude a vital piece of evidence and weaken the prosecution's case.

Crime scenes and murder investigations are a team effort. I was the photographic expert at the scene, so I advised the SIO or the lab sergeant if I thought aerial photographs would prove valuable to the overall investigation, or if I thought the Serious Crimes Unit from the Forensic Science Laboratory should attend with their specialist equipment, lasers, chemical treatments etc. At each scene I decided the type of film to use, which lenses to use, how to light the scene and the angle of shots, to avoid unwanted reflections or harsh shadows that might obscure or obliterate critical evidence. I decided the number of shots to take at each scene, and at the printing stage, chose which shots to include in the final photographic album used in court. Despite the enormous pressure from detectives and forensic colleagues to move the process along, taking the time to contemplate was critical. I shut out distractions and focused.

Every scene was unique. There was no set length of time it took me to photograph a crime scene. It all depended on the complexity of the scene, the hazards to the forensic teams, difficulty of access to the scene, or if a scene consisted of a primary and secondary scene, or more (e.g. the location of where the murder took place and where members of the public found the body). If it was a terrorist attack with a bomb explosion, the debris field could be miles from the site of the explosion. The scene could take days to photograph, even with several photographers working together. The same applied to train derailments and river boat accidents. Or if a scene was contaminated, or burnt out, or if the weather was atrocious, or there were other dangers at the scene that could slow access or processing – a large press pack might be present and require management, or distressed and hysterical relatives of the victims could come to the scene.

I mentally ran through a list of questions while I walked around the scene. Those extra few minutes taken to absorb the scene allowed a myriad of thoughts and questions to run through my mind. It gave me an opportunity to note the location of potential evidence, and to plan mentally how I would photograph the scene to tell the story of what happened in a series of images. I asked myself, what did I notice when I first entered the scene? How did it smell? What was the lighting like? Was there any sign of forced entry? Were there signs of a struggle? Had the perpetrator robbed the victim? Had someone staged the scene to look like a robbery or burglary? Were there attempts at cleaning up the crime scene? Did I smell bleach or other chemicals? I always treated the crime scene as a 3D scene, both at indoor and at outdoor scenes. I checked what was above my head, around the walls, on the ceiling and behind doors. Looking up at crime scenes often yielded valuable evidence – blood spatter patterns, bullet holes, or items, such as clothing or weapons, in tree branches or on window ledges – that might prove crucial to the investigation. During my walk through I examined the ground or floor, on which I was about to walk, with a powerful torch, to avoid stepping on any fragile trace evidence or shoeprints that might prove crucial to the investigation. Even in daylight, I shone my CSI torch obliquely across wooden, tiled or linoleum floors to search for shoemarks barely visible under normal lighting conditions.

At a murder scene, I photographed all rooms in the house or flat, not just the room where the decedent lay. It took ten hours or more to photograph the most basic murder scene, and more complex scenes could take thirty or more hours, or sometimes even days, with hundreds or thousands of images shot to document every detail. All entrances and exits, and all evidence of a struggle – torn off fingernails, scuff marks on the walls and doors, blood stains etc. – were photographed.

Each scene dictated how I told the story of what had happened. I could not move anything to make my photography tasks easier. I had to work around furniture and other obstacles, all the while checking the floor for any evidence or hazards to avoid stepping on them. Hoarded scenes also posed great challenges. Crowds of onlookers caused problems when trying to get establishing shots of the exterior of a scene. Imagine the opening scene of a movie. It gives the viewer a clear idea of where they are. The establishing shots tell the judge and jurors where they are in the broadest sense, outside a private residence, in the woods, on the twentieth floor of a block of flats. Depending on the scene, I took shots of the surrounding streets or areas adjacent. Because the decedent at any scene provided investigators with a valuable source of evidence, I shot close-up photographs of the victim's face, injuries, bullet holes, stab wounds, bruises and defence wounds in situ. I also shot photos of evidence on, near or under the body, to show its relationship to the body and the environment where the body lay.

Every scene presented a fresh set of challenges. *Was it safe? Would someone attack me? Would I have my equipment stolen?* I often worked alone in some of the roughest and most dangerous areas of London with high murder and crime rates. Several of my colleagues were beaten and robbed of their equipment at scenes they attended alone.

I had to undertake a wide variety of specialist work that was uniquely required of photographers working in a major metropolis. I had to be able to photograph anything, anytime, anywhere, under any kind of conditions, in all weathers. Most commercial photographers don't contend with such technical and logistical challenges in their work on a regular basis. They have full control over the shooting environment. Not so with a police photographer, who must develop the highest level of technical skills across a wide variety of photographic and imaging disciplines to take photographs in high pressure environments and under adverse conditions. Forensic photography requires a photographer to have a strong command of a multitude of techniques, equipment and imaging know-how. As Edward M. Robbins wisely said in one of his books, 'the modern forensic photographer must be part chemist, physicist, colour expert, mechanic, lighting technician, computer geek, artist, communicator and investigator, in order to be successful.' I could add: aerial photographer; public order photographer; surveillance photography expert; and much more besides.

The volume and seriousness of crimes in London provided me with an opportunity to develop expertise across a wide range of forensic photographic areas. And I learned a great deal from the forensic scientists at the scenes and in the lab, when I worked side by side with them. During my secondment to the MPS Forensic Science Laboratory I had an opportunity to use lasers, peripheral cameras and a variety of light sources, as well as biological methods to reveal fingermarks for photography – all skills that proved invaluable to any major crime investigation. These practices occurred in London far more than in other parts of England and Wales, because the MPS had the lab and police budget for research and development (R&D) that many other police services did not have at that time.

When I joined the scene of crime team, I had to take a police driving test before I was issued with an unmarked police van; and a limited amount of photographic and safety equipment. Although assigned to one area of the city on a specific police division, the duty officer could send me to any division of the MPS and any location within the United Kingdom or overseas, if necessary.

* * *

'What coping methods did you use?' Sarah asks me during one of our sessions together. She sits quietly opposite me, comfortable in the silence between us while I contemplate my answer.

'I went dancing with some of the other photographers and lost myself in the loud night club music. I didn't drink much, so it never appealed to me as a coping mechanism. If I went to the pub with police officers after a *bad scene*, they encouraged me to have a pint of beer or a glass of spirits, but I refused. Being a woman, I think it was easier for me to refuse, than it was for my male colleagues to say no to a pint of beer. After a while they stopped asking, and bought me a pint of orange juice. It was never an issue for me after that.'

'How about your colleagues, what did they do to cope?' Sarah asks.

'Everyone had a different coping mechanism, although nobody talked about coping mechanisms. Some turned to alcohol to lessen the pain, and take the edge off after a bad scene. The pub was a refuge for some, I suppose. Others smoked heavily; some ran for miles every day until they didn't have an ounce of fat left on them. Some suggested I should think of the decedents as a carcass, rather than a person. The thought horrified me, but I knew they meant well.'

'I see,' says Sarah thoughtfully.

'Probably not the healthiest coping methods, thinking back on it,' I add.

'How did you think of the dead bodies you photographed?' she asks.

'When I photographed homicide victims, to me they were not a carcass. To me, they were someone's cherished loved one, someone's mother, father, sister, brother, someone's husband, wife, or partner. Hours before, they'd been a living, breathing human being, with a life of possibilities stretching out ahead of them. I could not diminish them by thinking of them as merely a lump of flesh and bone. Each dead person deserved my respect. They deserved the best I could give. I kept them company, sometimes so quickly after their death that I could still feel the terror in the room, their fear, mingled with the sweet metallic smell of their blood that I inhaled and could taste on the back of my tongue when I swallowed.'

I've always felt it was *my privilege* to speak for the dead. Dead people were with me day and night. We were fine together. I'd learned to live with them. They were a part of my life and that would never change. I thought back to my first crime scene with little Elsie, and how it was not so much fear that I'd felt at seeing her dead body, but more a profound sadness at the thought of her dying alone.

To me, it was personal. I bent down to talk to them. To comfort them. To let them know *I'm here now and I'm going to speak for you, because you will never have the chance to speak for yourself. They mattered to me. Every one of them.*

3

Men Killing Men

Swimming Pool Murder

It's hard to imagine a more innocuous place for a murder than a public swimming pool. But on a hot summer day, the duty officer sent me to photograph a murder scene at a North London leisure centre. I'd always thought of a public pool as a fun place where children splashed about. A place of safety. A place of relaxation. A place to keep fit. To rest mind and body in the warmth and comfort of the water. But on a sunny July day, a London swimming pool turned into a blood bath, and the site of a vicious and brutal murder.

Two men, Johann Muller, a 47-year-old university professor, and Costas Georgiou, a 25-year-old café worker, regularly swam lengths at the pool. They did not know one another. When they swam lengths that day, they accidentally banged heads, and began to argue over the collision.

Witnesses told police that Johann called Costas *a bloody fool* for not looking where he was going in the water and the men traded insults. More than eighty people in the

54

pool watched in disbelief while the argument grew more heated. No one intervened. Ultimately, Costas left the pool and went back to the changing rooms, got dressed and hung around. Johann sat on the edge of the pool for a while after the altercation. He finished swimming his lengths, and left the pool. He took a shower before returning to the changing rooms. The still enraged Costas began arguing with Johann once more. Still in his swimming trunks, Johann stood his ground. But he had no idea Costas had grabbed an eight-inch Nato combat knife from his sports bag prior to their second confrontation. The two men traded blows. In the crowded changing room, Costas stabbed Johann three times in the chest in a frenzied attack, severing the main artery to Johann's heart. Costas ran from the swimming pool, leaving the husband and father bleeding to death on the changing-room floor. By the time I reached the scene an ambulance had taken Johann's body away, but the heavily bloodstained floor and detritus from their attempts to save his life were evident among the bloody footprints. While I worked, police prevented people from leaving the scene, so they could take witness testimony immediately. And at that stage it wasn't clear if the killer had remained at the scene among the crowd of people in the leisure centre.

After I'd photographed the bloodstained changing room and several fingermarks in blood on various surfaces, I identified additional bloody fingermarks on the underside inner curve of a silver handrail that ran along the wall of the changing room. The pattern of bloody handprints and fingermarks showed the direction of travel towards the exit door of the changing rooms. They were likely to be the killer's prints; left when he fled the scene in a hurry and grabbed the silver handrail. His bloody fingerprints and handprints were all along the length of the handrail. I knew these marks had tremendous evidential value. I made a judgement call that to photograph the assailant's fingermarks in the victim's blood, I needed the additional expert support of my colleagues from the Serious Crimes Unit at the Forensic Science Lab. Between us, we spent hours carefully lighting and photographing all the fingerprints in blood on that handrail. Some of the prints were on the inside surface and looked to be of good quality, when I used a small mirror to view them. It was time-consuming and they were challenging to photograph. But with the SCUs lighting and specialist photography equipment and techniques we were able to photograph all the marks prior to fingerprint officers lifting the prints or swabbing them for evidence.

The detective leading the murder hunt spoke to me after I'd finished all the photography.

'Anyone who takes a commando knife with him to a swimming pool and uses it to kill someone has got to be demented,' he said.

'I can't fathom why someone would bring a knife with them when they're going for a swim,' I said. 'Although nothing surprises me any more.'

'Carrying a weapon like that can only lead to devastating results,' he said.

I nodded in agreement. 'It's hard to comprehend how two grown men could fight to the death about an accidental bumping of heads in a public pool. Because of the knife, a trivial row ended in a senseless death.'

Later that afternoon I photographed Johann's forensic post-mortem. It proved to be a challenging mental and emotional leap to make. From a scene at a swimming pool so full of life, to the grimness of a mortuary within a few hours. When I photographed close-ups of Johann's face, his blue eyes were open. It was such an intimate and heartbreaking experience, looking through my camera lens into the eyes of a murder victim. There's nothing more intimate than that. It stays with you forever.

After the murder, Costas Georgiou borrowed money from his father, under false pretenses, and fled the country. But when his law-abiding father heard the news reports of the murder, he called police to say he suspected his son might be the killer. Acting on the father's tips, police captured Costas Georgiou after a five-day manhunt and authorities extradited him back to the UK. During his trial, he denied murder and claimed he killed Johann Muller in self-defence. The jury found him guilty of murder and sentenced him to a ten-year minimum prison term for the brutal and frenzied killing. Upon his release, after serving only ten years, he told the probation service he was moving overseas – but he never left the country. And it would appear they never checked the veracity of his claim. In fact, he remained living at the same flat he'd lived in prior to murdering Johann Muller. There he began a secret life as an under-world armourer, converting a massive arsenal of weapons and making thousands of bullets, using the metalwork skills he'd honed in prison. Ordering the parts on the internet led to his downfall. Border officials intercepted a parcel addressed to him that contained a bullet mould, and notified police who discovered the weapons production line at his flat.

Ten years after his release from jail for the murder of Johann Muller, Costas Georgiou stood before a court once again. After police found his stash of 36 guns buried in Epping Forest, he admitted to eleven firearms offences. A court jailed him for a minimum of seven years for manufacturing a cache of deadly weapons in his flat.

I shuddered at the thought that Costas had moved on from military knives to manufacturing his own guns and bullets, especially after hearing what he'd hidden in Epping Forest. Having seen the level of violence at the Muller murder scene, I feared for the life of anyone who crossed his path and caused him even the slightest offence.

Lonely Millionaire

The black-and-yellow handled screwdriver that stuck out of the victim's forehead caught my attention first. I'd seen all sorts of weapons used in murders but this was new to me. The killer had embedded a screwdriver into the centre of the victim's forehead with such viciousness that it went in right up to the hilt. None of the shank of the screwdriver was visible, only the handle. The decedent lay on his back in the hallway, just beyond the vestibule of his grand multi-million-pound home. Splayed out on the hall carpet like a sacrificial offering to the gods, a halo of blood pooled around his body, soaking the hallway carpet red.

When I arrived at the scene in the middle of the night, we didn't know much about the victim, but while I worked through the night, police discovered more details. The victim lived alone and was 66 years old. His name was Aaron Katz. He had fled Nazi Germany when he was a young man and became a successful London businessman. Separated from his wife, he had planned to sell his home and join members of his family in Australia later that year. A hotelier by trade, he was a multi-millionaire, who owned several London hotels and properties. On the evening of his murder, he had planned to meet friends for dinner in central London, but he never showed up. Thinking this was out of character for him, his friends alerted police. Firefighters broke into his home to discover the gory scene.

His killer had unleashed a tremendous murderous rage on Aaron Katz. He had knifed him 78 times, in his face, back, chest and neck, and then cut his throat. The grisly tableau was beyond horrific. The hall carpet squished with his blood when I stepped over his body. Where the decedent lay made me think he'd opened the door to his killer and a blitz attack followed. The screwdriver through his forehead had felled him instantly. He didn't have time to fight back or protect himself from the killer's vicious onslaught.

When FBI profilers from Quantico gave a presentation to SO3 photographers and police, at Scotland Yard, they told us that when a killer damages the victim's face, and literally tries to obliterate it with so many stab wounds, it's deeply personal, and most likely the killer knows the victim, or has some emotional connection to them. The face represents the essence of the person. Obliterating the face may be symbolic of obliterating the person. Multiple stabbing homicides, with such overkill, were often sex-related, with a jealousy motive, particularly in the murders of women. I'd photographed a lot of overkill in the murders of women killed by men – repeatedly stabbing, beating, or bludgeoning a victim even after death – but this was the first time I'd seen such a rage-fuelled horrific murder where the victim and the killer were both male. From the injuries the victim sustained, I suspected the decedent had some type of relationship with his killer. It takes time to stab a victim 78 times and cut their throat. That made me wonder if the killer felt confident nobody would disturb him during the time it took to inflict such injuries. Perhaps he knew the victim lived alone in a secluded residence, so he felt confident he would not be disturbed during the murder.

How could this man have deserved such a vile, terrifying and horrific death? I wondered while I did my walk through of the scene. I knew that photographing a mansion of that size would keep me working through to the next day and I was not wrong. It was a six-bedroomed mansion, with numerous bathrooms, and other nooks and crannies. Not long after I arrived, Peter, one of my videographer colleagues, turned up. The lush grounds of the mansion took up almost an entire block of one of London's most affluent and expensive neighbourhoods. I remember thinking that the beauty of the well-tended, flower-filled gardens, and the manicured lawn, seemed a striking contrast to the ugliness and the horror that I'd witnessed inside the house.

As Peter and I made our way up through the house, we soon discovered a treasure trove of hoarded possessions. This added an enormous challenge for us, in terms of navigating the hoard without disturbing the scene. In the victim's bedroom there was a narrow, cleared pathway that led directly to one side of the bed. The entire room was knee-deep in paperwork, newspapers, business magazines, reports, invoices and every manner of paper imaginable, along with many opened and unopened bottles of wine. Stacks and stacks of paper piled high, right up to the top of the mattress level. Papers also covered half of his bed, dozens of small piles. Only a small strip of the bed, where the victim slept, was devoid of piles of paper. In the opulence of this grand mansion a pervasive sense of loneliness seeped from the walls. The decedent had cocooned himself in one room, in a mansion that could have housed a dozen people. All the other rooms stood lifeless and loveless in the darkness and silence. All that space, all that money, and all those valuable possessions took the place of love, perhaps. The thought saddened me.

When we climbed higher into the upper levels of the house, furniture, artwork, antiques, mirrors, paintings and all sorts of valuables lay strewn about and piled up haphazardly. They filled every landing and every room we opened. We had to squeeze past the precarious piles, hoping they would not collapse on top of us while we worked. I knew it would be a challenge to discover whether the killer had stolen items from the victim, because the hoard made it virtually impossible to tell if items were missing.

Once we had a clear idea of what we were up against, I began my photography of the scene, followed closely by Peter shooting video. Photographing a treasure-chest of a scene like that was rare. Most of the murders I photographed were in run-down flats and houses in the roughest and poorest neighbourhoods of London. This murder took me into another world. The world of a multi-millionaire's opulence. And yet, for all his wealth, he met a grisly premature death, not unlike those victims on the council estates of London.

In the weeks following the murder I read in news reports that police had a prime suspect named Trevor Miller, of no fixed address. Trevor had lived for a time at one of the hotels owned by the decedent. The Department of Social Security had housed people who needed temporary accommodation in his hotels. Trevor Miller had also worked as a gardener for Aaron Katz in the past. According to police, Trevor knew that the victim had left his hotel that night with a large amount of cash. He went to rob his former employer at his luxury home. When the victim confronted him on the doorstep, Trevor thought Aaron had recognised him and launched his violent onslaught.

In the days following the murder, police launched an extensive search for the suspect. Trevor Miller called the police and confessed to the killing, saying he wanted to give himself up. He said he could not remember how many times he had stabbed the decedent. During the trial at the Old Bailey the judge postponed sentencing until he received a medical report on Trevor Miller. The judge said that although a mandatory sentence for murder was life, he had a statutory duty to consider a minimum recommendation. A court sentenced Trevor Miller to life in prison for the brutal murder of his former employer. He had killed Aaron Katz to rob him of £300 in cash, some silver, a watch, a radio, a cigar case and two wallets. Such a brutal and senseless murder, for such a paltry haul.

Over the years I learned that people will kill another person for the most insignificant of reasons. One man murdered his son for leaving the lights on in the rooms he was no longer using. The father had stuck notes underneath the light switches all around the house; reminders to switch off the light. But they proved of no value. His son kept leaving the lights on when he went from room to room, and his father stabbed him to death over it. Cheating at a card game seemed to be a popular excuse for killing another person. One scene I attended, a card-playing companion murdered a man he accused of cheating. He killed him with a Stanley knife he had altered to fit two blades side by side, separated by a matchstick. Known as a *Matchstick Stanley*, this made the double-bladed knife especially lethal when drawn suddenly across another man's throat in a fit of anger. If the person survived the attack, the gap between the two blades, caused by the addition of one or two matchsticks, made stitching the two separate slash wounds complex and challenging, so at the very least the *Matchstick Stanley* victim would bear the scars and disfigurement from the attack.

* * *

Professional Hit Men (Contract Killings)

Over the years I photographed several professional hits, usually associated with organised crime or gangs. The MO of these types of murders was overkill and brutality. The nature of the murder had to send a clear message to anyone who dared to cheat, disobey, or cross the gangland boss, or the Chinese Triad gang members or the Russian Mafia, or the East End gangsters. The torture and murder varied, but the level of cruelty left no doubt the murders were professional killings, not a run-of-the-mill murder. Gangland murders were especially brutal. Often the assailant tortured the victim mercilessly before they shot, stabbed or strangled them to death. They often chose 'overkill' to send a clear message to others. They didn't use only one method to kill a person, they used several combined. The Triads favoured using a machete to slice the victim's feet down the middle, between the big toe and the second toe, all the way back to where the ankle joined the foot. They also sliced the Achilles tendon at the back of the ankles, or the tendons at the back of the knees, with a machete or a knife, so the victim, if they survived, walked with a limp, or never walked again. A visible sign of their punishment. Once they'd finished torturing the victim, they often beat them to within an inch of death, and then shot them or strangled them, and then threw them into the river etc.

At one of the gangland murder scenes, the victim had been drinking in a crowded pub in the East End of London on a Saturday. He was a man in his early thirties.

His killer found him in the crowd and shot him at close range in the buttock and upper thigh. Two shots in close succession. Nobody moved. Nobody heard the gun shots because of the silencer. This was no amateur. Burning pain was the first indication something was wrong. The bullets tore through the victim's body and tumbled around until they burst out the exit wounds. The killer knew the din of conversation and the loud music would mask his gunshots. This gave him time to make his escape unnoticed. The victim didn't scream or beg for help. In shock, he pushed his way through the throng towards the door, as if nothing had happened. He left the pub and staggered, bleeding profusely, through the streets of London alone, in his desperate search for help. Blood pumped from his gunshot wounds, weakening him at every step until he collapsed on the rain-soaked street. His bright red blood ran in rainy rivulets into the nearby gutter. Ruby red streaks, a stark contrast to the wet grey pavement. He almost made it to the car park attendant's booth, but there was nobody on duty that day. He fell in the street and died face down in the rain. After the scene, I went to the mortuary to photograph his forensic post-mortem. When the lab sergeant undressed him, we found his wallet. I photographed his wallet and the other possessions he had on him. Then came the heart-crushing moment. When I focused my lens on his open wallet, I saw photographs of his smiling beautiful blonde baby daughters. So sad. Their daddy taken from them in a matter of seconds. Two gunshots. And it was all over.

* * *

Another professional hit I photographed was particularly horrific. A knock came on the door of the victim's flat in the middle of the day. The young couple in the flat came to open the door together. The killer blasted the victim in the face at point blank range and the sawn-off double-barrelled shotgun blew his head to pieces. The force of the gunshots splattered his head, teeth, skin and hair all over the wall, the radiator and the small hallway. His girlfriend had previously been his brother's wife. But he started a relationship with her when his brother went to prison for a long stretch. The victim had been involved in the drug business. The killer, dressed in black from head to toe, was a professional. He took out his target in seconds. The force of the blast at such close range decapitated the victim, splashing his blood onto his girlfriend's face and clothing, as she'd been standing next to him when he opened the door. She told the police she stood frozen to the spot and waited for death, paralysed by the shock and terror of what had happened. The killer had momentarily turned the shotgun in her direction, but left the scene and did not harm her. He was a professional. He'd come for one person. And he made a good job of that assassination. The hitman didn't say a word. Ominous in black leather biker clothing and a black visored motorbike helmet, he turned and walked away calmly. He made his getaway on the back of a waiting motorbike. I never discovered the outcome of this case.

In fatal shootings, firearms/ballistics experts from the MPS Lab attended my scenes and post-mortems, to analyse evidence, make weapons safe etc. Having a ballistics expert attend a crime scene and post-mortem provided us with vital information about the bullet trajectory, the range shots were fired from, the positions of the killer and the victim at the time of the shooting and if the shooter was left- or right-handed, among other things. At the time, the MPS were the only police service that sent firearms/ballistics experts to crime scenes and post-mortems. Collaboration between a firearms expert and a forensic pathologist or lab sergeants helped to produce a more accurate and reliable interpretation of wounds from a firearm. At the post-mortem the firearms expert could determine the trajectory of the bullets fired at a victim, after the pathologist inserted steel rods (like giant knitting needles) into the entry wounds on the decedent and threaded them gently through the path the bullet took through the body. In one shooting post-mortem the decedent had been shot so many times that by the insertion of the last steel rod, the body looked like a ball of wool with a dozen long needles stuck through it. A challenging site to witness and photograph. Having a firearms/ballistics expert attend my shooting murder scenes helped us assess the type of weapon fired, the number of shots fired, the angle of the shots and a lot more besides. These experts were an enormous benefit for investigating teams.

Sadly, it's highly unlikely you'll see a firearms/ballistics expert at scenes in England and Wales these days. Police budget cutbacks have consequences.

One Punch Can Kill

On a sunny afternoon, I arrived at a factory in the East End of London. A request had come through to the duty office for a photographer to attend a suspicious death scene. Police had cordoned off the back yard of the factory with crime scene tape. A solitary uniformed officer stood on cordon duty. There wasn't much to see by way of blood or the usual tell-tale signs of a violent death that I'd become accustomed to finding on my arrival. The freight and delivery area of the factory stood empty and silent. After I photographed the yard where the incident took place, I went indoors to take photographs of the makeshift canteen area where the young, mostly male, factory workers had been playing cards together during their lunch break. Half-eaten food and half-empty cups of tea stood abandoned on the lunchroom tables. Frozen in time, the card game and the chairs pushed back from the table, some overturned, stood where they were when the argument began.

Briefed before I arrived at a scene, I had an idea of what to expect. Although what the duty officer told me and what awaited me were often two different things. Getting a briefing on scene helped, although I preferred to enter a scene with few preconceptions and an open mind. This allowed the scene and the physical evidence to speak to me.

On this occasion, the decedent was a 19-year-old man. He'd been playing cards with his workmates during their lunch hour and one of them accused him of cheating. The argument escalated quickly. The accuser challenged the victim. 'Let's go outside and settle this,' he taunted. The victim, not wanting to seem weak in front of his male workmates, foolishly agreed. The group spilled out into the factory yard. Both sides urged their two colleagues to *fight, fight, fight*. The accuser threw the first punch. The force of the punch knocked the victim to the ground. He cracked his head on the pavement. One punch. That's all it took to kill him. He died in the ambulance on the way to the hospital. His post-mortem awaited me later that day at Valleywood Mortuary.

Dressed in scrubs and white rubber boots and prepped for the post-mortem, I waited outside the autopsy suite with the pathologist while the mortician retrieved the decedent's body from the fridge. I told him what I knew of the case and the scene, because he had not attended. To all outward appearances the decedent's body looked unremarkable, with few visible signs of trauma. I knew from previous experience of one punch death cases that he might have a skull fracture and a big brain bleed from his head smashing into the concrete with such force. A hard blow could have torn an artery and caused him to go into cardiac arrest. On impact, his brain would have bounced back and forth against his skull. We'd know more when the pathologist opened his skull.

From witness testimony we knew that our victim lost consciousness after the first punch. The pathologist said the impact of his head smacking the ground equated to the same force as someone hitting him over the head with a lump of concrete. For some reason, people don't readily imagine injuries not caused by knives or guns as lethal. And yet, punching someone in the head, even once, can prove lethal, or can cause serious brain injuries and life-altering disability for the victim. They don't think that a sucker punch or a coward punch can take a life. Fists are dangerous weapons, especially when used by young men between the ages of 18 and 25, when alcohol is involved.

Once I'd photographed the victim clothed and unclothed, and any injuries, marks, tattoos or other distinguishing features, the pathologist made the first incision. It's hard to watch the first time you see a pathologist putting the sharp point of a scalpel into the skin of a human being. Then watching while he cuts the skin in a Y incision from the collar bones, right down the front of the body to the pubic bone. It becomes less shocking the more you watch it, but somehow it feels like a forbidden act. Allowing us to see inside the pink glistening hidden recesses of their brain and body. Inside the private places of another human being.

The pathologist suspected the victim might have suffered spinal cord damage, so he chose to remove the complete spinal cord for examination. To reach the spinal cord meant removing all the organs in the body cavity until we could see the spinal column from the front. Although an interesting post-mortem to observe, it proved challenging and tiring to photograph due to the tight confines of the autopsy room, and the challenge of photographing the spinal cord in its entirety, from brain stem to tail bone. When I finally saw the spinal cord, I thought it quite beautiful. It looked like a thick, long silky white shoelace. Although I'd seen hundreds of post-mortems by the time I photographed that young man's autopsy, I'd never seen an entire body cavity eviscerated. Watching the pathologist remove all the organs proved fascinating and horrifying in equal measure.

It seems unimaginable that a single punch could be fatal. Fist fights on TV and in the movies seem effortless and give the impression that a person's head can withstand a pummelling. That is not true. In movie and TV fight scenes, stunt men and women expertly choreograph fights, and faux punches, move by move. These scenes don't reflect reality in any way, but they may influence young viewers into thinking that this is how things work. Something similar happens with guns. But in the real world, the consequences of a single punch, or a single gunshot, can be devastating and deadly. I hope that reading about this case might give young men pause for thought, and may prevent even one more of these needless and tragic deaths.

4

Mortuary Mondays

My introduction to Riverview Mortuary came in the form of a man whose killers had thrown him to his death under an 18-wheel juggernaut. With his head bagged tightly to preserve vital forensic evidence, the image of that man's face, squashed and straining against the blood-soaked plastic bag, like vacuum-packed meat from a butcher's shop, has never left me.

Riverview Mortuary was the kind of building you could have driven past a million times and never noticed. It stood like an outcast on the perimeter of Riverview Walk churchyard, hidden from view by towering trees that dwarfed the dowdy flat-roofed building. A wall of faded folding steel doors spanned the rear entrance, the only telltale sign of the mortuary hidden beneath the house-like red-bricked structure. Built atop an ancient burial pit, seven thousand souls still called this place home.

I parked my van on the forecourt, in front of the battle-ship grey shutters. The stench of decomposing bodies, a nauseating blend of rotten meat and disinfectant, hung in the air. Entering through the forbidding black gates marked *No Public Access* I climbed the stairs to the mortuary office and rang the bell.

Creepy Mo, as the SO3 photographers had nicknamed him, appeared to be the only other living soul at the mortuary when I arrived. *Were they locking people out or locking people in?* Mo slid back the bolts on the heavy door, top and bottom. He stood before me in white wellington (rubber) boots, with a long green rubber apron over jeans and a faded blue t-shirt. Skinny and reeking of smoke, his sunken cheeks, yellow teeth and prison pallor gave him a cadaverous look. *A man tempting fate by working in such a place.*

'Make yourself at home while we wait for the others,' Mo said, while he descended the stairs in front of me. He meant well, but I could never feel at home in any mortuary, no matter how many times I visited them. *I shuddered to think how he could live there, night after night. As the years had passed, he'd begun to resemble the dead people he lived with.*

Overflowing brown wooden desks filled the cramped mortuary office. The book of the dead lay open. Years of entries in the finest penmanship graced the lined grey pages of the leather-bound tome. Every death diligently documented. Sad but fascinating reading for a police photographer with time on her hands.

Quiet for a Monday morning. It won't last. Soon pale men in black suits, in vans with tinted windows, would deliver the dead. Hidden from view behind shuttered steel doors they disgorged the dead into the waiting hands of the live-in mortician.

After I dumped my camera bag and tripod in the office, I made my way past the wall of stainless-steel fridges to the changing rooms. I stripped to my underwear, put on scrubs and donned a waxed paper suit and white wellington boots. By the time I returned to the post-mortem examination room, Mo had already wheeled in six bodies and parked them along the walls. A virtual traffic jam of cadavers awaiting the forensic patholo-gist's attention. Sun streamed in through the oblong windows atop the beige tiled walls that still adorned one of London's oldest mortuaries. A single ribbon of dark green tiles transported me back in time to Victorian swimming baths. I could almost smell the water and hear the splash of the swimmers.

Mo clanged around. He grabbed small and large surgical implements from various glass cabinets that spanned one wall. He displayed his impressive collection of delicate and brutish surgical instruments with pride. He laid them in lines, on a stainless-steel tray covered in a blue surgical towel. Over the years I witnessed many trays of instruments clang and clatter across the tiled floor when rookie police officers knocked them over in their haste to escape before vomiting or fainting in front of their colleagues.

Mo, a man of few words, left me to my thoughts. I never needed to force conversation in his presence. I left him to his work while we waited for the lab sergeant, the investigating officers and the pathologist to arrive. When Mo left the exam room, I walked around slowly and looked at each of the pale naked bodies on the sturdy silver gurneys. I felt no fear. I felt no revulsion. I felt no sadness. A tranquil atmosphere filled the air. *Something was missing. Their shells remained but their essence had vanished.*

Male, Aged 43, Unlawful Killing

London-born Thomas Bowen, a 43-year-old resident of Australia, was the first post-mortem (PM) I ever photographed. Although I'd known what to expect before I attended my first forensic post-mortem, and had seen thousands of post-mortem photographs, it was the overpowering smell of the mortuary, a vile blend of death, decomposition and disinfectant, that was a punch to the guts. No photographs or words can capture the unexpected sensory element. An especially gruesome first PM added to the stress of that day. A jolt of nausea shot through me when the mortician brought Thomas's body into the autopsy suite. But with a quick dash outside for some fresh air, to gather my emotions and quell the powerful urge to vomit, or make a run for it, I managed to make it through my first PM without fainting or vomiting, and I never looked back. Don't get me wrong, forensic post-mortems take a lot of getting used to, no matter how strong a stomach you may have. They can be extremely smelly, bloody and gory and they can take up to twelve hours or more to complete, in some cases.

My job that day was to photograph Thomas's forensic post-mortem to document the injuries, both external and internal, his killers had inflicted upon him. Thugs had killed him during a summer holiday visit to his parents in London. Out for a drive on a sunny June day, Thomas, in a rental vehicle, was driving through a neighbourhood in East London. His elderly parents followed in their vehicle behind him, with his father at the wheel. Three youths drove his parents' car off the road after a trivial driving dispute escalated into road rage. When both vehicles stopped at a traffic light, the youths jumped out of their car to intimidate the elderly driver. Thomas saw the argument in his rear-view mirror and stopped his vehicle. He ran back to help his father. But the youths, in their twenties, turned on him, and threw him under the wheels of an oncoming 32-ton juggernaut, while his parents watched in horror. Thomas died at the scene. The youths sped away, abandoning their stolen vehicle nearby.

When Thomas's body arrived at the mortuary, Mo weighed and measured him, noted his general state of health and characteristics, and then wheeled him into the autopsy room. Still in a white plastic body sheet, the mortician laid him on the floor on a metal gurney. It's challenging to photograph an average-sized human being from ground level, so I photographed him on the floor for the full-length clothed shots. Some mortuaries had a step ladder, to give the photographer a higher viewpoint, but in most cases a fully extended tripod had to suffice. The lab sergeant then opened the body sheet and I took shots of Thomas, fully clothed, front and back, still with his head and hands covered in plastic bags. At many homicide scenes, the SOCO or lab sergeant will cover the hands and head of the decedent, with plastic or paper bags, sealed around the neck and the wrists. While this is not a pleasant procedure to witness, it's necessary to protect and preserve evidence that might dislodge when undertakers remove the body from the scene.

The lab sergeant then examined the body sheet to confirm that no evidence had dislodged from Thomas's body or clothing during transportation to the mortuary. Torn off buttons, broken fingernails, bullets, teeth, the tip of a knife blade, paint chips, soil, gravel, wood splinters or other debris have been known to dislodge from a victim's body or clothing and end up in the body sheet or body bag, so it's critical not to miss anything. The mortician and lab sergeant lifted Thomas off the sheet and onto the autopsy examination table and the lab sergeant removed the plastic bags from Thomas's head and hands.

To simplify matters, there are basically two main parts to a forensic post-mortem. The external examination of the body, clothed and unclothed, during which time several hair samples and swabs are taken from all orifices, and body temperature is also taken. A note is made of the degree of rigor and state of decomposition and general state of the body. Underneath the decedent's fingernails are scraped, then the nails are cut and bagged as evidence. Scrapings from under a victim's fingernails often provide a rich source of evidence for investigators. I never liked watching a decedent having their fingernails cut with scissors. Somehow, I imagined the lab sergeant would accidentally catch Thomas's skin and cause him pain. Involuntarily I clenched my fingers into fists at the thought while I watched. I squirmed more about this, and watching the pathologist use a syringe to remove the vitreous fluid from a decedent's eyes (as they did back in the day, to help gauge the post-mortem interval, (PMI: the time between death and the discovery/examination of the body), than I did watching much more gory aspects of post-mortems, like first incisions and the evisceration of organs in a block, or removal of the tongue.

The second stage of the PM is when the dissection begins. Forensic pathologists dissect cadavers with the precision of a surgeon, contrary to what people might imagine. It starts with a Y incision that runs from behind both ears down the middle of the chest to the pubic bone. This body length opening facilitates the internal examination of the body, once the rib cage breast plate is taken off. During the internal examination, blood, urine and stomach contents are all retrieved systematically and the organs are removed for weighing and detailed examination, and samples from each retained. The skull is also opened to reveal and remove the brain.

The pathologist examined Thomas's clothing methodically for any tiny paint chips, vehicle carpet fibres or clothing fibres, broken fingernails, or other foreign objects from Thomas's killers, or their vehicle, that would link the suspects to Thomas. I took shots of any findings as the autopsy progressed. All the while, the pathologist dictated his notes into a microphone hanging above the autopsy table. He searched Thomas's pockets for a wallet etc. I photographed these items and the lab sergeant bagged them as evidence. Identifying the victim quickly is of paramount importance in a suspicious death or murder investigation. On this occasion, sadly Thomas's parents were witnesses to his death, so we had no ID issues.

He then examined Thomas's hair and head, looking and feeling for any skull depressions, or wounds to the skull or face, and any items of evidence that might have lodged in Thomas's hair, mouth, nose, or ears. This can be challenging if the victim's face or skull has suffered considerable damage, as in Thomas's case. The pathologist or mortician shaves the hair surrounding any head injury that's discovered on a decedent, so the injury can be seen clearly in the photographs. The pathologist noted Thomas's injuries and I photographed anything needed during the slow and lengthy examination.

Those who've never been to a forensic PM might imagine that the forensic pathologist would take their own photographs. In the MPS district they don't. The pathologist's expertise is not in photography, and specialist photography at that. The pathologist is an expert focused on discovering the manner of death, the cause of death and the identity of the decedent. The photographs of the autopsy are as critical to the case as the crime scene photographs, so it's imperative they are of the highest quality. If the photographs are substandard in any way, this may cause issues for the pathologist when they give evidence in court. An expert who has photographed hundreds or thousands of autopsies will produce results that a forensic pathologist is unlikely to attain taking their own photographs. During an autopsy the pathologist is elbow deep in blood and viscera, and is wearing two pairs of latex gloves, arm protector sleeves etc. It's a messy business, eviscerating an adult human being. If they took their own photographs, they'd need to de-glove every time they took a photograph, and re-glove after they'd taken a few shots. This would make an already time-consuming process untenable for busy pathologists, in a large metropolis like London. This arrangement would not suit investigation teams waiting for a pathologist's report. The pathologists expect high-quality crime scene photographs and PM photographs to assist them during their report writing on each case. They study the photographs in detail. A fast turnaround of quality prints (or digital images) is necessary to enable them to write their report and present their findings to the investigative team in a timely manner.

After the mortician removed Thomas's clothes, I took photographs of his naked body, front and back. The pathologist then began his external examination, starting at Thomas's head and working down his body to the feet. Every centimetre of skin was methodically checked for bruises, scars, needle puncture marks, any injury or tattoo. Nothing can be missed. Every injury to the body is carefully measured and photographed with scale tape to show extent and depth of the injury. Precise measurements from a fixed point are incredibly important in homicide cases. I won't elaborate on the horrifying injuries Thomas sustained in the attack. It was a gory and bloody sight and not easily forgotten.

A forensic pathologist's work begins at the crime scene, not at the mortuary as you might think. Ideally, they should visit the scene and examine the body in situ, before it's moved or disturbed in any way. The pathologist's visit to the crime scene is a critical part of their work. The scene tells them the story of what happened. A scene visit helps to better explain their findings at autopsy. At a scene, the pathologist notes the position of the body, any weapons, blood spatter etc. They take the decedent's body temperature, either rectally or via a small incision through which they place a steel thermometer into the decedent's liver. They take the ambient temperature at the scene, to help establish time of death.

The pathologist, like the forensic photographer, is one of the few people allowed beyond the crime scene tape.

At most of my scenes, the pathologists dictated notes into a small recording device while they examined the deceased, as I stood in silence next to them. Notes made on scene, with the body in situ, help the pathologist enormously when they pair these with the scene and the autopsy photographs. Once the pathologist completes their scene examination, they permit the body's removal to the mortuary for further forensic examination. Ultimately the undertakers deliver the body to the nearest public mortuary where the pathologist conducts a forensic post-mortem. In the case of murder or suspicious deaths, the pathologist generally preferred to conduct the PM directly after the scene visit. All suspicious, unexpected, or unnatural deaths, e.g. homicide, suicide or accidents necessitate a legal investigation and the forensic post-mortem is a critical piece of the evidence-gathering process.

In England and Wales forensic pathology is a service provided to the police and coroners to assist in the investigation of homicides or suspicious deaths. Unlike in some other countries, Home Office-registered forensic pathologists are *independent of the police,* coroners and the Home Office. They are self-employed or employed within a group practice, or employed by a university hospital or hospital trust. Forensic pathologists are on call for crime scene visits 24/7/365. In the MPS, we were fortunate to have them available to us regularly, because they were based in the city, at one of the major hospitals.

In time, I became accustomed to the sights and smells of London's public mortuaries. Most Monday mornings

I'd drive straight to the mortuary, spending all day there photographing several forensic post-mortems of the victims of suspicious deaths and murders that had happened over the weekend. Although initially I dreaded mortuary Mondays, in time I found the process an extraordinary learning experience. With only a small group of Home Office forensic pathologists serving the London Metropolitan police district, I soon got to know each of them well. Working closely together at scenes, and then at the mortuary, most enthusiastically pointed out interesting or unusual findings to me while we worked side by side for hours, sometimes only the two of us and the mortician, in the autopsy suite, detectives having hastily dispersed before the pathologist's scalpel made the first incision.

At the trial, a year after Thomas's unlawful killing, his heartbroken mother testified that she saw the three men deliberately throw her son to his death under the wheels of the juggernaut. She tearfully told the court that she could not understand why it had happened. She said she woke at night with the same nightmare in which she saw the scene of Thomas's violent death play out over and over. No parent should ever have to witness thugs throw their son to his death under the wheels of a juggernaut. Ultimately, a jury cleared the three men of Thomas's unlawful killing. To this day, I will never understand how those three killers walked free after committing such a heinous and horrific crime. Neither Thomas nor his family received the justice they deserved.

* * *

Although there was no such thing as a typical week for a police photographer on scenes of crime duty in London, Mondays were busy days for the team at the public mortuaries across London. Forensic post-mortems can take anywhere between seven to twelve hours to complete, so I smelled revolting by the time the day was over. The smells of the mortuary clung to my hair, my clothes and my camera equipment. Before attending another scene, I asked to go home and take a quick shower. But it was not always possible. One day, after spending the morning at the mortuary, I drove to the forensic science lab to drop off an item to the SCU. By lunchtime I was ravenous, so I went to the canteen for lunch. By then, I'd forgotten how badly I smelled. I'd become accustomed to the smell and no longer noticed it. The lab canteen bustled with activity. Scientists and police officers stood in the long queue. I joined them and waited with my tray. Soon people shot me strange looks. Those ahead of me turned round and sniffed the air like a cadaver dog, trying to discover where the foul smell was coming from. At first, I didn't register, but when people behind me left a big gap between us, realisation dawned. It was me they were smelling and moving away from. They knew that smell from the scenes they'd attended. The smell of death and decomposition is unique. It's not easily forgotten, once you've smelled it once. I tried not to laugh. I silently acknowledged my apology with a head nod and a smile. A shrugged shoulder told them, I'm hungry and I'm not leaving until I'm fed. Sorry about the smell. Often it wasn't possible to go home for a shower. So, the next people I met had to suffer the putrid smell when I visited their police station or their home. Sometimes, it couldn't be helped.

Never Throw an Ornament at Your Husband

Life at the mortuary wasn't all grim and gruesomeness. I have many tragic but humorous tales from London's mortuaries. One such tale happened at Redcliff mortuary.

It's hard to imagine that a person could find themselves on a mortuary slab because someone hit them on the head with a small ornament, the kind you might find on a mantelpiece in your granny's home. In one case I photographed, a woman threw an ornament at her husband during an argument and he died from a brain bleed after the fight. At the PM we discovered he had an unusually thin eggshell-skull. The minute the pathologist said that, I had a vision of a cheap Easter egg, a thin one, not a luxury Easter egg that was thick and hard to crack. I shook off the image. The suspect had an argument with her husband and it escalated. She had no intention of killing him, and yet she did. In the heat of an argument, she grabbed a small ornament from the mantelpiece and threw it at her husband with some force. It hit its target and injured him, much to her surprise. They calmed down and thought nothing more of it, and they forgot about his head injury. But later that day he took a turn for the worse. His head injury had caused a bleed in his brain and he died.

During that PM the doorbell rang. With only three of us at the mortuary, and the forensic pathologist and mortician both fully occupied, I offered to answer the door. When I opened it, I found a nervous-looking man standing back from the doorstep. With eyes wide and a suspicious look on his face, he told me he was an electrician. He'd come to repair a light fitting on the front exterior wall of the mortuary. The quickest way to the light fixture was through the mortuary to the other side of the building. So, I invited him in. But he refused to set foot inside the mortuary. I reassured him there was nothing to see and nothing to fear. No matter what I said, I could not convince him to step over the threshold. He was adamant. In the end I asked him to come back later when the mortician was free to help him. He seemed to fear that somehow death would rub off on him. And if he came into the mortuary, he might never leave. I smiled when I shut the door and went back to work in the autopsy room. The pathologist and the mortician laughed when I shared the story. I suspect he never returned to the mortuary and that light fitting remained broken. But the lesson that day was, never throw an ornament at your spouse or partner, or anything else for that matter. It never ends well. And it's not worth the heartache.

5

Men Killing Women

Once Was Not Enough

'Her mother found her,' Geoff said, with a heavy sigh, his face taut with disgust. Detective Chief Superintendent Geoff Scott and I had worked together on many murders over the years. He was a bear of a man with a pot belly and a tender heart. I liked him. Geoff and I talked about the case, in hushed tones, while we waited outside the scene for the fire service to arrive. Early on that cold November morning, clouds, black and brewing, rolled across a darkening sky.

The crowd of onlookers grew when the fire engine arrived. The red-and-silver rig, big as a railway carriage, dwarfed the cars parked in the narrow road of red-bricked houses. The throbbing growl of the diesel engine vibrated everything in its path. High-pitched hydraulics hissed as sleeping ladders awoke. A radio squawked from its cab. A cacophony of sound crashed around in the quiet of a stunned silent street.

Haggard women in slippers smoked furiously while they whispered with shocked neighbours. Others stretched their flimsy cardigans tightly across their chests. Hands hidden under armpits; shoulders hunched high in self-protection. Shivering in the cold, but unwilling to leave, their pale anxious faces stared at me from beyond the crime scene tape. Rumours rippled through the restless crowd. Old and young, confused and concerned, their worried faces pleaded for answers. *Were they safe? Were their children safe? Who could have done this? Would they be next?*

Bloody footprints, visible on the bare wooden stair treads, told a harrowing tale of the victim's last movements. With only one way in to the two-storey house, and to protect this vital blood evidence, myself and the forensic team entered the flat through an upstairs kitchen window via a fire ladder bucket. The fire crew positioned the rig effortlessly. With the flick of a switch, four outriggers extended to stabilise the unit. Soon we heard a shout from the fire officer in charge. 'We're ready when you are. Who's first? Either of you afraid of heights?' he asked. We shook our heads no. He motioned to us to climb on board the rig. Jim, the lab sergeant, went first, and I followed. With Jim on the platform, the telescopic ladder glided upwards while I watched. The bucket stopped next to the kitchen window ledge, about 24 feet off the ground. With a little help from the officer on the platform, Jim's bulk disappeared through the open window. He laid down a set of aluminium stepping plates to build a bridge across the blood-stained kitchen floor. This allowed us to do a walk through, without destroying any evidence where the perpetrator or victim had walked.

The fire engine bucket vibrated from side to side while I watched it descend and come to a halt. I stepped on board. Through the mesh floor and open railed platform, I could see into the distance above the rooftops, and the curious crowd gathered below. I'd never entered a crime scene from the platform of a fire bucket before. Although I had no fear of heights, because I'd been flying regularly with the Air Support Unit, a fire engine bucket is a different experience altogether. My heart raced from a quick jolt of adrenaline, when the firefighter hoisted us up in the air. The rain pelted down on us, but it didn't deter the watching crowd. The fire officer helped me over the gap between the platform and the window ledge. I climbed through the small kitchen window and stepped down onto the plates Jim had set down for us. It was a challenge to try to climb through a window without touching the frame or the ledge, or allowing my clothing to brush against anything. I stood for a moment to catch my breath and steady myself before making my way across the foot plates on the blood-stained kitchen floor. Ahead of me, I could see Lorraine, partially clothed and lying face down on the landing. Her bloodstained feet pointed towards me. She lay right outside the threshold of the kitchen, blocking the pathway into the rest of the flat. Stepping over Lorraine's body, I joined Jim on the far side of the landing. At murder and suspicious death scenes, we sometimes had to step over decedents to access the rest of the scene. It never felt good. It felt disrespectful, but we had no alternative at many scenes.

Jim, a tall Scotsman of few words, with intelligent eyes and a crooked smile, had spent thousands of hours with me at crime scenes. We had an easy rapport. We walked through the scene to assess it forensically before I took photographs. Once we'd completed the walk through, Jim made himself scarce, and I began my work.

Before I shot a single photograph, I took time to absorb what the entire scene, and what the physical and trace evidence told me. Every scene spoke to me. I looked for anything odd or out of place or anything that didn't seem to belong. I ran through a list of questions in my head.

Were there signs of forced entry? No. With no splintered wood on the front door, no jemmy marks, no broken locks, no smashed windows, this told me Lorraine opened the door and probably knew her killer and had had no reason to distrust him. On the night Lorraine's killer struck, she'd been getting ready for a *girls' night out* with her mum and her friends. Her boyfriend, who shared the flat with her, had also gone out with his pals. When Lorraine didn't turn up, her mother phoned but got no answer. Worried about Lorraine, she went to Lorraine's flat, let herself in and found Lorraine's body.

Had it been a blitz attack? No. The evidence didn't indicate a blitz attack. I'd photographed many blitz attack murders over the years. These types of attacks are so sudden, so totally unexpected, that the killer takes the victim by surprise. The victim has no time to react, protect, or defend themselves. It's all over in seconds. Blitz attack murders, with either guns or knives or other sharp implements, often take place on a doorstep, the moment the unsuspecting victim opens the door to their killer or assailant.

Was it a burglary or a robbery? The killer had not stolen any valuables. The TV was still in place. He hadn't ransacked the flat looking for items to steal. Lorraine's handbag lay undisturbed on a chair in the living room, with her purse in full view. The motive wasn't robbery or burglary.

Did the killer leave trace evidence: shoemarks, a torn off button, a shred of clothing, fingernail fragments, skin or hair fibres, semen, vomit, blood or saliva? Yes. He'd struggled with Lorraine and raped her, so fibres from his clothing, his bodily fluids and his skin cells under her nails where she scratched at him during the attack were all evidence we collected.

Had there been a struggle? Yes. Lorraine's broken red fingernails lay scattered about the scene. They stood out against the beige carpet. I noticed them when I walked from room to room. To the untrained eye, these fragments of fingernails might have gone unnoticed in the deep piled carpet. To an experienced crime scene photographer, the message was clear. Lorraine had fought for her life, breaking off most of her fingernails during the ferocious struggle with her killer.

Did the killer bring a weapon to the scene or leave a weapon behind? Lorraine's killer used a large kitchen knife to kill her. The bloodstained knife appeared to fit the empty space in the knife block on her kitchen counter. We suspected Lorraine reached for the knife to ward off her killer's sexual advances when he became more threatening. Or Lorraine's killer grabbed the knife on impulse when she rejected his sexual advances. The fact that her killer had not brought a weapon to the scene suggested he had not planned her killing. Although there had been some degree of premeditation. Nobody else was home with Lorraine that night. He knew this, and took advantage of the opportunity to have her all to himself.

What did the choice of weapon tell me? A knife is a weapon that is an up close and personal weapon. You must be close to the victim to stab them that number of times. It's close contact cruelty, and infliction of pain, it's visceral, unlike a gun. It suggests a personal connection with the victim. Stabbing Lorraine and cutting her throat told me her killer had some emotional connection to her. When she refused his sexual advances, he flew into a rage. Stabbing Lorraine more than 48 times demonstrated overkill in this sexually motivated killing. It showed the killer's attempt to dominate Lorraine, and his desire for her destruction and obliteration. Stabbing someone and cutting their throat is a rage-filled personal way of killing another human being.

Was this a sexually motivated killing? Yes. What did Lorraine's body tell me? Her partially clothed body lay face down on the landing. Her killer had stabbed her dozens of times and cut her throat. He had inflicted *overkill* injuries on Lorraine that went far beyond those necessary to kill her. The evidence of overkill in this sexually motivated killing was clear. The level of cruelty her killer demonstrated by stabbing Lorraine so many times showed his need for possession, to have dominance, power and complete control over her. The number of injuries, their distribution and the type of weapon used to inflict wounds provides a great deal of information with respect to the killer's motivation and relationship to the victim. Judging by the disarray of Lorraine's clothing, it strongly suggested her killer had raped or sexually assaulted her. The decedent in every homicide case is a rich source of evidence, and at a scene I always spent a lot of time with the body, making sure I missed nothing in my photographs.

Meticulous examination of her clothing was critical, as items of clothing may provide valuable forensic evidence and may also offer clues to the killer's motivation. Whether the victim's clothing is damaged or in disarray may provide clues to the motive for the murder. The victim's clothing, or lack of, also gives investigators an indication of what the victim was doing prior to their death. In some of my sexually motivated murder cases, killers staged the female victim. They left clothing pulled over the victim's head to reveal their bare breasts, or pulled down the decedent's clothing to their knees or ankles to expose their genitals. Sometimes the killer removed lower garments completely, and left the victim with legs splayed. It added insult to injury. It's a vile and chilling sight to witness, especially as a woman. The killer telegraphs his contempt and misogyny through his final efforts to degrade his female victims in death.

The blood trail of bare feet told the horrific tale of Lorraine's final movements. I walked down the bare wooden steps towards the front door, shining my torch on each step. Each tread had bloody footprints on them. Each footprint led down the stairs. Bleeding profusely and unable to shout for help or use the phone because of her throat injuries, she bravely made it down the stairs to leave the flat to find help. Her bloody footprints told me she was upright when she went down the stairs. When I reached the halfway point on the staircase, I noticed an odd pattern in the footprints. They ended behind the front door and we already knew there were none outside the front door. The direction of the footprints changed. They turned round and went back up the stairs. Her footprints were almost solid blood, like she'd stepped into a tray of dark red paint and walked it all over the stairs. I'd never seen anything like it before. Suddenly the horror dawned on me. I knew what had happened. When Lorraine's killer fled, she struggled courageously to stay alive. Despite her horrifying injuries and her enormous blood loss, she had a strong will to live. But when she opened the front door, her killer was standing right in front of her, and confronted her yet again. Although he'd left the scene, he decided to return to make sure he'd killed Lorraine, so she could not identify him.

A chill ran through me at the thought of this happening to her. Standing in the tiny space behind the door I could feel her shock and horror when she saw her killer's face again. Once was not enough to terrorise her. Once was not enough to rape and humiliate her. Once was not enough to finish her off. And she was so close to reaching safety and help. She'd fought in vain to push the door closed against him, to keep him out. But in her weakened state he'd overpowered her and chased her up the stairs. She'd run into the back bedroom to hide from him, but he caught her. Then he began his second assault on her. This time he intended to finish the rape he hadn't managed on his first attempt. He pushed her onto the bed. The blood patterns told the cruel tale. But during her battle to fend him off they fell onto the bedroom floor. The assault and the savagery continued.

Her killer fled and Lorraine collapsed on the landing and lay dying, alone.

I wanted to tell the story of her courage and her will to survive, despite the most brutal of assaults. I've never forgotten Lorraine. I've never forgotten her courage. I've never forgotten how close she came to getting the help she so desperately wanted. It was heartbreaking to read the story of her last moments in her own bloody footprints.

Police caught Lorraine's killer not long after her death. He was a friend of Lorraine's boyfriend and he knew she would be alone that night, because her boyfriend had told him he was going out with friends. He went to see Lorraine to make his move, but he'd flown into a rage when she rejected his advances and he stabbed her in a frenzy of anger. He received an eight-year sentence for Lorraine's savage and brutal killing. One of the reasons behind this lenient sentence was that he had not brought a weapon to the scene, but used a weapon he found at the scene. If he'd brought a weapon to the scene, his starting minimum term sentence would likely have been considerably higher. He probably only served four years and was released on parole. His lenient sentence disgusted me. A wholly inadequate sentence for such a violent and despicable crime. Yet another man, who killed a woman in his twenties, set free to kill again. Not on any offenders' register. Nobody keeping track of him. And I've no doubt he went on to coercively control, abuse, rape and kill other women, after taking Lorraine's life.

This was a case that made me ask why I bothered. If men could rape and kill and terrorise women with impunity, and receive such a lenient sentence, it was a slap in the face for all of us who worked so hard to fight for justice for Lorraine. It was an insult to her family. An eight-year prison sentence for stabbing a woman 48 times, for cutting her throat, for attempting to rape her and returning to the scene to attempt the rape a second time, and inflicting more terror and injuries on her. Lorraine did not receive the justice she deserved. This case secured in my mind the fact that women's lives don't matter. That day, the level of anger at the scene was palpable. Friends and neighbours wanted to find Lorraine's killer, to mete out some justice of their own. Police hoped to find him before the locals did. Fortunately for him, they did. Lorraine's brutal killing never even made the newspapers, like so many of the so-called *domestic homicides* I'd photographed.

In the years since Lorraine's vicious killing, men have done little to prevent male violence against women and girls. They barely acknowledge that if men are perpetrating this violence against women (and against boys and men), that it's the men with the problem. Men claim it's *not all men* who are sexually harassing, raping and murdering women, and they also claim not to know any perpetrators. It doesn't add up. Recent crime statistics show that between April 2020 and March 2021, 177 women were murdered in England and Wales. Of those, men murdered 109, 10 were killed by a woman, and in 58 cases the suspect was unknown. Since 2020 sex-based violence against women and girls (femicide) has reached epidemic proportions around the world. A recent UN (2022) report stated that an estimated 81,000 women and girls, around the world, were intentionally killed in

2021. Of those women and girls killed in 2021, 45,000 were killed by their intimate (mostly male) partners. On average more than five women and girls are murdered every hour, by someone in their own family.

Where is the outrage by men? The silence is deafening. Men need to step up and examine the complex causes of this widespread problem. They need to self-reflect on their own behaviours. They need to take ownership of it, and do better. Up to now women and organisations run by women, have fought the good fight. Most recently a campaign called Killed Women was founded by two mothers whose daughters were murdered by their male partners. The burden to effect change in the criminal justice system should not be carried by these families who are already suffering extraordinary pain at the loss of their loved ones. As Dr Jackson Katz said in his TED talk about violence against women, 'it is a men's issue. And we need "more than a few good men" to end the cycle of violence against women.' He is not wrong.

* * *

'How did you find relief from what you saw, after a day attending murder scenes or other distressing incidents,' Sarah, my therapist, asks.

'The average person arrives home and shouts into the house from the hallway, as they kick off their shoes, "Hi sweetie, I'm home," or some version of that. And the response from their partner might go something like, "Hey, how was your day? Are you hungry?" and the usual reply might be, "Oh the traffic was slow; my boss was being a nightmare and the photocopier broke down. How about you?" That's where it gets tricky for a police photographer. Imagine blurting out the horrors of the day to your partner over dinner – it might go something like this: "Oh, it wasn't too bad, it started with a gangland killing. Some bloke got his head shot off when he opened his front door. The force of the double-barrel shotgun blast decapitated him, and his brains and teeth splattered all over the hallway. After that scene, I went to photograph a 92-year-old woman in hospital. A giant brute of a man had raped and beaten her. He'd only been released from prison days before the attack. And then I went to photograph . . ." Well, you get the point.

'How do you think the average person would respond to hearing these stories while they're eating their dinner?

'Probably not good dinner conversation,' I continue before she has a chance to answer.

I wanted to go home and not dwell on it, because I needed the mental and physical respite from the grimness of the day. I didn't want to recall, ad nauseam, what I'd seen each day, because I knew it would start all over again the following day. I'd already lived through it once. I knew the murders would keep coming. The violence against women. The rage-filled hatred that took another's life for the most trivial and mundane of reasons. Every 30 seconds in London a crime is committed. We only photographed the most serious of those. More than 20,000 scenes to photograph each year. That's a lot to carry.

Sarah nods her understanding and encourages me to continue sharing.

'Why spread the horror? Why inflict these grim tales on those we love? Why clutter their minds with horrific scenes? Then they must carry them, like I carry them. And not only that, a police photographer's work is highly confidential. Speaking about cases while they are still active could have caused a prosecution to fail, or provided an advantage to the killer if information about the scene, that police had withheld from the public, was revealed inadvertently.

'So, it left you with a heavy burden to carry, alone,' she says, as she studies me and waits for my reply.

'Yes, I suppose it did. It's a lonely place. It's only other police photographers, police officers, ER nurses and doctors, forensic pathologists, CSIs and paramedics who have any idea what you've seen and experienced. So naturally you gravitate to those people for your friendships and relationships, which I suppose cuts you off from the *other outside world* in a way. There was my grim London, and another London where people were rarely exposed to such horror, cruelty and rage-filled violence. I'm glad about that.'

'Tell me more about that,' Sarah asks.

'Often, after I'd attended a night of horrific murder scenes, I would stop at a lake in my division.'

Silence in the early hours of the morning. The streets feel different, like the city's been abandoned. The hum of traffic has disappeared, the jets are quiet. London sleeps, after a fashion. Trains rattle and squeal in the distance, like ghosts clanking their chains, haunting the night. Then the dawn chorus, my early morning symphony. Incongruous sounds of life and nature, the sun rising as it always does, oblivious to the pain and suffering I've witnessed and photographed. Life goes on, no matter what. Day follows night and the mood of the night is hard to shift.

'I'd take my camera and tripod out of my van to shoot photographs of the white rowing boats that floated and creaked on the lake in the dawn mist that rose off the water. Although exhausted, I sat on the bonnet of my van, alone in the silence, and felt relieved that those who were still sleeping soundly had no idea of the horror I had spent the entire night photographing. Somehow, photographing the beauty of the lake and the boats at dawn felt like an antidote to the grimness, the violence and darkness of the night before.'

'What do you think the darkness takes from you?' she asks, when my eyes fill with tears.

To Love, Honour and Decapitate

Often male violence against women involves more than one individual. The controversial term 'Honour Killing' describes the murders, primarily of women, who have allegedly brought shame or dishonour on their families. These so-called 'Honour Killings' differ from other domestic murders in several ways. But there is *no honour* in honour killings. Multiple family members conspire and plan these honour killings, at a family meeting. Both male and female family members are usually involved. Prior to the killing they may threaten the intended victim with death, numerous times, if they believe a daughter (and occasionally a son) has dishonoured their family. Family members are complicit in the murder and they may include the victim's father, mother, brothers, sisters, cousins and uncles. Perpetrators of these heinous torture, rape and murder crimes often face no backlash from their families or communities. On the contrary, families and communities often consider these murders justifiable and praise and celebrate the actions of the perpetrators. Over the years I photographed many honour killings, but one stood out in my memory.

St Jude's Tower, a 21-storey block of council flats, on the notorious Brookvale Estate, in Northeast London, loomed out of the darkness, towering over the two-storey houses surrounding it. A brutal-looking concrete edifice, with piss-smelling stairwells that a cold wind whipped around, even in summer, it was one of three drab high-rise towers I visited often, to photograph murders, suspicious deaths, arsons, gang killings, rapes, shootings and suicides. Faded ribbons of blue-and-white crime scene tape, torn hastily from lamp posts, fluttered in the wind; evidence of repeated police presence on the estate.

Built in the early 1960s, St Anne's Tower, St Jude's Tower and St George's Tower, each containing 120 flats, dominated the skyline and dwarfed the twenty-three low-rise blocks in their orbit. During daylight hours the Brookvale Estate, the size of a small English town, with five thousand residents, was almost as treacherous as it was at night, but for different reasons. Residents threw things at us from their balconies – once a toilet pot came crashing down not far from where I'd parked – when they recognised my white unmarked police photographer's van arrive on their territory. The duty officer warned us all, 'Never park close to the base of the towers, or a flying fridge could land on you.' People would throw anything they could lay their hands on at the police, including flowerpots, microwaves, toilet tanks and, yes, even fridges. At night the Brookvale Estate was a no-go area for police personnel working alone. The duty officer had warned me when I took his call to attend this homicide. 'Be careful, and call for a police escort when you reach the scene. Don't exit your van until they come to meet you,' he said. I heeded his warnings. He did not give them lightly. He'd worked London's treacherous and violent council estates for years. He knew the dangers. And so did I.

Light rain fell while I drove into the car park of St Jude's Tower. The concrete monster, with dozens of square yellow eyes, stared down at me. At 2 a.m., the deserted slick streets shone in the rain under orange lamp lights. The drug dealing gangs had called it a night. I radioed officers on scene, to request an escort to the scene on the eighteenth floor. It didn't take long for two uniformed officers to find me. The three of us dashed across the car park to avoid a soaking.

I put on a pair of latex gloves before I entered the lift, out of habit. I instinctively held my breath for the duration of the ride up to the eighteenth floor in the piss- and alcohol-smelling lift. I never put my camera gear, or tripod, down on a lift floor in a council estate, no matter how heavy it was, or how tired I felt. I never leaned against the vandal-proof silver walls, to avoid getting infected or contaminating my clothes or hair. Residents sprayed the lifts with chunks of vomit in the corners, or left bloodstains on the doors and walls, or urinated on their journey home from a night of heavy drinking. In some, residents smeared the lift walls with excrement, both animal and human, or hocked a loogie on the lift buttons for a laugh. I never understood why people behaved this way in their own lifts, in their own homes. But they did. Alcohol abuse and drugs played a big part in this anti-social behaviour. For the decent people who lived in these estates, who could not afford housing elsewhere, their lives were plagued with misery. The council allowed these estates to fall into disrepair. Residents, desperate for a move from their black mouldy ceilings and water-stained walls, set fire to their flats in the vain hope of a council approved move to another location. I photographed dozens of these arsons over the years, some that sadly turned fatal. When residents weren't battling black mould and tea-stained leaks dripping down their walls, they were running the gauntlet with drug gangs, often children and teenagers, who terrorised them on their daily trips to and from their flats, just for the fun of it. Thugs robbed residents at knifepoint in the dark concrete detritus-filled stairwells, where they'd smashed the light fixtures to gain an advantage on the unsuspecting victim who walked into their dark trap.

In the dingy hallway outside the flat, officers told me what they knew about the victim and occupant who lived there with her three young children. In her late twenties, and estranged from her husband, she shared custody of the children with him. After she took out an injunction against him for his violent behaviour, a court still permitted him to visit the children at the flat on weekends. It was during one of these visits that he killed her.

I changed into my crime scene gear and did a walk through while I waited for the lab sergeant to arrive. The victim lay on the bloodstained carpeted bedroom floor in the dark. I shone my torch around the room and over her body. The blood-soaked knife used to kill her lay beside her body next to the bed which sat directly on the floor, because it had no legs attached. Lying on her back in the tiny room, I could tell she'd fought courageously for her life, judging by the defence injuries on her body. I thought about her three children, who were in the flat when their father killed their mother in front of them.

He had severed her head, almost completely. Through the gaping neck wound I could see her spinal column, which was all that attached her head to her body. Judging by the savagery of her neck wounds, I got the impression he had tried hard to remove her head; to take it with him as a trophy. He had also stabbed her several times in her neck and in her stomach. I tried to comprehend the strength and rage it must have taken to inflict such injuries while I stood in the doorway looking at the victim's body. From the eighteenth-floor window of the small bedroom, I could see the lights of London shimmering in the distance. The silence and beauty of the nightscape a stark contrast to the horror of the brutal and gory scene before me.

It wasn't long before the lab sergeant arrived. He shouted in the doorway to me, and I spoke with him while he kitted up. I filled him in on what we knew and I got to work. I photographed the entire flat and paid particular attention to the bedroom where the victim lay, and to the kitchen, where the killer had taken the weapon from a kitchen drawer that stood partially open. You rarely see police photographers on TV dramas photographing much more than the body. Protocol dictated that at every scene I attended, I photographed every room in the scene, not only the room where the victim lay. A fight or argument might begin in another room, and spill over to where the victim ends up lying dead. After the fact, detectives interviewing suspects might discover relevant evidence located in another room in the flat, but they may not discover this until later in the investigation. By photographing the entire flat, evidence or potential evidence in every room is available to investigators.

Compared to other suspicious death scenes I'd attended, it didn't take long to photograph, including all the standard shots of the victim, close-ups of her face, her throat wound and stab wounds to her body, and the position of the weapon. In most of the flat there were no signs of a struggle. It appeared that the victim had run from another part of the flat, into the small bedroom, to escape her attacker, but he'd overpowered her and pushed his way into the bedroom where he trapped her and began his violent onslaught.

Once I'd finished my initial shots, the lab sergeant began his work while I waited nearby, in case he needed additional photographs. While we worked together, officers updated us on the door-to-door enquiries in the block; the whereabouts of the victim's husband; and other information they'd discovered from neighbours and relatives.

The victim and her husband were both Muslims and had an arranged marriage. Born and raised in Pakistan, and a devout Muslim, the victim's husband rigidly observed his culture's patriarchal and feudal traditions. He adhered to these cultural norms in his everyday life. By contrast, his wife, born and raised in Birmingham, to a Pakistani family, didn't observe the same traditions her husband observed. This appeared to be a source of conflict in their marriage. Although living separately, with a divorce pending, her husband became enraged when he discovered his estranged wife had started dating other men.

After killing her, he took their three young children to the home of one of his relatives and boasted about killing his wife to friends and family members. He claimed his wife had brought shame on him and dishonour to his family. He told relatives that he'd killed his wife to restore his and his family's honour.

This was the first honour killing I photographed in my career, but sadly not the last. A court sentenced him to six years in jail for brutally killing his wife. Yet another lenient sentence for a despicable crime. And sadly, these crimes continue worldwide, to this day, with impunity.

* * *

'When the nightmares come, they're always the same,' I tell Sarah. In the early days of therapy, the drowning nightmares were the most common, but as time went by, the nightmare that came most often was the one where I'm at a scene in a strange place. A different place each time. But in every dream, someone has been badly hurt, shot, or stabbed or thrown off a roof. I run to help them, and a crowd gathers. I shout to the bystanders to *call an ambulance*, and *someone bring me a blanket* and things like that. But nobody moves. The crowd stands and stares, as if they can't hear or see me. I shout louder, in a frantic tone, *call an ambulance*, but still nothing happens. I know that without immediate help the person will die, and yet nobody helps me. It's at that frantic moment that I wake up, breathless, heart racing and sometimes it's the sound of my own sobbing that wakes me up.

'What do you think the nightmares mean?' Sarah asks gently.

'I'm not sure,' I reply. Sarah sits patiently as I contemplate my answer. 'I suppose I'm finally expressing my thoughts and feelings through writing my book, and talking with you, so I'm no longer repressing them. When I think about it, the police photographer always arrives when it's too late to save a life, but often quite quickly after death. Maybe that's why I dream about trying to save people. Maybe it's a response to seeing so much death, that I had no control over. Maybe it's a kind of *putting it right* in my dreams.

'What do you think is the significance of the crowd of onlookers who won't help you?' Sarah asks.

'I don't know,' I say, while I consider her question. She sits calmly in silence and waits for my response.

'At so many scenes I attended, neighbours and people nearby heard the victim's screams while they were being killed, but nobody did anything about it. They never called the police. They never went to help the victim. They turned up the sound on their TVs and didn't want to become involved,' I said.

'How did that make you feel?' she asks.

'It made me so angry,' I say.

'Tell me more about that,' she asks.

'Because people could have saved a life and they didn't,' I reply.

'Once I went to a homicide scene at a six-storey block of council flats. The kind where the front doors of the flats open onto landings facing into a courtyard on three sides, in a U-shape. Sounds echo around those flats and the wind whistles up through the stairwells. There was always a dog barking in the distance, and the sound of police sirens wailing day and night. At this scene I photographed a woman whose boyfriend beat her to death with a motorbike chain. She screamed and screamed in terror and pain. She screamed for her life, yet nobody did a thing. Nobody called the police. Nobody went to her aid. Her screams echoed through the courtyard of the flats, and people heard her screams. I knew they did. Because they willingly told police officers this during the house-to-house enquiries.

'When I arrived at the scene, the residents stood in silence, on all six balconies, and stared, eerily, like a scene from a creepy movie. After I'd taken the photographs, I walked out of the scene, followed by the undertakers who carried the woman's body in a white body bag on a gurney. The residents had waited while I worked, and until we brought the body out,' I said, feeling my anger rising as I spoke.

'What really annoyed me was the fact that they never did a thing to save her life. *They listened to her murder.* Now they stood in silence when we walked past them to the waiting undertaker's van. I felt their shame. I wanted to scream at the top of my lungs at them, *Why the fuck didn't you do something to save this woman's life?* But I didn't. I walked past them and didn't look back. I couldn't bring myself to look at them, I was so disgusted. I knew at an intellectual level why they behaved the way they did. They lived in a vicious, cruel environment and they didn't want to risk their own lives to save the life of a stranger. I got that, but it didn't make it any easier to swallow.'

'Did this happen often?' Sarah asks.

'Sadly, yes. This wasn't the only case I photographed where neighbours or witnesses stood by and did nothing,' I reply. I think back to all the scenes where someone heard or saw someone murdering another human being and didn't call for help or intervene in any way.

'It happened more often than you might imagine,' I add.

'That must have felt frustrating for you and the detectives working the case.'

'Yes, it was. We were all doing our best to find justice for the victim and their family. But people would witness crimes and refuse to cooperate with detectives, or share any information during house-to-house enquiries. I found it shocking and inexcusable, because they deliberately deprived families and murder victims of the justice they deserved.'

6

No Monsters, Only Men

Prying Lenses

A factory owner discovered an abandoned vehicle containing the bodies of friends and roommates Olivia (29) and Anna (32). They had been dead for 36 hours when I arrived at the scene. Inside the car, the battered, partially clothed bodies of the two friends lay slumped. One victim, propped up in the front passenger seat, leaned against the door, her head resting on the window. The second victim sat slumped in the seat directly behind. Both women's eyes were open and stared vacantly into space. Because the body in the front passenger seat leaned on the door, we had to be careful when we opened it, to ensure we didn't lose any evidence, or allow the body to fall out of the vehicle. During that July, the city sweltered in a heatwave, so the victim's bodies had bloated and discoloured. A pungent smell wafted out of the vehicle when we opened the doors.

Women instinctively guard against the possibility of stranger danger. Fearful of a faceless evil man that lurks in the dark shadows of every street, every car park and every alleyway at night. And yet stranger murders are rare. Psychotic or sociopathic *monsters* kill only a small percentage of women on the streets of towns and cities. My experience photographing the murders of hundreds of women confirmed that women are more likely to find their killer in their own home, and their killer is more likely to have a familiar face.

Society counsels women to fear for their safety more in public places than in their own homes. Media coverage has saturated women's psyches with the monster myth. A belief that it's violent strangers, who prowl the streets waiting to strike at an opportune moment, who commit most murders. Stranger danger articles sell newspapers. They make good headlines. But they distract women's attention from the catalogue of carnage of domestic homicides and intimate partner violence happening daily around the world.

In the aftermath of homicide, news articles and broadcasters speculate on a litany of reasons why individuals commit murder. Killers are often labelled *beasts* or *monsters*. It's deeply unsettling for the average person to consider that the most ordinary of people are quite capable of committing the most sickening and extraordinary acts of savagery, cruelty and violence. Although the media label these perpetrators *beasts, animals, monstrous* or *monsters*, they're often unremarkable men when you come face to face with them. They look like your average guy next door. And that is the most frightening thing of all. You would not pick them out on the street.

* * *

When I stopped at the first set of traffic lights on the north side of Blackfriars Bridge, there was a loud bang. A crunch of metal and a squeal of tyres turned heads in my direction. The impact jolted me forwards in my seat. A man driving a red Ford estate car had run into the back of my unmarked police van. Although the accident was minor, protocol dictated I report it and follow police procedures. I cursed under my breath and grabbed my radio handset to call for a traffic unit to come to the crash scene. While speaking to the Met police dispatcher, the driver of the other vehicle jumped out of his car and marched towards me. He was a stocky little balding man in a white shirt, a grey cardigan and trousers that bunched up around his ankles. In my side mirror, I could see his mouth moving before I could hear what he was saying. The loud whoosh of passing rush hour traffic drowned him out. I knew by his scowling ruddy face that he'd be trouble. I stepped out of my van to speak with him.

'You stopped too suddenly,' he began accusingly, 'it's your fault I crashed into you,' he shouted, before I had a chance to say a single word. He continued blaming me for the accident. His adrenaline had kicked in, and his bluster soon turned to panic. 'My boss is going to kill me for crashing my new company car,' he said.

When I finally managed to interject, I calmly told him, 'You've run into the back of an unmarked Metropolitan Police vehicle.' I paused to let that sink in. He suddenly stopped shouting and grew visibly paler when the words registered in his mind. His demeanour changed immediately. I offered to call an ambulance for him. I told him I'd radioed for the police, who were on their way. Before he had a chance to say much more, two City of London police officers arrived, on lights and sirens. A traffic officer on a motorbike and one in a police car. The traffic officer, dressed in a high-viz yellow jacket, asked if I needed medical attention. I explained what had happened and identified myself as a Met Police photographer on my way to a double murder scene. The other officer took the little man aside to take his statement.

'I'll have to breathalyse you,' he said, 'but we'll send you on your way as fast as we can.'

'Blow into this mouthpiece until I tell you to stop,' came the instruction from the towering leather-clad traffic officer while he held the breathalyser to my mouth. While I stood blowing into the short white plastic tube, all I could think about was the murder scene that awaited me. While a police officer breathalysed me on the roadside, a detective chief superintendent, murder squad detectives, a lab sergeant and a forensic pathologist waited for me to arrive to photograph their scene. After what seemed like an eternity the officer told me my result was negative and I could go on my way. He was professional, understanding and gracious. In my rear-view mirror I could see the little man standing between two towering police officers, his mouth moving and hands gesturing wildly. Now he was *their* problem, not mine.

Paparazzi lenses peeked out of several windows above the crime scene. I couldn't believe it when I saw the lenses trained on the scene below. *How had nobody spotted the paps?* Someone had invited the press photographers into the offices above the scene before the police cordoned off the street. A phone call to the newspapers before a phone call to the police seemed the most likely explanation. People called the newspapers first, if they thought they could make a quick buck, with no consideration for the pain and misery their actions might cause the families and friends of the victims. I was livid to see the paps inside the crime scene cordon. 'Get those bastards and their cameras out of those windows and check to see if they've shot any film of our scene,' I instructed the uniformed officers. They dashed into the factory and frog marched the paps beyond the cordon. Then they moved the cordon further back to protect the scene from their prying lenses. But our scene was all over the news that night, and in the national newspapers the next day. Although the tabloid newspapers splashed photographs of myself and the female forensic pathologist across the front pages, fortunately they did not publish any photographs of the victims, to my great relief.

The crime scene was a small locked car, a boxy four-door sedan parked in a quiet side street in North London. On the left side of the road stood a group of low-rise industrial buildings, mostly small factories, and workshops with offices above. On the right side, a tree-lined ravine led down a steep overgrown embankment to two sets of railway tracks, invisible from street level. Tall dense trees pressed against the six-foot fence, topped with barbed wire to keep out intruders. The geography of the small North London street, cordoned off at both ends of the block, gave us a small measure of privacy for the work we needed to conduct at such a public scene.

Once police had ejected the press photographers from the building, we continued with our tasks. We had a traffic officer open the vehicle with a slim-jim, a 24-inch thin strip of metal used to unlock vehicle doors without a key or lock pick.

A murder scene in a vehicle is technically more challenging to photograph than a murder scene in a home or other premises, where there's more room to manoeuvre around the victims while in situ, without moving anything and destroying or damaging vital evidence. Although I knew either myself or a colleague would photograph the decedents at the mortuary, the scene photographs of the victims in situ were equally, if not more, important. It was imperative to photograph the exact position of each body, any obvious marks on the victims, and any potential murder weapon found in the vehicle. In the cramped quarters and with the pungent smell of decomposition and the heat of the day, it made for an uncomfortable situation. My heart broke to see two women so callously discarded, on public display. One of the victims was partially clothed, the other wore shorts and a blue t-shirt. It seemed like a strange scene from the moment I saw the two bodies. It didn't add up. Experience told me this was unlikely to be the primary site of the killings. Strangulation marks on the necks of both victims, and injuries to both suggested it would have been challenging for the killer to strangle two women in such a confined space, without anyone hearing the commotion or witnessing the attack, or without one of the victims escaping. It appeared that he had murdered the decedents elsewhere and moved them post-mortem to distance himself from the victims and the primary crime scene. I knew from the state of decomposition that the women had been dead for quite some time. Considering it didn't take long for police to run the number plate and discover the name and address of the vehicle's owner, who was one of the victims, it told us the killer wasn't the smartest of criminals.

While myself and the female forensic pathologist worked, investigating officers told us they'd traced the vehicle to an address 300 yards across the rail tracks from our scene. Once police discovered the primary scene, the OIC called for another crime scene photographer to attend the flat where the victims lived, which was good forensic practice. Attending both the primary and secondary scene might have exposed us to accusations of cross contaminating the scenes with trace evidence from one scene carried to another. When my photographer colleague at the primary scene started work, he relayed information to us, which was helpful. When news of the murders broke on TV that night, people came forward to share what they'd seen. Pieces of the puzzle began to fit together to explain the two bodies in the car. Witnesses told police they'd seen the vehicle parked in different locations, without the driver, but didn't report it because they thought the two women were sleeping. I marvelled at the audacity of the killer. He had murdered two women, one he'd lived with for eight years, and then drove their dead and rapidly decomposing bodies around, parking in different places, then changing his mind and returning to drive his victims to another location, and another, until he finally drove them through the Monday morning rush hour traffic and abandoned the car a stone's throw from where he'd killed both women. The callousness of his actions painted a picture of a remorseless, cold-blooded calculating man, with little respect for women.

While we waited for a crime scene tent to arrive, I began taking photographs of Olivia and Anna. Then the pathologist examined them both, which proved challenging in the confined space of the small car. She made notes into a recording device and asked me for specific photographs while she worked. In such a tight space, I ended up leaning into the vehicle within inches of each victim's face to capture the shots I needed. It was heart-wrenching to be that close to the dead women's faces, who both had their eyes open. Forensic pathologists do not close the victim's eyelids at scenes, as they often do in crime dramas. Every touch of the victim's bodies potentially destroys critical evidence.

Until the tent arrived, we couldn't remove the bodies in full view of all the spectators at either end of the street cordon. It made life more difficult at an already challenging and distressing scene. We made a concerted effort to hang tarps on either end of the road to thwart the gawkers. But people are persistent in their efforts to see something gory, or a dead person. I experienced this at other scenes. Those kinds of sights don't leave you. It's often better not to see such things, unless it's your job to do so.

Once the crime scene tent arrived, we moved the bodies from the vehicle and laid each one, in turn, on a body sheet in the tent. This was a team effort and it gave Dr V and myself the privacy and time to examine each victim individually. The injuries to both women indicated they'd put up quite a struggle with their killer. I photographed the injuries they'd sustained in the attacks. I stood beside the pathologist while she recorded her notes into a tiny tape recorder, occasionally stopping to ask me to photograph specific items or parts of each body. We did the same for the second victim. We both sweltered in the oppressive heat of the foul-smelling tent and it didn't help that I felt so ill with a cold. I tried to put my discomfort out of my mind while I focused on my task, getting justice for these two women. Once the forensic pathologist had examined both bodies, we returned to the vehicle together to see if the killer had left any items or clues underneath the bodies. I photographed the vehicle's interior once more, to show it with the victims removed, and any possible evidence that had remained underneath each victim, or under their feet in the footwells.

When we finished our work at the scene, we had the bodies removed to the mortuary for forensic post-mortems. We had the vehicle covered and taken to the Serious Crimes Unit at the MPS Forensic Science Lab for additional forensic examination and additional specialist photography. The SCU examination included the use of filters and lasers and chemical treatments to find latent fingerprints on or in the vehicle, along with DNA evidence, hairs and fibres from the killer's clothing and more.

In the weeks following the murders, stories filled the newspapers with photographs and articles sharing every detail imaginable about the two dead women. In most articles the journalists referred to them as *girls*, although they were 32 and 29, which I thought disrespectful and inappropriate. It sent a subtle message that the victims were immature and irresponsible. I still see the same issue in today's newspaper reports of the murders of women in their twenties and thirties. By contrast, I never saw male murder victims I'd photographed referred to as a *boy* or *boys* in news articles about their murders. Journalists reporting these crimes need to do a much better job when reporting violence against women and girls. The language they use matters. Words matter.

I didn't consciously seek out newspaper articles for my murder scenes, because my scenes filled the pages on a weekly basis. It brought me more anguish, the more I knew, especially when the information about the murders was so inaccurate. But when I saw myself and the pathologist splashed all over the front of the newspapers, it was almost impossible not to notice photographs of the victims and read about their lives. It pained my heart to see both women looking so beautiful and vivacious in the newspaper photographs. They didn't look like that when I'd photographed them. Of the details that came out in the yards of newspaper coverage, one of the most heart-wrenching facts to learn was that Olivia had only moved into the flat with Anna three months before the murders. She wanted to move out of her parents' home in the countryside, to have greater independence and enjoy London life to the fullest. Both women worked for the same company and were friends, so it made good financial sense for them to live together.

The killer, once engaged to Anna, had come back to the flat on the day of the murders to pick up the last of his possessions. Anna had kept her relationship with him a secret. Her parents knew nothing of him until after the murders. He had a history of violence and abusive behaviour. Fifteen years before the murders a court had jailed him for grievous bodily harm and cruelty to a nine-month-old child. He'd put the child's feet in scalding water while looking after him. Arrogant, coercively controlling and jealous, he could not stand the idea of Anna going out with another man. She wanted him and his possessions gone for good. He didn't take kindly to her rejection and he argued with her. The argument escalated and he strangled Anna in a jealous rage late on the Saturday night. Neighbours heard two piercing screams on the night of the murders, during the time Anna fought for her life, but they didn't call the police or come to investigate. He then waited for her roommate to come home and when she discovered what he'd done to her friend, he killed her also. He left their two bodies in the hallway of the flat over the weekend while he went to his new girlfriend's home to support his alibi. Later that weekend, under cover of darkness, he moved both bodies into Anna's car and drove them around London. Five people had seen the dead women in the vehicle, and yet nobody reported the incident, or gave the bodies a second look. Ultimately, he abandoned the car at around 7 a.m. on the Monday morning, not far from the flat where he'd lived with Anna.

Within weeks police arrested Peter Short for the murders of Anna and Olivia. The case came to trial a year after the killings.

'He thought he was God's gift to women. Not once has he shown the slightest shame. Prison is truly where he belongs,' said the SIO when we left the Old Bailey on the last day of the trial. Peter Short was convicted of the brutal murders of his ex-fiancée and her roommate, and was given two life sentences. He sobbed uncontrollably in the dock when the jury foreperson read the verdict. The only words he spoke during the three-week trial were, 'I didn't kill anyone!' He showed no remorse for the killings and maintained his innocence, despite the overwhelming evidence against him. Court security had to carry him away to the cells. Two years after his imprisonment, he challenged his conviction at The Court of Appeal. They turned down his appeal.

As the parents of the murdered women walked through the throng of TV reporters outside the Old Bailey Courthouse, it made me think it was the victims' families that had been handed the life sentences. The families were also the killer's victims, but not in the same way, and rarely acknowledged as such. They lived, but the killer also ended their lives too. A life sentence in England, at that time, meant seventeen years in jail. It rarely meant life in prison. But the families of the two women he callously terrorised and murdered will never live a day without suffering the excruciating pain of their monumental loss. Too often we forget about a killer's *other victims*. Those left behind who have to deal with the death of their loved ones for the remainder of their lives. It's a heavy burden to carry.

After Thirty-five Years of Abuse

When I arrived at the scene, murder squad detectives were waiting for me. They briefed me while I changed into my protective clothing. In the kitchen of the flat, they were speaking with a woman dressed in a pink nightdress, housecoat and pink fluffy slippers. She was calm and cooperative. I soon discovered Caroline was the killer. She called the police and told them she'd killed her husband, once she was certain he was dead. Police arrived to find her waiting for them at the flat.

Caroline had finally had enough of her tormentor. After thirty-five years of taking his mental and physical abuse, she stabbed him while he slept. Arthur had physically and mentally tortured Caroline for decades, but lacking the financial resources to leave, she found herself forced to continue living with her abusive husband in their council flat in North London. Long since estranged from one another, Arthur lived upstairs and Caroline lived downstairs. Forced to share the communal kitchen and bathroom, life in the tight quarters must have been extremely challenging under the circumstances.

Arthur's death was the first I'd ever been to where a woman had killed a man. It was also a rare occurrence to meet a self-confessed killer at a scene. There were no signs of a struggle in the neat and tidy flat, and no indication a violent crime had occurred. The only thing noticeably out of place was the cutlery drawer Caroline (66) had removed and placed on the kitchen table. She told police she'd taken the cutlery drawer out to find the knife she'd used to kill her husband, while trying not to make noise that might wake Arthur. Caroline had not fled the scene after the killing. She had not flown into a violent rage. She had not stabbed Arthur multiple times, in a frenzy, like I'd seen at the murders of women by men. Her actions were not rage-fuelled. She had not killed Arthur while he was awake. She had not terrorised him or stabbed him multiple times in an act of overkill. If you could call any homicide humane, this was it. Caroline ended Arthur's life with one stab wound to his neck. He never saw it coming. After enduring thirty-five years of her husband's abuse, something had pushed her over the edge that night and turned her into a killer.

But this scene was different. Most homicide scenes I'd photographed over the years were gory, frenzied and horrifying. The level of violence brutal, and driven by rage, misogyny, hatred or jealousy. This was a 'quiet murder' if you could imagine such a thing. When I opened the door to Arthur's bedroom to take photographs, I found him in bed, lying in a semi-recumbent position, with the blankets pulled up to his chest, and his arms outside the covers. He had a book lying face down on his chest. Caroline had waited until he fell asleep. She crept up the stairs with the carving knife and opened his door quietly. She raised the knife and with great accuracy, plunged it into the right side of his neck directly above his collarbone. The black handle of the knife stuck out of his neck. The blade had gone all the way into his neck up to the hilt, eight inches deep. Otherwise, Arthur looked like he was sleeping. His face was pale, waxy and devoid of colour. I took photographs of the tiny bedroom. Then it came time to pull back the bedclothes to see where all the blood had gone. The Lab Sergeant working with me removed the bedspread that covered Arthur. We both gasped at the sight. 'So that's where all his blood went,' Chris said while we stood staring at the sight before us. I'd seen plenty of blood at scenes before but never an entire single bed soaked in blood. The red stain had spread out from Arthur's waxy-looking body. Arthur (70) looked as though every ounce of his blood had drained out into the sheets and mattress below; the top surface of his single bed was completely red, like someone had dipped the sheets in a bucket of blood. There was no blood anywhere else in the room. No evidence of a fight, and no defence wounds on Arthur's hands or arms. Caroline had severed the main artery in his neck with the knife blow, and he'd bled to death. Because she hadn't pulled the knife out of his neck, no blood had spurted up onto the walls or ceiling. Arthur looked like he was still alive.

As dawn broke, and officers arrested Caroline and took her from the scene, I was taking exterior shots of the block of flats to finish up my work. I remember thinking how rare a sight it was, to see police officers taking a woman into custody for murder, in handcuffs, still in her pink nightdress and slippers and an overcoat. When the case came to court, the jury heard the horrific details of Arthur's abuse that Caroline had endured for over thirty-five years. The court sentenced her to three years' probation.

I so often hear men on social media commenting that it's not only women; that men are also murdered by their partners or spouses. Yet Arthur's 'quiet murder' by his wife Caroline was the *only* case of a woman killing her husband that I *ever* photographed, in close to a decade of crime scene photography in London. And I don't recall any of my colleagues ever commenting on a case where they photographed a man killed by his wife or female partner. And they would have commented on this, because it was and is such a rare event.

I rarely hear men on social media willing to self-reflect; to ask themselves what they can do to individually or collectively change or eliminate this appalling level of male violence against women and girls (and against boys and men). Perhaps men are more afraid of other men than they are willing to admit. Maybe that's why they're unwilling to even acknowledge the levels of misogyny and sexism in their workplaces and in their social lives. Women are living in fear every day, and they've had enough. Thoughts and prayers after yet another murder of a woman *just walking home* ring hollow in the ears of the heartbroken families whose lives have been devastated by yet another misogynistic entitled man who has taken another woman's life. Male violence against women and girls is now at epidemic proportions, worldwide. Women are exhausted, trying to avoid men verbally abusing, sexually assaulting, stalking, kidnapping and murdering them when they are trying to go about their daily lives. Not to mention the ever-growing clear and present danger to women and girls from the incelosphere. Women are now under siege, both in the real world and in the virtual world. It's never been a more terrifying time to be a woman in a world increasingly filled with male rage, mass shooters and misogyny.

Men appear unwilling to accept the ugly truth of their level of violence against women and girls (and against men and boys). And the many decent men who are appalled remain silent and do not speak out against the bullying and coercively controlling men that shout the loudest in these online conversations. Men only need to look at the Counting Dead Women Twitter/X feed (and equivalent in other countries) and scroll through the names and photographs of women murdered by men, to see the epidemic proportions of femicide year after year. So many of these 'what aboutery men' expend an inordinate amount of energy contradicting and abusing women on social media, to refute the truth of male violence against women and girls. Their energy would be better spent joining the existing organisations like White Ribbon UK, or forming their own groups, or lending their support to other men who are campaigning and educating men and boys to try to reduce violence against women and girls. While it is true that more men than women are killed throughout the world, it is men doing most of the killing. Men are killing men. Men are killing boys. Men are killing girls. Men are killing women. From my extensive experience, women may hurt men, but they rarely kill them. The same applies to mass shootings. Recent research tells us that men perpetrate 98 per cent of mass shootings. And a high percentage of those mass shooters have a history of domestic violence and misogyny, and have killed a partner, spouse or family member prior to embarking on a shooting rampage. Why are men so violent? There are many theories. It's a complex issue and beyond the scope of this book. Violence against women and girls is *a men's issue*. So, it's men who need to step up and find solutions to prevent the violence against women and girls that fills our social media feeds and newspapers day after day, year after year, decade after decade.

Gotcha!

'I should have trusted my instincts,' she said, while I set up my camera and tripod to take photographs of the injuries a rapist had inflicted on her, a few hours earlier. While I loaded film, she told me what happened to her. 'I went to a local club with my friend. As the night wore on, I sensed a bloke watching me. It gave me the creeps. He never came over to talk to me, but he kept staring,' she said. I could feel her reliving the scene while she spoke. I waited until she came to a natural break in the conversation to begin my photography work. I felt it was important not to thwart survivors from telling me their stories, if they felt the need to. Some rape survivors were mute, terrorised and fearful, even of another woman. Some would not make any eye contact with me. I handled the photography of each rape case delicately and tactfully. The survivor's feelings were of paramount importance. I took my time with each woman and let them set the pace. While I photographed her injuries, she continued. 'My friend met a bloke she liked. She was having fun, so she wanted to stay until chucking out time. But I wanted to go home to my boyfriend. So, I decided to leave the club and catch a cab,' she said. Because I'd just photographed the club and the scene, I could vividly picture where she was talking about. The scene came to life again, through her words, and descriptions of what happened. 'When I left the club, I turned right, heading towards the main road, to flag down a cab,' she said. Although she lived within walking distance from the club, she thought that catching a cab would be safer, because she was by herself.

'I'd only left the club and walked a few hundred feet, when I sensed someone behind me. I turned and saw a man following me. I started walking faster. I could hear his footsteps getting closer. I thought he might cross the road or turn off, but he didn't. Suddenly, he pounced on me from behind. He dragged me into a grassy area behind the club . . .' She stopped talking. To take a breath. To regain her composure. I listened while she continued. I knew what was coming next, because I'd been there. I'd seen where he'd pounced on her. I'd seen where he'd dragged her from the well-lit street to an unlit grubby wasteland behind the club. While I continued to take her photographs, she described in detail how he'd terrorised her, humiliated her and raped her. She told me what he did to her. What he said to her. And how he smelled. Considering she'd survived a brutal experience and rape; she was kind and calm with me when I photographed her at her home. She showed me such generosity, early on that morning, making me tea and toast, because she knew I'd been out all night at other crime scenes, and at the scene of her rape. All the while, she insisted that she sensed her rapist was up to no good. She said she'd talked herself out of trusting her instincts. She kept repeating 'I should have trusted my instincts.' I agreed with her, but assured her that the rapist was the only one to blame for her rape. That she did nothing wrong. She was not to blame, in any way. Trusting my instincts had saved me from a similar fate, at the hands of a man on the London Underground, several years before I joined the police. Although my attacker was six feet tall, fortunately I managed to fight him off, because I'd taken karate classes for several years. After what seemed like an eternity of a struggle with him, in an empty Tube station corridor, he ran away. Having experienced a serious assault as a young woman, I had great empathy for any girl or woman who went through a similarly frightening and life-changing experience.

When I arrived at the rape scene, in the early hours of the morning, it was still dark. I walked around the cordoned-off perimeter, shining my torch across the grass where the assailant had raped the victim. While I contemplated the scene, as I always did before I took any photographs, I was reminded of how grubby and disgusting the places always were, where men raped and murdered women. Scenes flashed through my mind of other cases I'd photographed over the years. Flashes of women's pale bodies, so often dumped naked or partially clothed on a patch of wasteland, among the filth, the dog shit, broken bricks and bottles, tyres and other trash. A not-so-subtle reflection of how misogynistic men, who rape and murder women, truly feel about them. Men use and murder women, then dump them in a filthy place. On display, with no dignity even in death, after humiliating and terrorising them in their last moments of life. Snapping back from my thoughts to the scene before me, I noticed something on the ground a few feet away. A brown leather wallet stood out against the grass. Officers who'd cordoned off the scene hadn't noticed the wallet in the darkness, but in the full blast of my two powerful flashguns, I noticed it immediately. I shouted to the cordon officer, 'The bastard dropped his wallet. It must have fallen out of his trouser pocket when he pulled down his pants.' As an experienced police photographer, I knew it was dangerous to jump to any conclusions about any piece of evidence found at a scene, but I had a strong feeling, on that occasion, that it *was* the rapist's wallet. It's hard to describe the joy I felt at discovering the monumental blunder the rapist had made. I asked the cordon officer to call for a SOCO to attend the scene and document the wallet and take it into evidence. When the SOCO arrived, he opened the wallet in situ and I photographed the contents. In the wallet there were bank cards and the suspect's driver's licence, his name and address. It turned out that it *was* the rapist's wallet. Officers went to his home to arrest him on suspicion of rape. After the rape, the suspect had taken a train to the north of England, to try to distance himself from his crime and create an alibi. Police in the north of England took him into custody that same day, in a seamless collaboration with the MPS. Among the feelings of disgust and anger about this brutal rape and the ugliness of the scene, I felt a great sense of pride in my work and a sense of relief for the victim when I found the wallet. It was one of those rare gotcha moments to savour. I never discovered any more about this case, but it turned out to be a productive night's work. The hardest part for me was not being able to share the information about finding the wallet with the rape survivor when I went to photograph her after I'd photographed the scene. I didn't want to give her false hope in her vulnerable state. But I did ask officers to let her know right away that they had a strong suspect in custody. I hoped that at least knowing her rapist was off the streets may have given her some small amount of solace.

Summer Night of Terror

On a hot summer night in North London, windows gaped open to beat the heat. She was sleeping soundly, safe in her bed. Alone in a ground-floor flat. Her bed stood below a large sash window, open at the top to let air into her stifling hot bedroom. The next thing she felt was the weight of a man on top of her. He'd lowered the sash window silently and jumped down on her while she slept. He pressed his gloved hand hard over her mouth. Shocked into consciousness, she struggled to breathe. She opened her eyes to see a man wearing a black balaclava. He was sitting on her chest. His eyes were wild. He smelled of sweat and stale breath. She saw the glint of a large knife. The point of the blade inches from her face. The adrenaline rush kicked in. Sounds distorted. Her lungs felt like they'd burst from lack of oxygen. She tried to scream and struggle free, but his hand pressed harder over her mouth. He told her he wouldn't cut her throat if she did what he wanted. The smell of this stranger on top of her she'd never forget. She knew he intended to rape her and maybe kill her. Soon she realised he wasn't there *just* to rape and rob her, he was there for the thrill of terrifying her. She was certain he'd kill her if she didn't cooperate. So, she stopped screaming. She stopped struggling. He raped her, but that was not enough. He pulled her from her bed and bound her hands with cable ties. He wanted her to talk to him while he ransacked her home. He dragged her by her cuffed hands, with him, from room to room. The cable ties cut into her wrists when he pulled her around. Hours passed. Cold, naked and shivering from the shock, she talked to him for the entire duration, to keep him calm and to save her life. She could see dawn's blue light through the gap in the long curtains in her living room. *When will her nightmare end?* He stole her possessions and, finally, hours after he'd raped her, he left. But not before he pressed the tip of the knife into her neck and she felt a trickle of warm blood. He told her not to call the police because he'd be watching. And he'd know. And he'd come back to finish her off. This was the harrowing tale she told me when I arrived at the scene as dawn broke. Courageously and calmly, she talked me through what had happened and where. I marvelled at her courage and resourcefulness in the face of such a vicious and prolonged attack. Soon paramedics whisked her away and took her to a hospital for treatment and to gather forensic evidence of the rape. I saw her again, about a year later, when I went to court to testify at the trial. The evidence we gathered at that scene, and the level of detail about her attacker that she shared with police on that morning, and during her testimony at court, helped to secure a conviction against the rapist. He received a long prison sentence. I've never forgotten the courage and bravery that young woman showed during that night of terror.

* * *

'It drives my neighbour crazy,' I tell Sarah.

'I don't answer the door when he rings my doorbell. He doesn't understand why. But he doesn't know I used to be a police photographer.'

'Why don't you answer the door?' my therapist asks.

'Because I photographed too many people who'd still be alive today, if only they hadn't opened the door to their killer,' I reply.

'Tell me more about that,' Sarah continues calmly.

'Opening the door can be a more dangerous proposition than you might imagine. I photographed many blitz attack murders that would not have happened if the victim hadn't opened the door to their rapist or killer,' I say.

'I know it bothers people, but it doesn't bother me not to answer the door. If it's important, they'll leave a package on my doorstep, or a note on the door, or they'll call or text to let me know they visited,' I continue.

'What is it about the doorstep scenario that bothers you the most?' Sarah asks.

'I think the ring of the doorbell is triggering. It sends my adrenaline surging. So now I have a sign on the door that says "Don't knock" and people don't knock. I've figured out a way to have some peace and quiet,' I say.

Sarah smiles at my reply.

'If someone is really determined to kill you, they'll find a way. But if you can keep a strong door between you and a potential attacker or killer, they may move on to an easier target or at least you might buy yourself time to escape or call for help.'

7

Love, Lies and a Landfill Search

It took us seventeen days to find the first piece of Emma Taylor's dismembered body. Seventeen days of searching, in a stinking mountain of decomposing trash, for the pieces of a 23-year-old woman. Seventeen days searching Europe's largest landfill to recover the remains of a daughter, a sister, a wife, a friend, a mother, whose killer had callously thrown her out with the trash, like her life had no value.

My involvement in the case started weeks before, when Emma's parents reported her missing to police. On a weekend off, the duty officer asked me to go to SO3 HQ to copy and print a photograph of Emma for urgent distribution to police who had begun a missing persons investigation. Her smiling face stared back at me from the small black-and-white photographs that hurtled through the printing machine. While I stacked and chopped piles of prints, I'd seen her smiling face hundreds of times. I hoped my police colleagues would find her unharmed. But I knew how missing person cases had turned out in the past. Sadly, too many ended up as a murder scene for myself or one of my colleagues to photograph. Thirteen days after Emma was last seen alive, that photographer turned out to be me.

'Get yourself out to Mucking Marshes Landfill right away,' came the instruction from Charles, who assigned me the case on a sunny April morning.

'Where's that?' I asked. I knew London well, from driving to crime scenes day and night, but I'd never heard of Mucking Marshes Landfill.

'It's about 30 miles from central London as the crow flies. Point your van east and when you reach the North Sea, you know you've gone too far,' he said with a hint of mischief in his voice.

'What have they got for me?' I asked.

'They'll brief you when you arrive,' he said, and hung up the phone.

When I checked my map book, I discovered he wasn't far wrong. I'd be almost at the confluence of the Thames Estuary and the North Sea by the time I arrived in the village of Mucking in Essex, on the South East coast of England. *It'll make a nice change to escape the heat of the city for a day*, I thought to myself, while I prepared food and drink to take with me, because experience had taught me that once I arrived at a major scene, I often didn't have an opportunity to eat, drink or use the toilet.

After an hour's drive, I could see the sparkling waters of the Thames Estuary in the distance, as Mucking Marshes Landfill came into view. Three gigantic cranes on Mucking Wharf stood like sentinels, fierce mechanical dogs guarding access to the landfill at the water's edge. Giant pylons threaded across the landscape, carrying their drooping electricity cables to far-off towns and villages.

A mix of industrial chimneys, refineries and concrete vestiges of a wartime past blotted the landscape in an area once frequented by Victorians, who sought curative sea bathing on a day trip from London to the coast. A four-mile-long perimeter fence, topped with barbed wire, surrounded the mountain of London's waste that towered incongruously above the tranquil landscape of Mucking Flats and the Thames Estuary.

At the site security post, I identified myself to the guard on duty. He eyed me suspiciously but opened the barrier to let me through. It didn't take long to spot Peter's unmarked police Transit van, topped with its distinctive roof rack platform, that we used to shoot photographs and video from a higher vantage point. Peter, a principal photographic officer, a rank above me, was one of SO3's most experienced crime scene videographers. We'd worked at many murder scenes together and we got along well. Peter was a robust, perpetually suntanned man, with thinning silver hair, glasses and enormous strong hands. An experienced photographer from a military background, he took no nonsense from police officers who behaved badly, in his opinion. A quick good-natured punch to their upper arm was his reply to any unsuspecting detective or uniformed officer who bothered me at any of our scenes.

'Glad you could make it,' Peter bellowed while he walked towards me. 'What time do you call this?' he added with a smile. 'We've been waiting for you.'

'So, what have we got? And, *who* are they?' I asked. I nodded in the direction of about thirty men, all dressed in white crime scene suits and black rubber boots.

'They're undertakers,' he said, as if it were nothing out of the ordinary to come upon a large group of undertakers on a landfill site first thing in the morning.

'What are they doing here?' I asked. The group stared in my direction; eyes fixed on us while we spoke.

'They're here to help us find the body of a young lady who went missing from her home in West London,' Peter said.

'They're a bit pale and creepy,' I said, 'And why are they staring at me?'

Ever the joker, Peter didn't miss a beat. 'They're mentally measuring you up for a coffin,' came his reply. We laughed heartily together. I'd become accustomed to people staring at me when I arrived at murder scenes. Their expressions ranged from complete disbelief to a judgmental look that said *this is not a suitable job for a woman*.

'The SIO will brief us. Let's be having you,' Peter said in his cockney twang. We walked over to the group of men gathered nearby. I was the only woman in the team, but that was nothing new.

'Thanks for coming out today,' said the SIO in a loud voice. Standing on an upturned yellow plastic crate to give his briefing, DS Anderson introduced himself and our mission. 'We're here to find the dismembered body of Emma Taylor, a 23-year-old woman whose parents reported her missing,' he said. 'We're looking for six or more body parts, probably in black plastic bags.' Some of the group looked around. Black plastic bags by the thousands surrounded us, not to mention the green, pink, yellow, blue, orange and white bags strewn across the landfill as far as the eye could see.

'This will be a challenging and unpleasant job,' he continued, 'particularly in view of the heat wave that's forecast for the coming week.'

He gestured my way. 'This is the police photographer AJ, and the police videographer Peter. Next to him is our Lab Sergeant Jim. If you have any questions on the forensics, ask one of them. They're here to document the search, photograph, videotape and recover any evidence we find.' I raised my hand in a salute to acknowledge the group, Peter followed suit. Jim nodded to the team. The three of us had worked together before and had an easy shorthand, which was helpful in such challenging circumstances. It wasn't easy to hear DS Anderson over the screeching of gulls circling nearby, the gusting wind and the rumbling sound of the diggers and compactors working in the background, but he continued 'Thanks to Malcolm and the landfill team, we know where to start our search. Does anyone have any questions?'

'Are we expecting any cadaver dogs or cadets to help with the search,' Peter asked.

'Unfortunately, no. We asked the dog section if they'd let us have dogs and handlers but they said no. Same goes for police cadets from Hendon. They said the rat-infested tip was too hazardous because the risk of disease and infection was too great and could be fatal.' An embarrassed laugh rippled through the group. I thought to myself, *if it's too dangerous for the cadets, the dogs and the handlers, how is it not too dangerous for us?* No doubt the others were thinking something similar.

DS Anderson introduced Malcolm, the landfill manager. Malcolm would brief us on site safety and the dangers of a landfill search and guide us to where he believed we'd find Emma's remains. Malcolm had advised the heavy machinery drivers about our body recovery task. And he'd halted the dumping of any additional waste in our cordoned-off sectors of the landfill. With 12,000 tons of London's residential and commercial waste arriving at Mucking every week, it was critical to prevent any additional dumping on top of the tons of waste we intended to search.

'The moment you come through those gates,' Malcolm said, pointing to the entrance to the landfill 'safety must be your number one priority. I hope you're all vaccinated,' he continued. 'The landfill is a dangerous place with lots of hazards, besides heavy machinery, like this compactor, toppling over or reversing on top of you,' he said, pointing to a huge yellow compactor with enormous silver spikes on each wheel. 'It weighs 16 tonnes and can flatten 30 feet of landfill materials into a 10-foot pile. Don't step in its way. Or it'll flatten you. Any questions?' he asked. Heads shook *no*. He continued.

'Aside from the machinery and the rats, the tip is filled with dirty nappies, nails, razors, twisted metal, broken plastic, rotten wood, bricks and old appliances and anything else you can imagine,' he said. 'So, watch where you're walking. Piles of refuse are unstable under foot. The face of the dig is the smelliest and most dangerous place. A 30-foot wall of garbage can collapse under you, or on top of you when you least expect it, so be vigilant. Some of you will need to wear your high viz jackets so the drivers can spot you easily. Because you'll be working close to moving machinery, you'll need to wear hard hats, safety boots and gloves.'

Oh shit, I thought, *not on top of a crime scene suit*. It was going to be sweltering hot in all that gear standing still, never mind working outdoors in the heat, digging through mounds of stinking, oozing garbage.

'So, what's the deal with the gulls?' Jim asked.

'You'll have to contend with them. Nothing we can do about that,' Malcolm said. When I arrived at the landfill I noticed a large flock of circling gulls, their screeching ear-piercing calls hard to ignore. 'They scavenge for food where the diggers are working,' he continued. 'They'll dive bomb you to give you a warning. They're a bloody nuisance. If they feel threatened, they'll shit on you or vomit on you. Stand your ground,' he said.

We laughed, but you could tell people were thinking, *what the hell have I let myself in for?* By this point in the briefing, I wanted to jump back into my van and drive away. But we were there to do a job, to find the forensic evidence to convict a brutal killer and give Emma and her family the justice they deserved. Malcolm answered a few more questions from the group, then drew the briefing to a close. Now it was time to start work on our gruesome task.

After the safety briefing Peter and I walked back to our vehicles to change into our scene kit and discuss a strategy for the photography and videography. *Rubber boots were a nightmare to wear on hot days* I thought when I took mine out of my van. Not only were the steel-toed boots heavy due to the metal plates in the soles, but the soles were rigid. They made my feet ache after about an hour of wearing them. I climbed onto the roof of Peter's Transit van to look at what lay before us and to take some shots of the location for the case file. These establishing shots provided a wide view of the landfill and oriented the viewer to the scene. I knew I'd shoot some aerial photography also, but that would wait until the end of the search, when my shots would pinpoint locations of our grim discoveries.

The group were gathering some distance away, grabbing shovels and pitchforks in anticipation of beginning the search. Who better than a group of thirty undertakers to search for a body? They knew the smells and the sights of dead bodies, in every state of decomposition. We all knew *that smell*, the unique odour of a decomposing human being. We all knew how to recognise decomposing flesh, even hidden in a sea of trash. Between us all, we were the best team of people suited to such a search, morbid though that may sound.

I clambered off Peter's van roof and discreetly stripped down to my underwear and pulled on a crime scene suit and mask. I may have stripped off my clothing in public places more than anyone else I know. If a command-and-control trailer turned up at a scene, I had the luxury of changing inside the unit, but mostly it was in the street, or in the back of my van. Not ideal, especially for a woman. When the group dispersed, DS Anderson came over to speak with Peter, Jim and myself about the forensics and to share more backstory on the case. By this time, I'd figured out that Emma was likely the woman I'd seen in the photographs I'd printed for the missing persons investigation. A sadness washed over me at the thought of searching for her missing body parts, and not for the smiling woman I'd seen hundreds of times in that cherished family photograph.

'The last time Emma's parents saw her alive was several weeks ago,' DS Anderson said. 'Her mum said she went to visit her estranged husband Simon to ask for a divorce. Nobody's seen her since. They reported her missing and her father accompanied police to her flat to investigate. He had a key, but Simon had locked the door from the inside. Police opened the letterbox and smelled gas. They kicked in the door and found Simon slumped in the hall but still alive. Emma's two sons were unconscious in their beds. The quick thinking of police officers saved all three of their lives. Simon denied any involvement in Emma's presumed death, so we've got to find her body so the Crown Prosecution Service will be able to proceed with a murder charge.'

'What do we know about the husband?' Peter asked.

'They met when she was still a teenager. According to her parents and friends we've interviewed, Simon had a history of domestic violence and he regularly beat her. He threatened to kill her in the past. One of the witnesses said that she overheard Simon say in a fit of rage that he'd kill Emma and "cut her up". She moved back to her parents' home after he broke her jaw during an argument a few weeks before she went missing. Their marriage had been on the rocks for some time according to her mum and dad. Simon claims she ran away with her new boyfriend and abandoned him and their sons. His sob story doesn't add up. I think he dismembered her body and dumped it, piece by piece, into the rubbish chute at the flats. At this stage it's a hunch. Let's hope I'm right.'

Landfill searches are costly for police, often running into the hundreds of thousands of pounds. They require dozens of searchers to painstakingly sift through thousands of tons of trash, in the hope of recognising and recovering evidence. They need thorough pre-planning and they often take weeks.

DS Anderson had to convince his commanding officer that a landfill search would produce the evidence we needed to secure a conviction against Emma's killer. Not an easy task. But as a veteran murder squad detective, with thirty years in the job, his boss respected his professional opinion and authorised funding for the search. The first five days of the search cost £50,000. The Mucking tip covered hundreds of acres and over 2,000 tons of London's waste arrived there by barge every day. Searching is slow, backbreaking and hazardous. It's one of the more difficult searches made by forensic teams and investigators. DS Anderson had to plan for the equipment, personnel and tools needed to undertake the search: tarps, shovels, rakes, garbage bins, protective clothing, masks, gloves and so forth.

Although this was not the site of a murder, it was still a forensic search and a secondary crime scene related to a homicide. We treated it with the appropriate forensic protocols, despite the challenging environment. Searching a landfill for body parts might seem like madness. How could you possibly find pieces of a human being in among the tons of landfill waste? Although to the untrained eye, a landfill looks like thousands of tons of trash dumped in a haphazard heap up to 30 feet high, it's surprisingly ordered chaos. It's easy to imagine that once a person has thrown an item away, it's gone forever, but that's far from the case. Landfill searches have revealed crucial evidence for detectives, including murder weapons, contraband and human remains.

After two weeks up to our knees in the rat-infested stinking morass, we had searched through 1,500 tons of rubbish where we should have found Emma's remains. But we found no trace of her. I drove sixty miles round trip each day during the search that lasted 25 days. Every day was backbreaking work. The weather grew hotter day by day, and we battled the gulls circling and swooping aggressively at us. The piercing screech of fifty gulls is ear-splitting. The garbage kept coming to the tip, day after sweltering day. The loud rumbling sound of the trucks offloading their piles of waste not far from us grew annoying, and the stressful challenge of not falling over into the piles of stinking toxic garbage was a daily issue.

The landfill management had mapped their site on a complex grid to ensure workers spread London's garbage evenly throughout the site, to maximise capacity of the landfill. From detailed maps of the site, and given dates by DS Anderson, they were able to tell the locations where waste management drivers collected the rubbish, and could pinpoint where digger drivers deposited it on the landfill. Armed with that information, each day we assembled in the area marked for excavation. We worked in a grid pattern; the way police conduct a missing person search in open terrain. But this search proved considerably more challenging. The wall of garbage was 30 feet high in places, and the chance of being buried alive if the garbage collapsed on us, was an ever-present danger. We worked alongside a mechanical digger that was loud, and belched out black exhaust fumes, as it dug into the wall of slimy garbage and lifted shovels full of trash and dropped them onto our tarps. We picked through each shovelful with rakes, pitchforks and garden forks. We sifted through thousands of garbage bags to try to find the bags containing Emma's body parts. The site management were cooperative and helped in any way they could. They had given us specific details of where we needed to start our search, based on the information DS Anderson had provided them. Contrary to what it looks like in photographs, the landfill company knows where each square foot of garbage has come from, which houses, which flats, which area of the city. Days turned to weeks and we found nothing. We were beginning to lose hope of recovering any of Emma's body parts.

DS Anderson suspected something was amiss. He went back to the landfill company and expressed his frustrations about our search, double-checking to make sure we were searching in the right areas. He went to speak with the barge men, the workers who collected the bright yellow containers from the wharf in central London and transported them down the river to Mucking. This was where we finally discovered the issue that had prevented us from finding Emma's body parts until day seventeen of the search. The barge men had been working an overtime scam. Binmen collected garbage bins from Simon's block of flats every Friday. Landfill management protocols assigned waste from Friday collections to the area of the tip we'd been searching. But the barge men left behind several of the Friday containers at the wharf in central London, so they could claim overtime to sail those containers down the river to the tip on a Saturday instead, and receive higher pay for weekend work. The waste arriving on a Saturday went to a different location on the tip, far from where we were searching. Despite the barge men knowing we were searching for a woman's body; they kept their mouths shut. Only DS Anderson's good detective instincts and persistence finally got them to confess to their underhanded scheme and their shameful behaviour. DS Anderson was incandescent when he arrived on site to brief us on the morning he discovered the barge men's overtime scam. We were furious. Despite knowing how critical the search was for the victim's family and for the police, who were footing the enormous bill for the search, the barge men kept quiet, knowing full well their overtime racket would mean we'd never find Emma's body. They did the right thing in the end and came clean with DS Anderson, but only after he'd shamed them into telling the truth.

Murder squad officers briefed us daily while the investigation progressed. When news of the landfill search became public, we had a breakthrough. Simon confessed to killing his wife. He told police that in a fit of rage he'd grabbed Emma by the throat and *accidentally* strangled her. After which he stuffed her body in a cupboard in their flat while he figured out a way of disposing of her remains. Friends and family members had visited the flat in the days following Emma's disappearance. Simon put on a show for them, tearfully describing how she'd abandoned him and their two young sons, aged four and five, while Emma's dead body lay in a cupboard mere feet from where they sat.

After five days Emma's body started to decompose and smell putrid in the warm April weather. Determined to avoid a long prison sentence for his crime, he decided to dismember Emma's body in the bath, while his young sons slept in the next room. He used a hacksaw and two carving knives and it took him over ten hours to dismember Emma's body. He told detectives he'd cut Emma's body into six pieces and wrapped them in black plastic bags. He disposed of them via the rubbish chute at their block of flats, under cover of darkness.

In early May, police charged Simon Taylor with the murder of his estranged wife. Now the pressure was on for us to find Emma's body. After spending weeks searching in the sweltering heat, exhausted, filthy and tired, the news of Simon's admission gave us renewed energy and determination. We knew Emma's body was on the landfill somewhere and we would not stop until we found it.

We knew that if we found all six pieces of her body, we had some chance of making a positive identification, although it could be challenging. We'd look for distinguishing marks on the parts recovered: scars or tattoos etc. Because Emma hadn't been missing for long when we started the landfill search, we hoped her body might not be too decomposed. This would give us a better chance of making a visual identification. Discolouration and bloating from decomposition make people look quite different to the person they were in life, so this type of visual identification can be unreliable. Crime dramas show you fresh cadavers, but for me, the bloated, green, mottled foul-smelling cadavers were a more common reality.

At a scene like this one, police forensic personnel had to work well with forensic team members and detectives who were complete strangers until we all came together to solve a murder. It was imperative to collaborate with colleagues immediately and hit the ground running once all parties arrived on site. All murder investigations are a team effort. No single detective, and no single forensic expert can take credit for solving a murder. It's the team who solve a murder. Our team at Mucking understood the importance and value of what we were there to do, despite the revolting circumstances and the disgusting environment we worked in. That kind of singular focus helped us form a cohesive team over those weeks we spent on the landfill in the sweltering heat. We were there for Emma, and for her young sons, and for her family.

Ten days after police charged Simon with Emma's murder, and seventeen days after we began the dig at the landfill, we found the first part of her body. Over the following days we found several of her limbs but sadly we never recovered her head. After we'd found the dismembered parts of Emma's body, I called Jeff, the controller at the Air Support Unit (ASU) to request the helicopter so I could shoot aerial photographs of the site.

'Jeff, I need India 99 at the tip at Mucking for a rotors running pickup. A few quick circuits around the tip should do the trick,' I said. Jeff checked the weather while we spoke.

'That should be fine. Cloud base looks good. Give me a shout when you've found a suitable landing zone and

I'll send them to pick you up. They'll be with you in less than twenty, barring emergencies,' he said.

'Thanks Jeff, will do.'

I grabbed my flying kit bag from my vehicle and changed into my flameproof flight suit and boots in the back of Peter's van. I radioed the ASU for a pickup, then drove to an open field adjacent to the Mucking Tip that provided the perfect landing zone. I parked by the gated entrance to the field, and with camera bag slung over my shoulder I trekked through the knee-high grass to the centre of the field. Minutes later I heard the familiar thump, thump, thump of the aircraft approach. Its 16-inch rotor blades slapped the air loudly. I stood alone in the middle of the field and waved to the helicopter. When it grew closer, Brian flashed its white landing lights to acknowledge me. I put on my white flying helmet and flipped down the smoky-brown visor to protect my face from the powerful rotor wash. With its sleek fifty-foot fuselage, the impressive flying machine, dressed in full police livery, loomed large as it descended towards me. The sound waves from the 600 horsepower engines sent vibrations through me. The downwash from the rotor blades flattened the grass around me like a giant crop circle. I crouched down to avoid the helicopter blowing me off my feet. Adrenaline surged through me. The smell of the hot jet fuel grew stronger and the throbbing sound of the engines grew louder. It's a unique and overwhelming sensory experience to stand alone in a field while a huge helicopter comes right at you. Brian lowered the retractable landing gear and the helicopter came to rest. It bounced on its wheels while it settled on the soft grass right in front of me, with its rotors still running at full speed.

Brian gave me the thumbs up. I crouched low and ran under the main rotors towards the front of the helicopter. Unlatching the passenger door, I jumped aboard. Dumping my camera bag on the floor, I plugged in my helmet comms and greeted the crew. Brian waited until I'd climbed into my safety harness and secured it to the anchor point on the cabin floor before we took off.

'What are we doing today?' asked Andrew, the observer, while we did a reverse take-off from the open field. The grass beneath us swirled around in a circle as we climbed into the sky.

'I'm photographing the locations of where we found the dismembered remains of a murder victim,' I explained.

'Oh, that sounds awful, what's the story?' Andrew asked. I filled them in on more of the details while we circled.

'I need shots of the entire landfill, then closer shots of the flagged areas where we found the pieces of Emma's body,' I said.

'Ok, no problem,' said Brian. The helicopter orbited around the tip and climbed higher into the sky so I could photograph the entire site from various directions. Once we reached an altitude of 1,500 feet, Brian slowed our airspeed so I could safely remove the window. Shooting crime scene photographs through scratched Plexiglas wasn't an option. I undid the butterfly clips and slid the window down into the pocket in the helicopter's door. The cold wind from the open cabin window swirled around the aircraft like a vortex, powerful enough to suck everything out of the cabin if not bolted down or secured.

Like a well-oiled machine, I talked back and forth with the pilot. 'More to the left, keep coming around, bank harder, left, left, left, a little higher, hard left,' I instructed, until Brian positioned the aircraft in the exact spot needed to shoot all my photographs.

As we circled above the landfill, the noise drew stares from workers on the tip and residents nearby, who'd probably never seen the MPS helicopter in their neck of the woods before. Some shielded their eyes with their hands for a better view. The white-suited search crew on the tip stood leaning on their shovels while they watched me take my aerial photographs. From fifteen hundred feet above them, the body search team looked like tiny white ants.

'Thanks, I've got what I need,' I said. Securing the window, we circled back towards the tip.

'I'll drop you off as close to your van as possible,' Brian said as we came in for landing.

'That'd be great, thanks Brian,' I replied.

When the helicopter descended into the field, I could see a small group of men leaning on the gate next to where'd I'd parked my van. Mesmerised by the sight and the sound of the huge loud helicopter, they stared. I jumped out and walked towards them, while the helicopter took off behind me. When I flipped up my smoky-brown visor, took off my flying helmet and shook loose my long brown hair, they looked surprised. It never got old. *I'd seen that look many times*. They hadn't expected a woman to emerge from the helicopter in a navy flight suit, boots and a *Top Gun* helmet. I smiled as I greeted them. They didn't say a word, they simply opened the gate and let me pass.

In November that same year, Simon Taylor, an unemployed labourer, pleaded guilty to killing his estranged wife. The court sentenced him to three years for the killing and dismemberment of his ex-wife, one year for the attempted murder of his children, and one year for not giving Emma a Christian burial. In total, a five-year prison term despite the overwhelming evidence against him. Emma's family were appalled, disgusted and furious at the token sentence imposed on Simon Taylor, for the killing of their daughter and the attempted murder of their grandsons. The end of the trial should have closed a chapter in the sad and gruesome affair. But instead, the lenient sentence added insult to injury to Emma's grieving family. The judicial system had treated them despicably, only giving them notice of the trial 45 minutes before the case began at the Old Bailey, which meant they were unable to attend. Because Simon pleaded guilty, Emma's family had no opportunity to have their victim impact statements heard in court. The family felt let down by the justice system. To add additional pain, after Simon killed Emma, her belongings passed to him, which meant her family had to ask his permission to take anything from the flat where Emma and Simon had lived with their boys. After the trial, Emma's mother feared that the man who'd killed and dismembered her daughter would come out of prison and demand custody of her two grandsons, who he'd also tried to kill. In the agonising months after the trial, the family said the strongest support they received came from the investigating officers in the case. On that first Christmas after Emma's death, officers leading the enquiry bought bicycles for both boys for Christmas, at their own expense. These are the kind and selfless gestures police officers often make, that the public rarely hear about.

At the end of the trial the judge, yet another antiquated privileged old white man, added insult to injury when he explained the lenient sentence by telling the defendant 'I'm sure when you've completed your sentence you'll return to the community.' He went on to say that he thought Simon would be 'a worthwhile citizen again. You are not a man who is ever likely to do it again.' Not only did he impose a sentence far too lenient for the heinous and despicable crimes Simon committed against his wife, his sons and indirectly to Emma's family. His insensitive comments on the sentencing added insult to injury. The judge did not have the qualifications to make such a pronouncement on the potential danger Simon posed to other women. He had no evidence on which to base that opinion. The lenient sentence showed how little value the lives of murdered women held in the judicial system. I never discovered whether Simon went on to kill or abuse other women after his release from prison, but I'd put money on it that he did. Coercively controlling, violent men like Simon, with a long history of violence and psychological abuse, don't give up their power. They find another victim to abuse, control and kill.

There was nothing *normal* about spending 25 days on a landfill. As the lone woman on the site, searching for another woman's mutilated body parts, the experience left me angry, sad, repulsed and disgusted at the casual cruelty Simon had inflicted on Emma, and the callous disregard for the feelings of her family by the judge and the courts. While her mother, father, brother and her young sons may not have been physically imprisoned, Emma's killer imprisoned them mentally and emotionally through his vile actions. They faced a life sentence of sadness, heartbreak and pain and the loss of a loving mother, daughter and sister. Apart from Emma, there were five additional victims who received no justice.

Looking back on this scene now, I feel some small comfort knowing that although we never did find Emma's head or one of her arms, she is now resting in peace in a beautiful place. After fifty years, and 20 million tons of London's waste, Mucking Marshes landfill closed in 2010. The land on which we searched for Emma's dismembered body is now a nature reserve. Filled with birdsong, bees and butterflies, reedbeds, ponds and grasslands, it attracts cuckoos, skylarks and owls. What was once one of Europe's largest landfills, and a secondary crime scene, is now a haven for wildlife. The angry squawking gulls have gone. Only the sound of birdsong carried on the wind keeps Emma company. Nature has reclaimed this place of sadness.

8

Suicide

By His Own Hand

His mother discovered his body. He lived alone in a luxury flat in Canary Wharf. By the time I arrived at the scene, it was dark. There were no lights in the flat. The power company had cut off his electricity for non-payment. Police on scene requested a lighting rig so the scene examination could begin without delay.

I stood in the corridor outside the flat and changed into my PPE while we waited for the lighting rig to arrive. I entered the scene with the Lab Sergeant and we did a scene walk through together by torchlight. Then he left the scene and I continued my work alone. Scenes often had no ambient light, because of a fire, vandalism, or because there was no electricity, or bulbs were missing. It added an additional layer of technical difficulty to photography tasks. A portable torch in my kit proved invaluable for pitch black scenes. Its focused beam provided a powerful light source which allowed me to focus accurately. Using two or three powerful flashguns meant I could light any scene by using a *painting with light* technique to shoot all my photographs.

The victim, a man in his mid-twenties, lay in the middle of his bed. Covered with a duvet, he looked pale but peaceful. He looked like he was sleeping. I walked from room to room taking photographs, and sensed a palpable loneliness. The luxury flat lacked the most basic furniture and possessions. Even the curtain rails were bare. While I stood in the darkness, alone with the deceased, I could see the glittering lights of London in the distance. A million-dollar view. But inside the flat, the energy hung like a heavy sadness. Next to the bed where he lay stood a flimsy silver clothes rack, the kind used in a charity shop. A few items of clothing hung from the rack. The bare minimum. Two expensive suits, a couple of silk ties and several cuffed shirts. Two pairs of polished leather shoes stood neatly together below the overhanging clothes. From these clues, I guessed he was a city trader who'd fallen on hard times after the stock market crash. It looked like he'd sold, or had the furniture in his flat repossessed, apart from the large bed on which he lay. Once I'd finished my shots, we focused our attention on the decedent. By then the lighting rigs had arrived. When the lab sergeant pulled back the duvet, we discovered one bullet hole in the centre of the victim's chest. A small entry wound. No mess and no blood spatter, only a small hole torn through his clothing where he'd pressed the gun against the middle of his chest. A handgun lay on the right side of the decedent, furthest from the door. While we documented the remainder of the scene, we heard from investigating officers that his mother had come to visit him earlier in the evening. She had let herself in with her own key and called out to her son. When he didn't answer, she looked around the flat and found him on the bed. She said she didn't want to wake him, so she let him sleep. In the darkness, she pulled up the duvet in a loving gesture, and tiptoed out of the flat. *How could a mother find her son and not know he's dead?* Even to someone experienced in seeing dead bodies, he looked like he was sleeping. And in the darkness, the gun on the other side of his body was not easy to see, unless you went round that side of the bed. With the bed clothes removed, I photographed his body, his gunshot wound, and then together we turned him over. We were able to see the exit wound (which are generally larger than entry wounds) from the bullet that had torn through his chest, and had come out his back. But it was nowhere on the bed. We moved the mattress and the bed to discover the bullet had passed through the victim, then through the mattress, through the box-spring, through the carpet, and finally embedded itself in the floor underneath the carpet. Fortunately, the bullet had not gone through the floor and injured the occupant of the flat below. The gun he'd used to kill himself looked like one you might see in an old Wild West movie, but it did the job. It only took one bullet to kill him. It was a sad scene, to find this man who'd been riding high in a career that paid well. Ultimately to take his own life in a dark, cold, sparsely furnished flat. When we discovered more information, I learned he'd been a trader in the city, as I'd suspected from the clues in the flat. Since the downturn in the economy, his girlfriend had broken up with him, and he'd had his furniture and car repossessed. He'd sold everything of value that he possessed. A heartbreaking sight. He wasn't much older than me. *How could it have come to this?* I thought. A man with so much life left to live.

One in five UK police officers and operational staff have symptoms consistent with post-traumatic stress disorder, and over two thirds of those suffering with PTSD are unaware of their condition. A recent landmark study of almost 17,000 serving police and operational staff in the UK identified rates of PTSD and depression nearly five times higher than those of the wider UK population. With police personnel witnessing more than 200 critical incidents over the course of their police careers, and with the government slashing police budgets, it's not surprising that suicide rates among police officers and police staff are on the rise in both the US and the UK.

Training probationary police photographers was an integral part of my role as an experienced crime scene photographer. I also took probationary police officers to major crime scenes with me, so they gained first-hand experience of the photographer's role, the critical importance of scene protection and preservation, and an understanding of the role of various other forensic experts at the scene. On one of these training assignments with a new photographer, the duty officer assigned us to the suicide of a police officer. When we neared the address, Anthony became more jittery and anxious. I could hear the tightness in his voice when he peppered me with questions. I knew it would be a more challenging scene than others, in terms of emotional stress, because the death of a police officer by suicide impacts the entire police family. The details the duty officer gave me were minimal. All we knew was that a police officer had shot himself. His body was found in his garden shed. The lab sergeant and SOCO had attended the scene and found it consistent with a suicide. They requested a photographer because although a suspected suicide, we treated it like a murder, from a photographic perspective, to cover all our bases.

This was Anthony's first suspicious death scene, and I hoped it wouldn't be too gory, like many of the shooting deaths I'd photographed. It was the luck of the draw whether the duty officer sent a newbie photographer to a gory scene, or not. Some were much worse than others to start your career with.

When we reached the address, crowds of people and police cars filled the street in front of the house. Anthony gathered his gear and we made our presence known to the officer on duty outside. When we walked into the house, we saw a uniformed female officer standing in the middle of the living room holding a sobbing hysterical woman in a tight embrace. Although the female officer was a colleague of the decedent, she somehow found the strength to remain composed enough to comfort and console the dead officer's wife. These are the tender moments the public rarely witness. Poor Anthony nearly lost his composure. The raw and loud emotion of the grieving widow proved almost too much for him. He had a look of panic on his face and turned white. I thought he was going to collapse in front of me if I didn't do something fast. I remembered how I'd felt the first time

I saw a dead body at a scene. I wanted to be the reassuring figure for Anthony that Ian had been for me when I started on the scenes of crime team.

'Let's go to the back garden and start your shots,' I said, snapping him out of his focus on the grieving widow. I guided Anthony through the crowded house into the back garden where I knew the victim's body awaited us in the garden shed.

'Set up your gear. Let's do the shots from the end of the garden, looking towards the house first. That shot will include the garden shed also. Then we'll do some close-ups of the shed and deal with the body next.' Anthony nodded his agreement, without saying a word. His hands shook while he mounted his camera on the tripod. I pretended not to notice and stood patiently beside him. To distract him, I asked him to talk me through the photographs we'd need to document the scene comprehensively. Soon his hands stopped shaking and his voice grew stronger. He focused the camera and I checked each shot for sharp focus. The technical aspects of the scene took over and he calmed down by the time he finished the shots in the garden, and we moved on to the garden shed. Opening the door of a garden shed, knowing the person inside has shot themselves usually means a lot of splattered blood and brain matter, and it's never a pleasant sight. I held my breath when I opened the shed door. The scene wasn't gory, but it was heartwrenching. The decedent had fashioned a home-made gun out of the barest essentials. He had clamped the makeshift gun to his workbench. The barrel and trigger mechanism faced upwards. He sat on a chair beside the work bench and placed his mouth over the gun barrel and shot himself. The bullet went through his mouth, then through his head and came out the back of his skull. Although a small, stripped-down version of a gun, and not especially powerful, it still did the trick. It wasn't too gory, unlike many other shooting scenes I'd photographed. And for Anthony's sake, I felt relieved. He'd soon know the horror of shootings with sawn-off shotguns that blew heads clean off, and handguns that killed with one shot. At least this was a less horrifying scene with which to begin his career.

Once we'd finished the photographs in the garden, we went back into the house and took shots of the suicide note left on the dining room table. The dead officer had written a note to his wife, explaining the reasons for his death and saying he was sorry. He asked her not to come out to the garden shed. He had hoped to spare her the horror of seeing him dead. She had left the house to buy some groceries at a local supermarket. She hadn't been gone long, but in the meantime her husband had gone to the shed and shot himself. In seconds his life was over.

When the decedent's wife returned home, she found his note and naturally she ran out to the shed to see if she could save her husband's life, but it was too late. I remember her screams, through her tears, asking *Why, why, why. Why didn't he tell me things were so bad? Why didn't he talk to me? We could have sorted things out together*. Sadly, they were questions, with no answers, that she would live with for the rest of her life.

Police suicides are a sad testament to the high price some of my police colleagues paid for a career of exposure to life-threatening and horrific events, within the context of a macho culture where they felt unable or unwilling to share how bad they really felt. Or were unable to access confidential mental health resources before it was too late. Not a lot has changed for the better in the years since that police suicide, I'm sad to say. Police officers are still taking their own lives, now in greater numbers than ever. More needs to be done to protect the protectors.

Male, 50, Jumped Off Railway Bridge

I once photographed a man who died after he'd jumped from a railway bridge into the brambles and undergrowth 50 feet below. Way out in Greater London in the rolling countryside, I met officers at the closest access point to the scene, which was still quite a hike from the railway bridge. It meant leaving my van and gathering up my heavy equipment and trekking through overgrown fields of nettles and brambles to reach the spot where the victim's body lay. Torn clothing was a daily ritual because we had no police issued clothing back then. When I arrived at the bridge, I put my crime scene suit on and took establishing shots. These overview photographs give the viewer a sense of the location in broad strokes. They begin the story, and the remainder of the photographs walk the viewer through what happened in a logical sequence, so they can follow along as if they were at the scene.

On that roasting hot day, by the time I reached the broken body under the bridge, sweat ran down my back in my impermeable Tyvek suit and brambles had scraped my hands from pushing through the dense undergrowth to reach the decedent. The body was fresh (had not yet begun to decompose in any significant way), which suggested the decedent had died within the 24 hours prior to our arrival. Passengers on a passing train had seen him jump and raised the alarm. Otherwise, police would have never discovered his body, because it was well hidden from view in the dense undergrowth where he lay.

No doubt, he stood on the small wall contemplating his actions prior to leaping to his death. When I stood in the same position, looking down at his body, which I'd done with other suicide cases, I got a sense of what it would feel like to jump from that height. It's a visceral experience, standing in the footsteps of someone who has just taken their own life, particularly those that jump from high places, from windows or rooftops. Because I had to take shots looking down towards the ground, where they lay, broken and bloody below. It was impossible not to feel a mix of horror, and the gut wrench of wondering how desperate they must have been to go through with such a horrifying fall to their death. When I looked down to the ground before taking my shots, every fibre of my being screamed, don't fall.

Accessing crime scenes to reach the body was often a challenging and time-consuming effort, before even considering the smells, the sights, the injuries, or state of decomposition of the deceased. A police photographer must be fit and strong enough to manage physically challenging scenes. People end up dead in the strangest of places. And where the dead went, I went. On this occasion, it took me twenty minutes to reach the scene, and another ten minutes to clamber down through the dense brambles and steep overgrown terrain to reach the body.

It's no simple task to investigate a suspicious death outdoors, and especially one in the deep undergrowth. It's difficult to see the body, and it's difficult to discover items of evidence in the long grass and the dense shrubbery. Not to mention the confusion added to the scene by discarded litter thrown from passing trains that had trundled across the bridge overhead. It didn't take long for me to photograph the decedent and the areas adjacent to where he lay. Knowing that we would return this man's body to his family gave me a great sense of relief and peace, knowing they would not have to suffer the interminable thoughts about whether he was dead or alive, or if someone had harmed him and buried his body. There was always a pervasive sense of loneliness photographing a dead body in an isolated part of the countryside. The dead man had clearly thought through his suicide. He'd chosen carefully where he wanted to end his life. He knew that accessing the scene by ambulance would be challenging or next to impossible. He'd taken the time to choose that spot for its isolation. This was a profoundly sad thought. I never discovered why he decided to take his own life. We never did find a suicide note. It left me with unanswered questions. Another lonely death for the photographic archive.

Male, 45, Discovered Dead in Lake

On late turn one night, the duty officer assigned me to a suspicious death in a forest. Epping Forest is almost six thousand acres of ancient woodland that runs north to south on the eastern edge of North London. From Forest Gate in the south to Epping in the north, the forest is about twelve miles long in a north-south direction, but no more than two and a half miles wide from east to west. Epping Forest has more than a hundred lakes and ponds of varying sizes. Some of the lakes were manmade. The majority from gravel extraction, but several formed because of World War II bombs dropped by German bombers on the forest.

When the duty officer mentioned the word forest, I knew it would be a challenging scene to photograph deep in the pitch-black woods on a moonless night. I radioed police from my van, and asked them to position a car, with flashing lights, on the roadway closest to the track down to the scene. While I drove around the dark forest roads, I knew it would be a long trek to where the body lay and not much fun in the dark. I spotted the flashing blue lights of the police vehicle and pulled over next to them. They gave me a rundown of what to expect and suggested they drive ahead of me with their high beams on. Bumping and rattling along the rough track, we drove deeper and deeper into the woods. With every bump and pothole we hit, my camera gear rattled and slid from side to side in the back of my van. The forest track narrowed until the brambles and overhanging tree branches scraped eerily on the sides and roof of my van. At that point, we abandoned our vehicles and walked the rest of the way to the scene. I walked ahead, lighting our way with my powerful crime scene torch, so we didn't break an ankle on the rough terrain.

I heard deep male voices before I could see the investigating officers standing together in a group, at a clearing deep in the woods. When I turned off my torch to conserve power, I could barely see my hand in front of my face. I spoke with the SIO who explained that a man walking his dog had discovered our victim floating in the lake. His dog went to investigate. He'd barked and barked and would not return. This led the owner to search for his dog, which took him to the lake. The lake, hidden from view by dense shrubbery and overhanging trees was an eerie sight in the beam of my torch light. The water looked inky black in the darkness. I knew it was going to be a nightmare of a scene to investigate and photograph without the aid of lighting rigs. The Officer in Charge (OIC) had mentioned rigs were en route and should be arriving shortly. While I waited, I loaded my camera and donned my personal protective clothing. At that stage we didn't know much about the victim, apart from the fact that he appeared to be male. His body floated on the surface of the lake close to the edge. He was face down, with both arms spread out on either side of his body. He looked like a watery crucifixion. It was going to be a challenging scene to light with my flashguns due to the rough terrain and the overhanging trees and shrubbery. In a situation like that, where there was no ambient light, I used a technique called painting with light. Without getting too technical, it entailed setting up the camera on the tripod, checking the focus and turning the camera to a bulb setting. I used a shutter release cable to open the shutter without touching the camera, to avoid camera shake. I locked the cable release and let go. This freed up my hands and allowed me to use all my flash gun power to paint the scene with enough light to illuminate the victim, the lake surface, the nearby trees and the bank closest to the body. During a painting with light session, I fired ten or twenty flashes. How many I used depended on the size of the scene and whether there was any ambient light entering the camera from nearby street lights or the moon. I also used this painting with light technique at arsons, fatal fires and at fatal motor vehicle accidents. It's a skill every police photographer should master if they want to produce quality photographs under difficult lighting conditions. An on-camera flash, that we see on most digital 35mm cameras used at crime scenes these days, doesn't cut it.

Once I'd finished painting with light, and taken all my preliminary shots, it was the turn of the lab sergeant and officers to recover the man's body from the water. Not the most pleasant job, wading into the inky black water in darkness to recover a corpse. Not to mention a body wearing saturated clothes that added extra weight to the already heavy corpse. A bloated and decomposing body in water is slippery and hard to handle, but officers managed to pull the decedent's body up onto the bank. I photographed him again, and took close-ups of his face to aid in identification. The lake bank, littered with fallen trees, strewn with branches, and ankle-breaking holes, made working around the body a difficult task for all involved. In this type of terrain, it would have been easy to break an ankle in the darkness or end up in the lake by accident.

Once I'd finished the extra shots, officers searched the man's pockets for identification, and anything that would help us put the puzzle pieces together. I stood next to the decedent while they searched him, and I photographed the items recovered from his pockets. Among his possessions we found a soggy suicide note. *What a strange thing to do, to write a suicide note and put it in his pocket knowing he would drown himself.* But I suppose in his frame of mind, he probably didn't give the note a second thought, and put it in his pocket. Because so few people leave suicide notes, it seemed a shame not to know what his note said, because it was not fully legible having been in the water. Although some families may find comfort from a suicide note, others may not. At another suicide I photographed, the decedent took an overdose and lay on his bed to die. I photographed the scene as a possible murder. But once we'd moved the decedent off the bed and onto the body sheet, we found his suicide note folded up under the pillow he'd been resting on. It was the last shot on my roll of film for that scene. That was a sad and tragic case, where his family had accused him of being a paedophile.

I never discovered why the man in the lake had taken his own life. But with my work at the scene finished, it was back to bed for me, but not before a long hike back up the forest track in the dark, and then finding my way out of the forest with only a map book to guide me. We had no GPS back then. After these night scenes, I'd learned to return to bed and fall asleep quickly. Back then we didn't work shifts, so the night callouts were additional to a full day and evening of work, often non-stop with little sleep or food. With only four photographers on duty to cover the whole of London and Greater London, I tried to sleep between calls. I was often so exhausted when I returned home after a night call-out to a murder, that I'd arrive home, take off my boots and police jacket and fall onto the bed, still fully clothed. But sure enough, the phone would ring, and it wasn't long before I was back on the road again to yet another murder scene.

Adult Female, Age Unknown, Hanging in Bathroom

One especially memorable lonely death scene took me away from my usual East London territory and over to West London, to a scene I've never forgotten. When I drove into the estate of red-bricked low-rise flats, two uniformed police officers were waiting for me in a police car. They looked sheepish and embarrassed as they walked towards me. And I knew why.

Earlier that day, a resident, smelling a fetid odour from one of the flats, had called the police. The local station had sent two rookie officers to investigate. When they got no answer, they forced entry to check on the well-being of the occupant. The sparsely furnished flat appeared empty. The door to the small bathroom on the right side of the hallway gaped open. They thought the foul smell was coming from a blocked toilet in the flat. One of them held his nose, ran in, flushed the toilet, opened the window and ran out again. They called a locksmith to secure the flat. He came, replaced the lock on the front door and they all left. It wasn't long before frantic calls to the police station began. Neighbours in the adjacent block could see, through the open bathroom window, the horrific sight of a decomposing body hanging in the bathroom. The officers waiting for me were the ones who'd attended the scene earlier and missed the decomposing cadaver. *How did they miss a dead body? How did they not recognise that distinctive smell?*

I stifled the urge to laugh, as Owen and Stewart relayed their story to me, while I dressed in my crime scene garb and gathered up my photographic gear. I'd been in the job long enough to know their colleagues would have teased them mercilessly for their major oversight. I'd already laughed with the duty officer, when he gave me the assignment. *The teasing and the jibes were part of the job. They'd never make that mistake again in their careers.*

'How will we ever live it down?' Owen said earnestly, while we walked towards the entrance to the block of flats.

'We'll have to ask for a transfer to another station,' Stewart said, looking grave. Barely managing to keep from laughing, I said 'Everyone makes mistakes when they're new in the job. Your colleagues will soon forget about it,' I reassured them. I don't know how I kept a straight face. *A little white lie now and again never hurt anyone.*

When we entered the building, the stench of a decomposing body hung thick in the air. A strong enough smell to make the average person gag or vomit on the spot. *How could hundreds of people live in a building with that vile smell and do nothing about it?* An overwhelming stench, even on the ground-floor level. A putrid blend of stale urine, excrement, rotten cabbage, rotten eggs, rancid meat and fustiness. The smell, a blend of chemical compounds and gases produced by the body during decomposition. I suppose, if you've never been around a dead body, you might not recognise the smell of death and decomposition, but you'd know something was afoot. From experience, I knew it would be a horrible scene to photograph. From the smell alone, I knew the body would be in an advanced state of decomposition. I was not wrong.

All the flats in the five low-rise buildings appeared occupied. The group of apartment blocks, surrounded by manicured lawns and flower filled gardens, stood in an affluent area of West London. Not in a run-down council estate filled with abandoned flats, where I'd photographed similar cases. And where it might have been more likely to expect such a scene.

When we reached the fifth floor, the smell grew stronger when the lift doors opened. I stood by the entrance to the flat, loaded my camera with film, and set it on the tripod. I put on a crime scene suit, mask, overshoes and gloves, and pulled up my hood. Owen and Stewart waited outside. I could see from the threshold that a noticeable cluster of dead blowflies and pupal cases lay on the hallway floor of the flat. A familiar sign that a decomposing body is nearby.

I took photographs of the exterior of the flat and went inside alone to see the body and what my photographic challenges might be in such a small space. I stepped into the bathroom and closed the door behind me to see a full view of the victim. The officers didn't see the decedent on their first visit, because the bathroom door shielded her from view, because she hung almost behind it. Her bloated congested face was every shade of brown, green and red imaginable. From head to toe, enough maggots wriggled on her to give the impression of movement. Her purple protruding tongue and bugged-out eyes were a wriggling mass of pale fat maggots. The fly larvae were busily consuming her organs and tissues while I watched. Dozens of maggots crawled about on her head, face and body. I imagined I could hear them feeding noisily, like the buzzing from a busy beehive.

I stared at the decomposing, bloated and barely recognisable body of an unidentified woman, taking in all the details, especially the angle of the cord around her neck. She hung by a tight straining noose fashioned from a lamp's electrical cord. Fully dressed in a tweed skirt suit, and still wearing shoes, her legs dangled into the bath below. I knew enough about hanging, because I'd photographed many over the years, to understand that her death must have been a horrifying six or seven minutes of agonising slow strangulation, compared to a quick hanging death from a high point such as a tree, which causes the neck to break from the sudden force of the drop. The beige cord around her neck she'd secured tightly to a small metal pipe that ran along the top of the bathroom wall, above the bath. Judging by the stench and the state of putrefaction, I'd been correct in my assessment that she'd been hanging there for weeks, if not longer.

I told Owen and Stewart that I'd need one of them to assist me in the bathroom. They both recoiled in horror at my request. Owen agreed to help. Built like a barn door, he squeezed his burly frame into the bathroom next to me and shut the door. With a medium format Pentax 6x7 camera, a large tripod, two large Metz flashguns and three humans in the bathroom, it made for a tight squeeze. Neither of us were more than a few feet from the hanging woman. Sweat poured off Owen while he held the flashgun aloft at my instruction. Maggots dropped from the decedent into the empty bath. I watched them wriggle and fall while I focused my lens. I dripped with sweat, cooking inside my impermeable paper suit in the syrupy hot summer air. Sweat ran down my back and dripped from my forehead. I took the photographs quickly. Owen held his breath. I had barely enough distance to capture full-length shots of the woman's body on my 45mm wide-angle lens. My facemask proved little defence against the vile fetid smell. I could taste the dense air through my mask. Every breath I took was like inhaling the warm vomit of a drunk. Wedged against the sink by the window, the urge to retch was overwhelming. Even with the window ajar, the stench was revolting. But I'd learned, over time, that once you start to retch you start to cough, and once you start to cough you lose control of the urge to vomit. I found that controlled breathing helped me. After the full-length shots, I told Owen he could leave. I didn't want him vomiting on my scene, to make matters worse. He handed me my flashgun and wrenched open the bathroom door and ran out. I closed the door, changed lenses, and took close-up shots of the decedent's face, the noose around her neck and the knot in the cord. All-important shots in any hanging case. By the time I'd finished taking the photographs, I thought my lungs would burst. I found Owen and Stewart on the balcony of the flat leaning over the railing. Owen looked a little green around the gills.

We stood talking together in the sparsely furnished living room while we waited for the undertakers and a locksmith to arrive. A lab sergeant had visited the scene earlier, done his due diligence, and determined the case a suicide. As was common practice for the MPS, I photographed the scene as if it were a homicide. Always a wise insurance policy against anything untoward arising at the PM to indicate a cause of death other than suicide. Most often, I was the person who spent the longest time with the decedent/s at crime scenes, despite what you might see on the police TV dramas, where the police photographer is on screen for seconds and other forensic professionals and detectives are on screen for long periods. Detectives in the MPS did not trample all over the scene, because we restricted scene access to a chosen few and most first officers on scene did a great job of keeping scenes cordoned off and protected. That comes from good training and strict scene protocols. Instead of trampling all over our scenes, detectives studied the photographs and video shot at the scene during their investigation of the case.

'Sad, isn't it, how she died alone and nobody missed her?' I said.

I walked into the hallway and grabbed a handful of letters from the pile strewn about behind the door. I wiped off the dust and fly casings to reveal the name of the occupant. With each lonely death, I discovered another life story. This one belonged to Georgina Bell.

She had lived and died alone in this bleak and dreary place. *Where had she come from? Why no family photographs, no books, no plants, no pets, nothing?* A barren beige wasteland of a flat. Four walls and a roof over her head but no evidence of love, contentment or a life well lived. She'd been someone's daughter, sister, mother, friend or lover once. *Where were they now? Why did she die alone? Yet another invisible, frightened, forgotten soul.*

Male, Aged 19, Defenestration

When I arrived at the hotel on Sapphire Square, I didn't see anything out of the ordinary. But when I looked up at the hotel, a giant tower more than twenty storeys tall, perched on a plinth that housed the ground-floor reception, I could see people looking out of all the windows of the tower. With over 400 guest rooms in the hotel, I had quite an audience for this scene. The guests and uniformed hotel staff pressed their foreheads against the glass panes while they looked down at the scene below, where the decedent's body lay. I could see from the ground level that someone had broken a window in the stairwell of the twentieth floor, as most of the pane was missing.

A man in his late teens had thrown himself out the window. His body landed on the narrow ledge at the side of the tower, on the roof of the ground-floor level of the hotel. A few feet further out and his body would have landed in the street below. This would have been a harrowing experience, not to mention fatal if he'd landed on anyone walking along the street. The decedent, an obese man, took up most of the ledge. Where he landed and how his body lay didn't leave me much room to move past him so I could take shots from all angles. Splattered brain matter clung to the wall next to where he lay. A large halo of blood spread out under his head. Blood from a head wound is different from blood from the body. It's always much thicker and more like a heavy red sticky syrup. I needed to step over his body to take the necessary photographs from various aspects so a jury wouldn't be confused about what and where they were looking. I put my gloved hand out to steady myself so I didn't fall off the edge of the rooftop. When I touched the wall of the building something squished through the fingers of my gloves. I knew I'd put my hand in his brain matter, but my focus was safely climbing over his body to the other side, so I kept going, trying not to slip on his blood and brain matter that covered the ledge he lay on. No police photographer ever wanted to become a second victim at a scene, and none of us ever wanted to appear in another police photographer's photographs. This thought ran through my head at that moment. People in the adjacent buildings stood gaping open-mouthed while I worked. A morbid curiosity compelled them to keep looking at a sight they would remember forever.

After I finished my shots on the ledge, I went to the twentieth floor of the skyscraper to photograph the stairwell window he'd smashed to jump from that floor. Looking down from the twentieth floor I took shots of his body on the ledge below. Although I had no fear of heights, leaning out that window, held securely by two police officers, was not an experience I wanted to repeat. I saw the decedent's last view before he jumped – that always felt eerie and sad.

Falling from that height to the ground takes less time than it has taken you to read this sentence. And the impact with the ground is something akin to being hit by a car travelling at over 80 miles per hour.

I photographed far too many men who took their own lives. The leading cause of death for men in the UK, under the age of 45, is suicide. The increase in male suicide rates around the world is a complex and multifaceted issue with a myriad of contributing factors. To try to tackle this problem, we need to reduce the stigma around mental health, raise awareness of the epidemic of male suicide, and make it easier for men to get help when they need it. We need to challenge expectations of traditional masculinity that discourage men from expressing their emotions or seeking help when they are experiencing mental health issues.

Female, Age Unknown, Suicide by Drowning

A man on his way to work saw her body floating in the water when he cycled past on the canal towpath. He raised the alarm and two uniformed police officers and a lab sergeant attended. By the time I arrived, blue-and-white crime scene tape cordoned off a large section of the towpath, and morning commuters were irritable about the detour. And they weren't shy about letting us know how much it inconvenienced them to take an alternative route. They had a callous disregard for the fact that a human being had died, and the cordoned-off area was an active crime scene.

I put on my white crime scene suit and PPE and made my way along the towpath with my camera bag and tripod. When I reached the lab sergeant, he filled me in on what he knew, and we walked to the spot where the body was still floating in the canal. I took photographs of the decedent *in situ* and the scene along the canal bank, and shots from the nearby bridge and canal bank on the opposite side. While taking the scene photographs, I noticed we were within the shadow of a tall tower block. We later discovered the decedent lived there. I'd visited that high-crime tower on numerous occasions to photograph murders and suicides, drug dealer shootings and victims of muggings and GBH. I'd heard the horror stories from residents. It had become a living hell for the original, and mostly elderly, occupants once the drug dealers had moved in and started plying their trade.

The lab sergeant used a long-handled boat hook to carefully float the body towards the bank without causing any damage to it, but the reeds and the bank edge vegetation posed a barrier to pulling the waterlogged decedent onto the towpath. A dead body is unwieldy at the best of times, and heavy enough without wet clothing that makes the body heavier, and harder to handle. Not to mention if the body has been in water for quite some time, it becomes jelly-like and bloated, and limbs may detach during retrieval which is an unpleasant and traumatising experience for those of us undertaking the recovery.

Fortunately, in this case the body was *fresh*. We didn't have to contend with the additional challenges of recovering a decomposed cadaver. I helped the lab sergeant and the officers on scene, and between us we managed to remove the woman's body from the canal. Both police officers fared less well than myself or the lab sergeant in our wellington boots, and they ended up with soaked shoes, socks and trousers for their efforts. We placed the decedent on a large white plastic sheet on the towpath. I took more photographs of her, full-length back and front, and close-up shots of her face to aid in identification. Then the lab sergeant examined the decedent closely. In drowning deaths, the water, tides, marine life and other scavengers can take a toll on *floaters* as they are known. Cold water slows the decomposition process, but when the seasons change and the water temperature rises, decomposition speeds up. Gases from decomposition build up inside the body and cause it to become more buoyant and float to the surface. *Floaters* were some of the worst cases I photographed, either at the scene or at the PM, because of the vile smell, the bloated body, the discolouration, the bursting and vascular marbling of the skin, the swollen genitalia and the sloughing of skin from the hands and feet. Not to mention the dirt and vegetation that adheres to the body, tangles in the decedent's hair, and abrasions or lacerations from the body striking rocks or other debris in the water. Bodies recovered from the water after some time would be almost unrecognisable to loved ones. TV crime dramas have misled people into believing that bodies recovered from the water look like the person did in life, but that is so far from the truth. The shock of viewing and identifying a drowned loved one would stay with you forever. This is often why police advise family members not to view the body in these cases.

When I looked through my lens to focus the close-up shots of her face, her expression seemed peaceful; she didn't have a look of terror, which somehow made her death seem not so awful, in the scheme of good or bad deaths. A foamy froth exuding from her mouth and nose told me she was still alive when she submerged. The froth (sometimes tinged with blood) looks like the bubbly foam you'd see on a beach when the waves rush out. It results from the victim inhaling water which mixes with air and lung mucus to produce the froth/foam that bubbles out of the decedent's mouth and nose. Suicide by drowning is not the most common method of suicide, but it happens more often than people might think. It's not reported in the newspapers as often as more *newsworthy* deaths. It doesn't take long to drown – from a few seconds to a few minutes. People attach themselves to all manner of heavy objects, like dumb-bells, heavy chains, anchors, or breeze blocks to make sure they'll sink into the water. It's even possible to drown yourself in a tiny rain puddle, if you happen to fall face down into one while you're drunk, and lie in the water long enough. And men who stop to pee into the canal after a long night of drinking . . . They also end up drowning. Sadly, we have the photographs in the archive to prove it.

Dressed in a buttoned-up beige camel coat and a floral-patterned headscarf, she was tiny and still had one shoe on. She looked like she'd been on her way to church, or to the corner shop for a pint of milk and a newspaper. She'd tied her hands with white electrical cord, the sort you'd see on a lamp in someone's home. Of all the suspicious deaths I'd seen, I'd not seen a death by drowning where the victim had tied their own hands. But nothing surprised me. The lab sergeant, with his vast forensic and scene experience considered this a suicide. Seeing her hands tied securely made me realise how much she must have wanted to *not change her mind* when she hit the cold water after jumping from the bridge, or wading into the water from the reeds along the canal bank. I photographed it as if it were a murder, and once the post-mortem was completed, and no foul play discovered, we would file those images away. We never took anything for granted at a scene. What might look like a murder can be a natural causes or accidental death and what looks like a suicide could well be a murder. The photographs and attendance of a lab sergeant in all suspicious death cases made sure nothing was missed.

The thought of the victim sinking into the dank waters of a London canal littered with shopping trolleys, old tyres, shoes and other detritus filled me with horror, and a sense of sadness and despair. I could imagine the filthy water filling her mouth and nose and the sense of panic this must have caused inside her. The gasping for breath. Swallowing the cold water. I couldn't help wondering if she did change her mind when she sank into the cold canal water, but could not save herself.

I couldn't fathom how desperate she must have been to end her own life. This tidy little woman seemed out of place. Not dressed for death. I could picture her life, her tiny frame, scurrying to the local shops, a nervous little person, living in a dangerous and gloomy tower block on a squalid council estate. I'd met lonely souls like her over the years. They often became prisoners in their own homes, in threatening towers where they had lived happily for years before the drug gangs and the violence took over. Poverty kept them prisoner and loneliness drove them to despair.

When I visited to take their photographs, because gangs of thug kids on the estate had beaten or robbed them for the fun of it, they were too afraid to open the door to anyone. I had to keep knocking and shouting through the letterbox, I'm the police photographer, I've come to take your photograph. Eventually I managed to charm most of them to the door to show them my police ID through the glass or through the letterbox. This convinced them it was safe to open the door. I'm sure it helped that I was a young woman with a trusting face and a friendly smile. I was less threatening to them than a male photographer or visitor, because often men had attacked them.

It wasn't long before I'd taken all the necessary photographs and made my way back to my van to go to my next assignment. The jobs kept coming, one after another. The pace relentless. It didn't leave me time to dwell on the previous one. I needed to be mentally and physically ready for the next challenge.

In a busy city like London, and especially in the high crime area I worked, I rarely had time for contemplation. I had to *get on with it* and put each scene behind me when I stripped off my crime scene garb. The next scene or victim waited for me, and each was another mystery, another person or victim whose life had intersected with crime and brutality.

Sometimes I met officers I'd attended these scenes with, and they'd tell me the outcome of their investigation. If they'd found a suicide note at the victim's home or if the family told them their loved one had been depressed. I never found out what happened in this case. Over the years I had to accept, and live with, half told tales. I still wonder why that tidy little woman killed herself in an East London canal on that chilly Monday morning.

Man, Mid-twenties, Hanging in Park

To witness a human being hanging from a tree, swinging in the breeze, is a horrifying sight on any day. There was something incongruous about this man choosing a lovely part of the park, and on such a beautiful day, to hang himself. He hadn't chosen a secluded part of the park. On that hot sunny morning the juxtaposition of such a horrific sight in the flower-filled surroundings made it an especially sad sight. He looked like he'd been on his way to work, judging by his clothes. In a crisp white shirt and suit trousers, he'd hung himself with his own black leather belt. The leaves were in bloom and the grass a lush green. As scenes went, this was a quick one to photograph. It had already been ruled a suicide. But I photographed the scene in case detectives uncovered additional evidence subsequently. I never learned much about the decedent's backstory, but I could not dwell on it, or it would have driven me crazy. All I knew was what I saw and photographed on the day. Knowing more sometimes helped to make sense of such a tragic scene and other times it became more of a burden. It could play on your mind. On the day I photographed this hanging, calls were non-stop. I had other scenes to attend once I'd taken the pictures. There were always people waiting for a photographer. Driving in heavy London traffic took a toll. Going from scene to scene, day and night was exhausting. The lack of food and lack of sleep, and the physical exhaustion made us all more emotionally vulnerable.

When you go from scene to scene, non-stop, you need to shake off the last one and mentally prepare yourself for the next. You must keep looking forward, and moving forward. In the end, I never did find out why he decided to take his own life. He was only in his mid-to late twenties, not much older than I was at the time I took the photographs. The questions remain.

Female, Aged 21, Suicide by Train

Train suicides were among the most horrific scenes I ever photographed. In high summer one year, the duty officer sent me to the scene of a suspicious death. He told me that a young woman had jumped in front of a London to Scotland express train. She was a 21-year-old medical student in her first few years of university. She'd been having trouble keeping up with her studies and had failed some of her courses. Her parents were both doctors and high achievers by all accounts. They wanted the best for her. The best schools, the best university, the best life as a doctor, but the pressure proved too much for her. She couldn't cope with the workload, and didn't want to disappoint her parents. She decided to end her life by jumping in front of a train speeding along the track at 85 miles per hour. Her body exploded when the train hit her. The force of the impact tore her clothes off. Her torn clothing, shredded large pieces of her skin, intestines and torso, and other pieces of her body, large and small, lay strewn along the railway tracks for hundreds of yards, and in the fields on either side of the embankment. Her blood splashed onto the driver's cab windows. I could imagine the shock and horror of that poor driver, when her body hit the train. The sight would have stayed with him forever. Passengers sat on the stopped train, impatiently waiting for it to continue its journey. Several craned their necks to try to see the gory sight. I saw them when I walked along the embankment to the front of the train. Thankfully most could not see what I could see, because their angle of view from the side windows of the train restricted their view ahead. I took all the necessary photographs quickly and efficiently, so the train could be on its way to appease the grumbling passengers. But before that could happen, we had to pick up the pieces of the victim. Usually, any police or forensic personnel on scene vanished when it came time to touch, collect pieces of, or lift a dead body. This scene was no different. So, when I finished my work, I helped the lone police officer to pick up the pieces of this young woman's body and put them into black garbage bags. While we walked along the tracks searching for human flesh, teeth, bone,

THE DARKROOM

shoes and clothing, in the sweltering sunshine, I asked him, 'What about all the smaller pieces?'

'Don't worry about those, the foxes and the birds will take care of them,' came his reply. A wave of sadness washed over me at the thought. I did not reply. The end of a young life. Tragic. Horrific. Over in an instant.

9

Fatal Fires

Playing with Fire – Matricide

A boy stood at the cordon watching while I worked outside the smouldering fire scene. Something unusual about his demeanour caught my attention, so I asked firefighters about him. They said he'd turned up at the scene soon after they'd arrived. He'd stood watching the flames, mesmerised, while they fought the blaze.

A fire scene always attracted attention from neighbours, kids and passers-by. Naturally, people are curious about what's happened in their neighbourhood. Drawn by the flashing lights and sirens of police cars and ambulances, they show up at scenes, as if by magic. They're fearful it might happen to them, so they stop, stare, ask questions, and when they've had enough, or the activity dies down, they move on.

When I arrived at the scene of this fatal fire, I didn't know a lot about the situation. Only that a woman and her son lived in the house. At any fatal fire or arson, it's critical for fire investigators and detectives to gather information about what happened *before* the fire started.

The fatal fire broke out in a red-bricked terraced house in a Northeast London suburb. House-to-house enquiries were already underway by the time I arrived. It's critical to question neighbours and witnesses quickly, while their memory of events is still fresh in their minds. The testimony of witnesses helps police and fire investigators to piece together a picture of what happened.

When firefighters extinguished the blaze, and said the scene was safe to enter, I did a walk through while I waited for the fire investigator to arrive. In a waxed paper suit, yellow hard hat and black wellington boots I explored the house, careful not to step on any critical evidence in the darkness. Protocol dictated that we wore steel-soled metal toe-capped boots at arsons. Although their stiff soles made my feet ache, after working in an arson scene for hours, they were preferable to a 3-inch nail through my foot, a common hazard at arsons.

Alone in the stillness of the smouldering house, I planned my shots while I walked from room to room. I looked for burn and smoke-damage patterns; for evidence of accelerant-pour patterns, or a melted container that had held flammable liquid. I scanned for evidence of unrelated small fires, or an obvious seat of the fire (where it most likely started), and for any incendiary devices, that would indicate arson. From working at hundreds of fatal fires alongside fire investigators, I'd learned a lot about arsons and fire investigation, which served me well when photographing fires.

Fire scenes that burnt at between 500 to 1,500 degrees centigrade, combined with the water hosed onto the premises created enormous photographic challenges.

Light from flashguns or torches does not penetrate smoke, and my lenses steamed up in the hot damp atmosphere, the way glasses do when a person walks from a cold to a hot environment. Water dripped from the ceilings in most fire scenes, yet another issue for camera and flash equipment, although my Pentax 6x7 proved to be a robust camera in challenging environments. To manage the camera fogging issue, I set up my equipment inside to allow time for the lens fogging to dissipate while I conducted my scene walk through. Flashguns could also cause an explosion in the atmosphere of a fire scene. There were plenty of safety hazards for a photographer at arsons. They were not everyone's favourite assignment.

Every crime scene told its own story. The sights, the sounds, the smells. The MPS treated every arson as though it were a homicide if police found a victim in the location. So, I photographed arsons and fatal fires in the same way I photographed murder scenes. Protocols did not permit anyone to move, disturb, or remove evidence from the scene prior to extensive photography. Once I'd photographed the entire scene, I then worked closely with the fire investigator. Because I needed to remain on site to photograph evidence when the fire investigator discovered it, it made sense to help with the dig. Although not strictly my job, I never hesitated to grab a shovel and aid in the *digging out* process under the supervision of the fire investigator. Digging out a fire scene refers to removing layers of debris until you reach the floor underneath. This often reveals pour patterns on a cleared floor that were not obvious when debris, ash and other detritus covered the floor. A fire investigation is a team effort. So, two people digging out helped us process the arson faster and more efficiently.

Smoke had licked its blackened tongue along the tops of the walls in the staircase and snaked its way into the front bedroom at the top of the stairs. Pour patterns on the staircase carpet were plain to see, snaking their way down the stairs from the front bedroom door. The bedroom where the victim lay had taken the brunt of the fire damage. Smoke had blackened the walls and ceiling. An adult female lay, charred and unrecognisable, in the front bedroom. She was lying on the floor in a gap between the bed and the window. The position of her body suggested she had tried to crawl along on the floor to escape the fire but smoke inhalation had killed her before she could reach the end of her bed. She never made it to the door of her bedroom.

The heat from fires makes everyday objects look other-worldly. The heat had half melted a plastic clock in the kitchen. It dripped down the wall like a Salvador Dali painting. A melted gooey blob of black plastic lay disfigured on a coffee table. Transformed by fire, it had once been a phone.

At fatal fires and arsons, I worked closely with police civilian fire investigators – forensic chemists from the MPS Forensic Science Laboratory. They investigated and reconstructed fire scenes, discovered what caused the fire, and located a fire's origin (the seat of the fire), the primary task in any fire investigation.

While I walked through the house I heard a familiar voice, calling out from the front door. Jodie, the sole female fire investigator at that time, had arrived. I'd worked with Jodie, a forensic chemist and trained fire investigator, at many arson scenes and fatal fires. Strong and fierce when she had to be, as a petite female, she too had to navigate the annoying and incessant questions at fatal fires and arsons, which usually began with the tedious starter, 'So, *you're* the fire investigator?' On one memorable occasion, Jodie and I were busy digging out the debris from the fire to search for burn patterns on the floor below the detritus. The male uniformed officer standing outside the door, on the street, watched us work. Then he began making sexist comments about female fire investigators. After about his third or fourth snide comment, I stopped shovelling to wait for Jodie's response. And she didn't disappoint. 'Oh,' she said. 'I wasn't aware you needed a penis to use a shovel.' I laughed out loud at the barb, and we went back to digging out. The officer didn't say another word to us for the remainder of his cordon duty shift.

Although a rare occurrence, sometimes it's a child who sets fire to a house and a parent is the victim. Children set fires for a variety of reasons. Some light fires to express feelings of anger or emotional distress. Although no parent wants to believe their child might kill them, (committing parricide), some children do commit callous acts of violence against a parent.

Criminals frequently used fires to cover up homicides or other violent crimes, due to an erroneous belief that burning a scene, or a body, destroys the evidence of the homicide. In most cases, it does not. Business owners set fires to claim insurance, public housing tenants set fires to finagle a move to a larger property. Disgruntled coercively controlling ex-spouses set fire to the homes of their once beloved spouses and children, often resulting in multiple fatalities. I photographed far too many of these heartbreaking *domestic homicide* fatal fire scenes, and they hardly made the newspapers.

During the house-to-house enquiries, neighbours had told police that the victim's twelve-year-old son was a fire bug. 'He's been a bloody menace in the neighbourhood, setting small fires here and there.' The neighbours and their kids had started to consider him a nuisance kid with no self-control. A boy obsessed with fire. His mum, a nurse at a local hospital, had grounded him for setting small fires that locals had complained about. When she returned home from her night shift at the hospital, he'd asked her if he could go over to a friend's house to play. She refused his request because of his recent bad behaviour. She insisted he stay in the house and play in the garden while she slept. She was trying to discipline him for his previous misdeeds to teach him a lesson. Unwilling to take no for an answer, he threw a temper tantrum. Neighbours had heard the shouting. His mother stood by her decision and ignored his histrionics. Exhausted after her night shift, she didn't have the energy to continue to argue with him. She went to bed and shut her bedroom door.

Angry that she'd forbidden him to leave the house to play with his friends, he'd gone to the garden shed and found a bottle of highly flammable turpentine. By the time he came back into the house, his mother had fallen asleep. In the stillness of the house, he'd crept up the stairs and sloshed the turpentine outside his mum's bedroom door, and down the stairs. He lit a match at the bottom of the staircase, dropped the bottle and fled the scene to his friend's house nearby. The accelerant-soaked carpet on the stairs and landing quickly created a wall of fire and thick black smoke, blocking his mother's escape route. When the fire engines arrived, the boy came back to the house and stood across the road watching the house burn. While the blaze gathered strength his mother lay on the floor in the upstairs bedroom, overcome by the smoke.

When firefighters doused the fire, the boy began to grasp the magnitude of his actions. It didn't take long before tears spilled down his cheeks while he talked to us. 'I only wanted to scare her,' he said, through the tears. He didn't mean to kill her. He wanted to teach her a lesson. To frighten her a bit. To pay her back for telling him no. He thought she'd wake up when she smelled the smoke and she'd run out of the house. He didn't think she would die from smoke inhalation before she reached her bedroom door. It was a heartbreaking scene to witness, especially because he was an only child being raised by a single parent, a hard-working mother who was doing her best for her young son.

Because of the destructive nature of fire, arson scenes are particularly challenging to photograph, and investigate. Water pressure from fire hoses leaves ash and soot debris in soggy piles. The weight of hundreds of pounds of water hosed onto a fire can make the ceilings and walls unstable and at risk for collapse while you work. Everything inside the scene is pitch black or grey, and it's often hard to distinguish charred human remains from other debris. Arson scenes smell awful, a mixture of smoke and accelerants, of burnt synthetic materials, wood flooring, rugs and clothing. And the smell of a burnt human body is something you never forget. Burnt human hair was my least favourite smell.

Arson scenes are filthy, wet and sweltering hot after firefighters have extinguished the fire. The heat retained in a fire scene is hard to fathom until you've experienced it first-hand. Despite the challenges involved, the importance of thorough and accurate documentation and photography of fire scenes is perhaps the most critical aspect of every fire investigation.

Killer at the Cordon – Matricide

Killers sometimes start fires at a crime scene to cover up a homicide. But what they fail to realise is it takes a tremendous amount of heat (thermal energy) to burn an adult human body. Firefighters douse fires long before the body is fully incinerated, so the true cause of death is determined at the post-mortem. The pathologist can tell if the victim was dead before the fire started. If the victim was alive, soot particles show up in the airways or the lungs of the decedent, because the victim breathed in the smoke and particulate matter before they died.

At one fire I had an interesting but not unique experience. The victim was a middle-aged woman. Her killer had brutally beaten and strangled her to death. He tried to hide her body behind a sofa in the living room. Someone had moved all the furniture in the flat out from the walls. Someone had draped the furniture in plastic sheets – it looked like they had started decorating the place. But there were no paintbrushes or paint tins in sight, which was odd. When I'd finished photographing the interior of the scene and the victim, and most of my work was complete, I stood inside the crime scene tape to take shots of the exterior of the building. While I focused my camera, I heard the voice of a man behind me. I kept working and didn't pay him much attention. Crowds often gathered by the cordon and asked me questions or shouted abuse or smart remarks at me. I'd learned to shut them out mentally so I could finish my work in a timely manner. But this bystander persisted, so eventually I turned around to speak with him. He stood on the other side of the crime scene tape, mere feet from me. He was wearing a t-shirt and jeans but no shoes, socks or jacket, which struck me as odd considering how cool it was that day. Immediately something about him rang alarm bells in my head. Instinctively I knew something was off. I noticed pinprick-sized blood spatter on his t-shirt when we spoke. He asked me questions about why I was there? What had happened? I answered a few as vaguely as I could. Soon his questions took a strange turn. He started making comments about the scene, that only someone who'd been inside the scene would have known. I called the cordon officer, and suggested he take a statement. I let him know, discreetly, that this bystander was worth a closer look. I suspected he was the killer. He willingly accompanied the police officer away from the cordon, and I continued with my work. Before I left the scene, I spoke with the senior investigating officer and asked about the man who'd spoken to me at the cordon. It turned out he was the son of the decedent. And he was her killer. He'd told the police the voices in his head had made him kill his mother. When he'd spoken to me, he'd sounded disassociated from the crime, and yet his curiosity had brought him back to the scene. He'd initially fled in panic after killing his mother and setting fire to the flat they lived in. I later found out he suffered with paranoid schizophrenia and had not been home from hospital very long. His mother had agreed to care for him in the community. Sadly, he'd become paranoid once he'd stopped taking his medication. He'd mistaken his mother for an evil entity the voices in his head had commanded him to kill. I don't know what happened to him in the end. I'd imagine he served his sentence in a forensic psychiatric facility. It was a sad case because his mother had been his only friend and confidante, and she genuinely had a desire to care for her mentally ill son. Now he was alone in the world.

A Self-Immolation

As she closed her bedroom curtains, a retired nurse saw flames leaping into the night sky. On a building site across the road from her house, a man had set himself on fire right before her eyes. Still in her nightdress, she rushed downstairs to fill a bucket of water. By the time she'd crossed the road, sloshing water while she ran, it was too late.

She could not reach him, despite her best efforts. To end his life, he'd chosen a private spot, hidden from view, behind a wooden construction fence that ringed a vacant building site. He'd managed to squeeze through a gap in the fence that surrounded the site. His choice of location told the tale of a man who did not wish to be disturbed, a man who had not wished to be saved. The scene and witness statements helped us piece together what had taken place. Earlier that evening the decedent had walked to a nearby petrol station and purchased and filled a plastic fuel can. From there he walked to the empty building site. He took off his greatcoat, his shoes and most of his clothes, and folded them neatly in two piles. In only jeans and a t-shirt, he doused himself in petrol, placed the container next to the piles of clothes and walked barefoot into the middle of the building site. He sat with his legs crossed in a yoga pose, set himself on fire and burnt to death. There were no signs he'd moved after the flames had engulfed him, although his hands had tightened into fists, which happens when muscles contract from the heat and dehydration, which gives the decedent the look of a boxer with clenched fists raised. His charred remains were localised to a small area in the centre of the site.

Over the years I'd photographed most methods of suicide, but self-immolation was a rare and surprising sight to see in London. While I photographed the scene in the darkness, and smoke continued to rise from the decedent, with each flashgun burst of light, the thought of dying engulfed in flames filled me with horror. *How painful must his death have been? What resolve it must have taken for him to remain calm for the length of time it took him to die. Had he not wanted to flail around or change his mind and try to escape the conflagration. How long did it take to die?* When the forensic pathologist arrived, I learned that extensive burning gives the victim initial pain, but the flames quickly burn away nerve endings and the parts of the body already burnt no longer feel pain. And yet I still cringed at the imagined pain the charred victim must have suffered. I couldn't imagine a more painful death, despite what the pathologist said.

The sight of a burnt body is shocking, but the smells of a burnt body are almost worse than the sight. Of all the smells at fatal fire scenes, the smell of burnt hair is one of the worst. It's a smell you never forget. I always thought burnt hair smelt like the perm lotion you smell wafting out of a hairdressing salon, but imagine it more like a burnt chemical smell. Burnt body smells are complex, because different parts of the body give off different odours. All the odours blend in a pungent, sickly sweet, meaty kind of smell, with metallic and chemical overtones.

Burnt hands contort into a pugilistic or boxer-like pose because when muscles shrink, they close the hands into fists. Muscle shrinkage also causes the knees to bend or the arms to flex. At many fire scenes, a person who died in the fire lying on the floor of a bedroom, looked like they were ready to leap up and run away, with their knees bent upwards, and the elbows bent and the hands clenched into fists, or missing completely, if they burned off. Skin splits on the head and near the joints. The soft tissues, muscles and fat contract from the heat, so the skin splits, often around the abdomen, and lengthwise along the muscles of the arms and legs. The internal organs shrink, but I often saw lengths of pink glistening intestines poking through the split skin, like a sausage on the grill where the casing splits and the sausage meat oozes out. None of it is pleasant to see, although I quickly became accustomed to it because I photographed hundreds, if not thousands of fatal fires over the years.

In time, I learned that the young man had set himself on fire because he'd lost his job, and his girlfriend had broken off their relationship. With no suicide note, we could not confirm or refute this hearsay. But no matter the motivation, his death saddened me and I've never forgotten it.

10

Laughter Kept Me Sane

People would often ask me, 'How did you stay sane in a job as distressing and stressful as that of a police photographer?' I survived partly because I had a good sense of humour. I laughed easily with colleagues and survivors alike, to release the tension and put people at ease. Having a resilient and playful nature helped enormously.

Hanging on for Dear Life

When I arrived at an arson scene, a large group of spectators had congregated behind the crime scene tape. Fire engines and police cars cluttered the car park in front of the flats. While I stood at the rear of my vehicle to change into my crime scene overalls, I noticed the smoke-stained window and blackened bricks above the window frame of a flat on the top floor of the building. On a drainpipe adjacent to the window of the burnt flat, I saw a pair of blue Y-fronts hanging from a bracket on the pipe. I thought it seemed a little odd, but I'd seen lots of weird things over the years, so didn't give it much thought. I gathered my camera gear and went into the scene and photographed the flat and the bedroom where the incident took place. The fire brigade had arrived quickly on scene which minimised fire damage to the flat in question. It didn't take me long to photograph the entire flat, including the bedroom where the fire had started. By the time I'd finished my work, officers had gathered witness statements from neighbours and already had a suspect in custody.

It transpired that the male victim had come home after working a night shift and gone to bed. His wife crept into the bedroom where he slept, and set light to the bedclothes, in the hope her husband would burn to death while he slept. She crept back out of the bedroom and locked the door behind her. Fortunately, for her husband, he woke up before the fire took hold. In a panic, he tried to escape through the bedroom door when the room started to fill with smoke. Finding the door locked, he had no choice but to exit by the single pivot window in the bedroom, which proved rather challenging under the circumstances. When the flames engulfed the room, wearing nothing but his underwear, he contorted his body to climb out of the third-floor window, with the intention of shinning down the drainpipe to safety.

In his haste to escape the smoke and flames, he managed to snag his underwear on a bracket that held the drainpipe to the building. Now well and truly stuck, when the fire service arrived, they discovered him dangling from the pipe, looking less than comfortable in his snagged underwear. When they raised the ladder to rescue him, they lifted him out of his underwear to save his life.

With the crowds gathered below, drawn by the sirens, I could only imagine how embarrassed he must have been to have found himself hanging by his underwear while he waited for the fire brigade to rescue him. Still, I thought, it's better stark naked and alive than burnt to a crisp in a smoky bedroom fire. I did laugh, I must admit. And no doubt so did the firefighters who rescued him. Not to mention the neighbours getting an eyeful. As arson scenes went, this was one of the more amusing and memorable ones. It wasn't all doom and gloom and bleakness. Laughter kept me sane in the mire of misery and chaos. It proved to be an important part of staying sane in the face of so much sadness, horror and violence. Although I laughed at the underpants situation, I did not laugh at the victim. From the actions of his wife, it appeared they had serious problems in their marriage. But she had not thought through her plan. She hadn't anticipated he'd climb out the bedroom window to escape. She hadn't secured it. No doubt a suitable punishment for the wife would have cooled her desire to set any further fires.

Bottoms Up

Many of the victims I photographed over the years were incredibly resilient, humorous and remarkably gracious considering what had happened to them. When I visited them at their homes to take photographs of their injuries, sometimes there were big surprises, other times funny moments and I laughed along with them. It put them at ease and made the whole process much less stressful and embarrassing for them. Laughter was an important way to relieve the tension in situations like this. I never laughed at the victims. I only laughed with them. Like the man who'd been stabbed in his bum. He lived in a high-rise flat, quite close to others nearby. I could see occupants in the other flats quite clearly from where I stood. When he told me he'd been stabbed in the bum, I asked if he'd prefer to have a male photographer take his photographs, but he said that wasn't necessary. He was comfortable with me taking the photographs. We stood in his sunny living room together. I set up my camera and he stood a few feet in front of the camera with his back to me, then he dropped his pants and under-wear and bent over. With his pants around his ankles, he started to laugh. I had visions of someone looking through his curtainless windows from the nearby flats and wondering what was going on. Bent over, and still smiling, he looked back at me through his parted legs and asked, 'Do you think I should hold my penis and testicles out of the way, so they're not showing in the photograph?'

'I think that would be a good idea,' I replied. I wanted to spare the poor man having photographs shown to the jury that included his penis and testicles, when that wasn't necessary. He duly held his penis and testicles out of the way, and I quickly shot all the photographs of his injury. He pulled up his pants and turned to face me and we burst out laughing together. I had many of these surprising and humorous experiences over the years with different victims. Another funny anecdote like this comes to mind, but this time the joke was on me.

Sorry, I Don't Speak Spanish

On a sunny summer morning, a petite smiling woman named Maria answered the door to us. Two detectives stood behind me like a pair of door-to-door salesmen, in light-coloured suits, both holding navy clipboards. We must have looked an odd sight when she opened the door. Her brown eyes sparkled and her wild dark hair hung carelessly about her shoulders. She greeted us in Spanish, although none of us spoke Spanish. I only knew one phrase, *Perdón, pero no hablo español*. But it didn't seem to matter, the woman's warm smile spoke volumes. Genuinely glad to see us, she gestured a welcome and invited us into her home. I'd come to the Victorian house in Notting Hill to photograph the scene of a break-in and assault, and the victim's injuries sustained in the attack. Her ex-boyfriend had broken in and assaulted her after their relationship had ended. I decided it would be best to photograph her injuries first and then upstairs, where the attack took place. The detectives with me offered to wait in the kitchen while I documented her injuries. The victim and I went into the front room. Judging by the furniture, the room doubled as a dining room and a living room. I closed the door behind us, put down my camera bag and extended the legs of my tripod. Maria was wearing a white t-shirt and blue denim dungarees, with a cardigan on top. Because she spoke no English, I mimed the action of moving the pine oblong table and two benches back towards the wall, so I'd have enough room to work. She seemed to understand, and together we repositioned the furniture. I indicated she should sit on the bench while I took photographs of her injuries. So far so good. She seemed to be following along and things were going fine. I spoke to her although I knew she didn't understand much English, but sometimes the sound of a soothing voice helps a victim to relax and cooperate. She smiled a beaming smile when I spoke with her. She didn't appear to understand a word I said, but she cooperated and seemed at ease in my presence. Although the detectives with me had advised me she spoke no English, I soon found out they hadn't exaggerated. The entire interaction with Maria took on the quality of a Marcel Marceau mime act. I wanted to laugh but resisted the urge. Documenting the injuries of an assault victim is no laughing matter. I had to ensure my photographs were exposed correctly, sharply in focus, with scale tape in each photograph so jury members could tell how large or small a bruise or injury was relative to the size of the victim. I could overlook nothing.

I smiled while I gestured. I pointed and used facial expressions – they were the only tools in my arsenal. Yes, I know what you're thinking, why didn't they bring an interpreter with them. They'd tried to find an interpreter, but none was available. We had to go ahead with the photography so I documented her bruises and injuries at the optimal time, once they were visible enough to be seen, but before they'd faded. So, back to the photographs. Maria seemed keen to help. All the while, I was conscious there were two detectives waiting in the kitchen, so the pressure to take the photographs quickly was greater than usual. Generally, I went to a victim's home by myself, so the pace of my work was set by the mood and disposition of the victim, their level of cooperation, or their level of distress and other factors, such as who else was in the residence with the victim. If they were distraught, they needed me to be patient and take my time with them. Building trust through a conversation and a pleasant demeanour moved the assignment forward. It's a lot to expect of an injured person, both physically and mentally. A police photographer (usually a man), a stranger, turns up on your doorstep soon after the most traumatic experience of your life. They ask you to trust them. To take off your clothes and to allow them to document your injuries, often in intimate places; your mashed faces, your stitched wounds, your black eyes and battered bodies. To be able to garner a survivor's trust is a gift. It takes a blend of assertiveness, warmth, charm, compassion and a genuine love of people.

Anyhow, back to Maria on the bench. I pointed to my camera bag and she nodded her understanding. I bent down to choose the right lens for the job. With my back to Maria, I concentrated on my gear and loading a roll of 120 film (ten shots per roll). It didn't take long. When I turned to face Maria, she was standing there stark naked, less than two feet in front of me. Not only was she naked, she had both arms outstretched, crucifixion style. My immediate response was to laugh, but I didn't. Smiling broadly at me, she looked relaxed and unselfconscious. I'd seen so many naked bodies over the years, both dead and alive, that the sight of a naked woman right in front of me wasn't a big deal, but it was a big surprise because her injuries were on her arms and legs and didn't require her to be naked. I managed to persuade her to put on some of her clothes and her underwear, so she didn't catch cold. I got the shots I needed in the end. Maria smiled and waved to us at the door when we left. I never did figure out why she took off all her clothes. People did the strangest and most unpredictable things in front of a police photographer and their camera and this was not the first example by any means. But it did add some levity to that day's work. I never mentioned it to the two detectives who accompanied me, but I'm sure they wondered why I was smiling broadly when we left Maria's house.

Fleaing the Scene

'Take off all your clothes, now,' I urged the two burly detectives. I stifled a laugh as I watched them flail around on the concrete walkway. Fleas jumped about in their hair and on their suits as they struggled in vain to brush them off. A mass attack by the small brown insects caused the two officers to run out of the suspicious death scene when they felt the first bites. There were dozens of fleas on each of them. They were easy to see against their light-coloured suits and shirts.

'Come on. Hurry up,' I urged. 'You need to strip off to stop them biting you.'

'We can't take our clothes off here. People will see us,' they pleaded.

'I've an idea,' I said.

I laughed to myself as I ran down three flights of stairs as fast as I could, back to my van to grab two white paper crime scene suits and a body sheet and evidence bags. Residents in the flats opposite who watched me racing away from the scene, in full crime scene regalia, must have wondered what on earth was going on. I hurried back to the flea-bitten officers.

'Quickly, put these on,' I said, while I ripped open two packages of paper suits and shook them loose.

'But we can't strip here, out in the open,' they implored, shy at the prospect of undressing in the middle of a London council estate. And in front of a female photographer, with a camera.

'Don't worry, I've seen it all before,' I said while I looked around us for somewhere suitable for them to undress. The enclosed stairwell landing at the end of the walkway offered the closest, best option. At least the decorative breezeblock construction afforded them partial privacy from the prying eyes of people in the opposite flats.

'The stairwell,' I said, pointing, 'that'll do, at least it's not too open and public.'

Without another word, we ran to the stairwell at the end of the third-floor balcony. I stood with my back to them, shielding their modesty with a white body sheet, as they undressed. I listened for the footfalls of unsuspecting residents on the concrete stairs above and below us. I had a vision of an elderly woman climbing the stairs with her heavy shopping bags and finding herself face to face with me in full crime scene coveralls plus two half-naked police detectives looking rather shifty. I couldn't resist the urge to laugh at the absurdity of the situation. Then they started to laugh. When I turned around, I realised they were laughing because the paper suits they'd squeezed into fitted a 5ft 4in person, and they were both six feet tall. The suits were a snug fit and left little to the imagination. Their hairy legs protruded about eight inches below the ends of the elasticated suit legs. An unforgettable sight. Two large police officers zipped into the most unflattering waxed paper suits. Underneath as naked as the day they were born.

We laughed so hard, the tears streamed down our faces. Once we'd composed ourselves, I helped them bag their clothing into two large evidence bags. In went their fancy tailored suits, then shirts, ties, socks, the lot. The body sheet came in handy that day, as a barrier to protect their modesty. Luckily, it was a warm summer morning, so no chance of them catching a cold.

'Let's have a photo, lads,' I said. After a half-hearted protest, they agreed, but only if I promised not to share the pictures with anyone. I took a few shots and promised them a print each, and that I'd destroy the negatives. I'm probably one of the rare people that convinced two Scotland Yard detectives to strip naked in public. And not be arrested for it.

Not long after, a van arrived from the police station to take them to the nearest hospital for fumigation and treatment for the intense itching caused by the bites. Not a prospect either of them relished. As they climbed into the back of a police van, I watched from the balcony above. I still had a scene to photograph. It was back to work for me. I'd been to enough hoard scenes over the years, that fleas were on my mental scene-safety check-list. I'd warned the two officers before they entered the flat, but they'd shrugged off my recommendations that they either wait outside or wear full protective clothing. It's always wise to listen to the sage advice of an experienced police photographer. If not, you live and learn. Or in their case you endure dozens of flea bites, you strip naked in public, you get hosed down and fumigated at the hospital, and then you learn.

Another officer arrived to provide a police presence at the scene while I worked. I suggested he wait outside while I photographed the dead man. He wisely agreed. He'd heard the flea story. I pulled up my hood, put on a mask and fresh latex gloves, taped at the wrists and ankles, and stepped into the fleapit to document the scene. An old man lay dead and decomposing among his cluttered possessions. From the entryway through to the living room, piles of black plastic bags, clothes, books, newspapers and all manner of bric-a-brac stood shoulder high. I picked my way through the narrow canyon of detritus to reach his body, all the while avoiding knocking into the precarious hoard with my tripod, balanced on my shoulder. The last thing I wanted was a flea-infested hoard falling on top of me. I took the necessary shots of the old man and moved on to document the remainder of the scene.

In the kitchen, the bedrooms and even in the bathroom and toilet the old man's hoarded possessions stood in piles up to the ceiling. He'd turned his entire flat into a pile of stinking detritus so dense it was difficult to open the doors into each room. I had to climb on the hoard to capture shots inside each room. I'd had plenty of practice, as I'd been to every manner of hoard situation in the past. Hoards where beer cans littered the entire room, so the bed, devoid of any sheets, floated in a 15-inch-high sea of empty beer cans and vodka bottles. I'd been to hoards where the occupants didn't throw away a single soiled nappy (diaper), but flung them into one of the spare rooms until the pile grew into a mountain of faeces and urine-filled nappies that I had to climb on to capture my photographs for a child abuse case. An unforgettable sight and smell.

Although assigned this case as a suspicious death scene, a lab sergeant had attended prior to my arrival. After an examination of the scene and the victim, he'd deemed the old man's death from natural causes, with no suspicious circumstances evident. However, as any experienced death investigator knows, it's always better to assume nothing, err on the side of caution and have the scene photographed. A wise precautionary measure in case the post-mortem uncovered any suspicious findings. In this case the pathologist ruled the old man's death consistent with natural causes.

Snowy Owl at Christmas

It was two days before Christmas when I went to a high-rise block of flats in the East End of London to photograph an assault victim. The grimness of recent work had ground me down. I wasn't feeling the spirit of Christmas at all, as many years I worked right through. Christmas was a busy time for police photographers in London. I felt exhausted and was running on fumes. Most of my visits to victims' homes were by pre-arrangement/appointment. I never wanted to climb twenty flights of stairs in a block of flats and find the victim had nipped out to the shops. This was back in the day before everyone had mobile phones plastered to their ears 24/7.

I rang the doorbell and waited. A young teenager invited me in. She shouted over her shoulder to her dad.

'It's for you Dad, the police photographer is here to take your picture.'

I walked into the flat to greet the family who'd been watching TV in the living room. The flat was neat and tidy, and warm and cozy. The family were friendly and welcoming. They offered me a cup of tea when I arrived. I politely refused because I still had more jobs to complete before I could go off duty for the night. And besides, when you go to so many filthy places, you're reluctant to put your lips to a cup. You don't know where it might have been or what it had been used for before they served you tea in it.

Standing in the living room was a huge *real* Christmas tree, fully decorated and lit up with strings of fairy lights. The atmosphere in the room was festive. I set up my tripod and loaded a roll of film. When I started to take photos of the victim's bruised face – muggers had punched and kicked him – his children asked me if I wanted to see their owl. *Was it a Christmas ornament? Was it a Christmas toy, I wondered?* 'Yes, I'd love to see your owl when I finish taking the pictures of your dad,' I said.

With the photographs of their dad's injuries complete, I turned to the kids and said, 'Ok, show me your owl.' They pointed to the Christmas tree.

And there it was, standing on a tree branch staring at me, unmoving, a huge white owl. I couldn't believe my eyes. A magnificent snowy owl (a female I subsequently learned) with large yellow eyes and smooth white feathers. It swivelled its head while it surveyed the scene. It wasn't nervous or bothered in any way. I was amazed it hadn't flapped around and freaked out when I used my two flashguns, because they could be noisy when they fired, and squeal a high pitch as they recharged.

I asked the kids to tell me the story of their snowy owl. They said they'd found it injured on their balcony after a storm, and they'd nursed it back to health. It didn't sound like they would be parting company with it any time soon. The visit with that family warmed my heart and filled me with Christmas cheer. It lifted my spirits on that night and has remained a fond memory for me. I wonder how the story ended? I guess I'll never know. But it was a lovely Christmas story and I've never forgotten those kids and their snowy owl.

11

From Cradle to Grave

Male, Less than 24 Hours Old, Neonaticide

He was a beautiful full-term baby boy. Ten tiny fingers and ten tiny toes. Perfect in every way, but sadly found dead. Discarded, like yesterday's rubbish. A woman walking her dog, early on a cold morning, discovered his naked body. She noticed a white plastic bag when her dog went to investigate. The small shopping bag, dumped in the gap between two parked cars, looked like a bag of rubbish, tied at the top. If it hadn't been for her dog, the baby's body may have remained undiscovered for longer. Thankfully foxes hadn't scavenged his body by the time we found him.

When I arrived, the lab sergeant was waiting for me to photograph the scene before he could undertake his work and move on to the mortuary with the baby's body. The scene didn't take long to photograph. I took some shots of the street, and some shots of the baby and the bag. Focusing my lens on the baby's face and body in the plastic bag upset me. Although I could grasp it intellectually, and see the baby's body through my viewfinder, it felt beyond my comprehension. My brain didn't want to let me believe the ugly truth of it. It defied all logic to photograph a baby only hours old, now dead and gone forever.

Although mothers killing their newborns is rare, this wasn't the first newborn homicide (neonaticide – the killing of an infant within the first 24 hours after birth) I'd photographed over the years. In other cases, young women *mostly*, left their babies on the steps of churches and convents, and other perceived *safe* locations, in the hope that a kind person discovered them before they succumbed to the cold. But sadly, nobody found these infants in time to save them.

Questions raced through my mind while I took photographs. *Why had she concealed her pregnancy? Was she fearful of telling her parents? Was she mentally ill? Was she in denial, or ashamed of her pregnancy? Was she a rape or incest victim?* I couldn't help thinking, there must have been a better way than this. Fostering, adopting, handing over the baby to a family member, or a friend. Anything would have been better than this. It's hard not to feel angry and disgusted at a scene like that, but it wasn't my place to judge. My job was to present the photographic evidence. To tell the story of this baby boy's death, without fear or favour, and to let the evidence speak for itself.

It wasn't long before the investigative team arrived at the mortuary. Post-mortems on children are emotionally distressing to photograph, but a PM on a neonate who had come into the world only a few hours before, broke my heart. I took the standard shots of the baby, back and front, and listened while the pathologist noted the condition of his body, his size, weight, the colour of his eyes, skin, hair and his height. The beautiful blue-eyed boy looked like he was sleeping. While the pathologist worked on his tiny body, I stood beside him to watch and take photographs when needed. A female officer, the first responder on scene, attended the PM, along with the lab sergeant, myself and a mortician. The first PM for her, I suspected. She stood near the wall, looking anxious, a few feet back from the autopsy table, as if the wall might hold her up if she buckled. Her face revealed her churning emotions. Tears welled up in her eyes as the PM progressed. I wanted to rip off my latex gloves and hug her. But I had work to do, so I couldn't comfort her. I nodded to the lab sergeant, and he took the hint. He went over to her, and gently guided her outside to take a breath of air and shed some tears.

Compared to the tiny boy's body in the centre of the adult-sized stainless-steel autopsy table, the male pathologist's hands and instruments looked enormous. As the autopsy continued, the pathologist noted impressions of finger marks on either side of the baby's temples. I photographed the marks on his soft skull. The position of the fingermarks told us his mother had gripped his head and pulled him out of her birth canal with force. This gave us a clue to the fear, panic and pain she must have endured, all alone, giving birth in secret. There were no other marks or injuries on the baby. His mother had not inflicted any wounds on him. He was a healthy, full-term beautiful baby boy. He died from exposure to the cold.

When the female officer and the lab sergeant left the autopsy suite, the pathologist held out his hand to me, and in it lay a tiny pink perfectly formed heart. On this occasion, I think the pathologist needed to break the silence and the tension through this action. While you may find this a horrifying thought, at many forensic post-mortems it was quite usual for a pathologist to hold out a brain or a liver or another organ to me, to look at, or invite me to look at something unusual inside the body or skull cavity, which I often did, with great interest. After all, I photographed the innermost depths of a decedent's open body cavity, and inside their skull, at most of my forensic post-mortems, to show how knife wounds had sliced through organs, and hit bone, or to show a mass of blood clots on the brain from a head wound, or holes in the skull from a gunshot. A police photographer works so closely with the forensic pathologist, they cannot stand far away from the autopsy table, or stand next to the autopsy table for hours and not engage. It's not feasible. Myself and many of my photographer colleagues chose to learn from each PM to add to our forensic expertise. It's a rare learning opportunity not afforded to many. This cumulative forensic knowledge proved valuable when we attended homicide and suspicious death scenes. On this occasion it was a *teachable moment for the photographer*, that disguised the pathologist's attempt to manage his own feelings about the autopsy he was performing. I looked closely at the small pink heart in his gloved hand. It was only the size of a walnut. It's impossible to explain how it felt to witness such a tragic and senseless loss of a new life. The cycle of his lifespan less than 24 hours from birth to death. I found it incomprehensible that anyone could so cruelly discard such a beautiful baby boy. Now, looking back with the benefit of age, knowledge and maturity, I understand more fully the complexity of these tragic concealment births, infanticide and neonaticide cases, and the challenges of identifying young women who are most at risk. There's a scarcity of research on neonaticide, and the UK does not keep any official records of how many mothers and fathers kill their children in the first 24 hours of life. Estimates range from between seven deaths per year to around 300 deaths in England and Wales. True figures are likely to be considerably higher. In the existing research, some suggest that those who kill a child in the first 24 hours of its life tend to be teenagers/young women, living with parents, bearing their first child; have low levels of education, living in abusive homes, and have concealed their pregnancy or denied their pregnancy to themselves because they lack emotional maturity and the financial resources to cope with a pregnancy. However, there is no consensus on this, which makes it challenging to assess and intervene with those most at risk.

The lab sergeant returned to the autopsy suite, followed by the female officer a few minutes later. It didn't take long to complete the autopsy, and we all went on our way. The police officers investigating this baby boy's death showed great kindness and compassion throughout. They were gravely concerned for the safety and welfare of the young mother. Because we had not found any placenta at the scene, officers did everything in their power to find her before she died from blood loss, or infection. Sadly,

I never discovered if they traced the young mother or not, or what happened in this neonaticide case.

Thankfully, these days, there are more solutions available to avert these tragic and senseless abandonment deaths. In several countries there are *safe haven* laws that allow people (usually women) to surrender their newborns at a police station, a fire station, or a hospital, without risk of prosecution. In other countries, mothers have an opportunity to leave their newborn in a safe, warm bed inside a *baby hatch*, or *baby box*, built into the walls of hospitals, churches, social centres, fire stations and police stations. Sensors, built into these hatches, alert the occupants that a newborn is in the box, and staff care for the baby immediately. Those surrendering a baby find a letter inside the box. It encourages them to seek medical help, and return to the location to speak with staff, without fear of prosecution, should they change their mind within a certain period after surrendering their baby. Although these *safe haven laws* and the baby boxes have been in operation for some time, sadly, too few women and girls are aware of these options, and needless and tragic deaths continue to happen.

Female, Aged 75, Robbery and Homicide

Children weren't only the victims in my cases, some were also killers. When I arrived at the scene, the OIC walked with me to a ground-floor flat that opened out to a neatly tended communal garden. The decedent lay in a pool of blood near the front door of her home. Her feet stuck out into the hallway. I could see them when we walked towards the scene. The position of her body told me she had opened the door to her assailant. There were no signs of forced entry to the front door, no jemmy marks or splintered wood. Her assailant killed her when she opened the door. In his attempt to rob her, he pushed her into the hallway, and barged past her into her flat, searching for money or anything valuable he could steal. She stumbled backwards into the downstairs cloakroom and struck her head on the corner of the small sink.

Powerfully built, and tall for his age, her fifteen-year-old killer ended her life in a second. One push from the adrenaline-filled teenager was all it took. He ransacked her flat but left with only a few pounds. He ran from the scene through the back door of the flat, and left the victim to die, bleeding and alone. He never went to her aid. If the door to her flat had not been left gaping open, police might not have discovered her body for some time.

As I walked through the scene photographing the entirety of the flat and the grounds, I remember thinking what a senseless death this was. Not only a waste of a precious life of someone loved, but also the waste of a teenager's life, and pain and misery for two families.

It's common for thieves to target old people, because they think they won't meet much resistance. The victims are too frail to fight back against robbers who may be carrying a weapon. But in some cases, the victims have lived through wars, and are feisty, and will fight back, which often doesn't end well. Robbers will often target a victim who is on their way home. They'll follow them to their home address and try to rob them, or assault them on their doorstep or in the hallway of their home. The shock of the assault is sometimes enough to cause the elderly person to have a heart attack or fall, causing fatal injuries for such frail individuals. The futility of this kind of loss of life made me so angry. His life ruined, and her life ended. Pain for his family. Pain for her family. And all for what. All for a few pounds.

Although this scene was sad and tragic on so many levels, I was thankful that there had been no indication that the teenage killer had raped the elderly victim. Sadly, this was not always the case.

Female, Aged 92, Assault and Rape

'I heard a noise downstairs,' Ethel told me. In the darkness, she'd turned to her husband in bed next to her. He was deaf and sound asleep. 'He'd been unwell, so I didn't want to wake him,' she continued. 'I thought the noise was next door's cat, in our back yard.' At 92, her joints were stiff. So, she sat on the side of their bed to steady herself for a moment. She slid her feet into her slippers and shuffled across the dark bedroom.

Out on the landing, she looked over the bannisters and saw a light from the kitchen spilling the length of the hallway below. 'I thought that Bill must have forgotten to turn off the kitchen light when he came up to bed,' she said. Holding the handrail, she crept slowly down the stairs. Some of the treads creaked under foot. When she turned towards the brightly lit kitchen, a large black figure filled the doorway. 'I couldn't see his face, it was in shadow, with the kitchen light behind him,' she continued. 'What are you doing in my house?' she shouted at him. He didn't answer. He lunged for her. He covered her mouth with his gloved hand and dragged her along the hallway, back into the kitchen where he beat, kicked and punched her mercilessly and then raped her. 'I told him I was a one-man woman. And that Bill was the only man for me,' she told me in a shaky voice. A frail bird of a woman, with snow-white hair, Ethel didn't stand a chance against a huge bear of a man. A brute, freed from prison only days before the rape, having served a sentence for sexual assault, burglary and other crimes.

Wearing a bulky dressing gown that dwarfed her, she sat in a wheelchair, in the overheated hospital ward where I photographed her. I could see her bruises before I reached her. Two purple-black swollen eyes, bruised hands, shins and forearms. Clearly in pain from the beating, and the rape that had caused internal injuries, she greeted me warmly nonetheless. I knelt to chat with her to explain how I'd go about taking her photographs for court. She held my hands while I spoke with her. Her thin wedding band loose on her ring finger, and blue thread veins visible through her paper-thin skin. A nurse helped to unclothe her gently while I worked my way through photographing all the bruises and injuries on her body. She winced in pain as we progressed with the photography. Every movement excruciating for the courageous elderly woman who sat before me.

She wasn't the first or the last rape survivor I photographed over the years. I'd photographed hundreds, of all different ages and backgrounds. They each told me their rape ordeal in detail while I photographed their injuries. Between myself and my colleagues we'd photographed the rapes of six-month-old baby girls, right up to this elderly lady at 92 years of age. I learned some time later, that police arrested the man who raped her. He went back to prison for eighteen years for the crimes he'd committed during his short release from prison.

Most of my rape cases involving elderly victims never made the newspapers. You might imagine that men raping elderly women is a vile, and rare, occurrence, but it's not. We're not talking about it. Why are we not talking about men raping elderly women? Because it's hard to even imagine that elderly women (and a small percentage of elderly men) could be victims of sexual violence, perpetrated at the hands of strangers, nursing-home staff, and by their own family members. The very people an elderly person should be able to trust. Often the perpetrators of these despicable sexual assaults and rapes are young men in their teens, and sometimes even a son or a close relative of the victim, shocking as that might seem. It's time to bring this hidden and oddly *taboo* issue, of sexual violence against elderly women, to light. Advanced age affords no protection against a man raping a woman (or another man). A common misconception is that rape is about sexual desire, provoked by women wearing revealing clothing, but it's not. The rape of elderly victims, children and even baby girls refute this stereotype. Rape is about power and control, anger, misogyny, hatred and humiliation. Sadly, many elderly survivors of rape are too ashamed to come forward. Too ashamed to report the rape to police or even tell their families, for fear their loved ones and others won't believe them. Many social workers, family members and health professionals miss the signs of rape in the elderly. Because people mistakenly perceive rape as a crime primarily against young women, support, legal and other services tend to cater to that group and not to women (and men) 60 years of age and older. There's a paucity of research on sexual violence against older women. And a lack of research on the psychological effects of rape, or the underlying motivations of the offenders that commit these heinous crimes. This needs to change. Our elderly members of society deserve better.

Care and Protection

It was not only the elderly and women who were the most vulnerable and defenceless victims. I photographed many care and protection cases that involved the suffering, abuse and deaths of children, babies and neonates. Children who had been, or were imminently, at risk of abuse or neglect by a caregiver. Child abuse could be physical, sexual or emotional. Neglect meant failing to provide the child with support for their health, welfare and safety. Including allowing the child to live in squalid conditions (mould, broken windows, no bed or bedding) or to live without adequate food, clothing, heat or medical care. In many of these cases, caregivers abused drugs and alcohol. They gave their child alcohol to keep them quiet, while they partied or got high. They often failed to keep their children safe from people who might abuse or exploit them. In these types of cases, police had permission to remove a child temporarily to a place of safety for up to 72 hours, without a court order. Police officers did their best to find a responsible grandparent or sibling to take care of the child, or children, for those 72 hours. During that period, I attended the home of the child to photograph evidence of neglect and abuse. I photographed empty filthy fridges, bare cupboards and squalid living arrangements, for presentation at court. Sometimes that work involved photographing a child at their home, or in a hospital, if the caregivers or parents had physically injured the child. In many cases the child's mother, father or caregiver turned up at the scene and screamed hysterically, hurling angry abuse at the officers and myself, which made photographing these scenes even more emotionally gruelling, and occasionally dangerous, when a hysterical parent tried to physically intervene while we worked.

I photographed numerous cases of horrific child abuse. It's hard to imagine that a caregiver or parent could starve a child to death in a city like London, but it happens. Such cruelty to a child in their short life; in one instance, forcing them to sleep in the bottom drawer of a chest of drawers, the child so emaciated she fitted into the drawer, although she was a toddler; and she died in that drawer, locked away in that prison of a room. I photographed far too many tragic cases where children lived and died in squalor, because they slipped through the cracks, with no social services intervention. I photographed flats and houses with no heat, no light and few possessions, where caregivers entertained strangers that posed a danger of sexual abuse to young children in that vulnerable position. I photographed flats where parents allowed dogs and cats to piss and shit all over the place, and children lived in that squalid environment. The animal fur so dense that a carpet of dog and cat hair covered the floors throughout the entire home. Some of those places were so grim and disgusting that the soles of my rubber boots literally stuck to the floor while I walked around taking photographs. They were the sort of places where you wiped your feet on the way out, not on the way in.

One, sadly memorable, case of child abuse that I've never forgotten was a little girl I photographed at one of London's hospitals in the East End of the city. After traipsing around, and losing my way in the overheated hospital, I finally found the ward I was looking for. I went to the nurses' station to let them know I was there to visit a child who needed her injuries photographed for a child abuse investigation. One of the nurses led me to a room nearby, while she went to find the child. I set up my camera and tripod and began loading film while I waited. When the door squeaked open, I turned to see a nurse carrying a little girl in her arms. She had her head buried deeply in the nurse's shoulder, so I couldn't see her face, but I could see her bandaged legs.

'She hasn't said a single word since she was brought in a few days ago,' the nurse explained to me while she held the child in her arms. Now facing me, the little girl didn't want to make eye contact. The nurse continued to relay the story of what had happened, in a quiet voice. 'Her mother switched on the electric rings on the cooker, pulled down her underwear and sat her on the hot rings because she'd been a *bad little girl*,' the nurse said, barely able to contain her disgust. 'The pain and the trauma of her burn injuries has caused her to be nonverbal,' she continued.

The little girl, a wide-eyed beauty, with light brown skin and a face the picture of innocence was four years old. I bent down to talk softly to her while she sat on the nurse's lap facing forwards. I took a roll of film out of my bag and handed it to her in its shiny wrapper. This was a way of getting her to put out her hand to me and to distract her from any fear she might have, seeing my tripod, camera and flashguns. I talked to her as she examined the shiny pack of film with curiosity. I needed her to trust me and to feel safe enough with me, so I could photograph her injuries. The nurse explained to her that I was going to take her photo and she'd need to take off her bandages. I knew that removing the bandages would be a painful ordeal with such nasty injuries to the backs of her thighs and to her buttocks. She cried in agony when the nurse removed the dressings from her wounds. It was hard to witness. I did my best to take the photographs quickly, all the while talking gently to her while I adjusted my camera exposures and re-loaded film. She sensed I was not there to harm her. I chatted away while I worked. She never said a word, but she calmed down and stopped wriggling and screaming. I'd photographed many child abuse injuries over the years, but this little girl's injuries shocked even me. Her mother had burned her with cigarettes. The circular small burn scars were all over her little legs and thighs and on her forearms and hands. Some of the cigarette burns were fresh and others old. Every time she *misbehaved*, her mother burned her with her cigarette. For the last few shots, the nurse laid her gently over her lap, face down, so I could photograph her little bum cheeks. The burn marks on both her bum cheeks were the exact shape of the coiled elements on an electric cooker. Larger rings, then medium sized rings and then smaller rings. It wasn't the sight that shocked me, but the capacity for cruelty shown to this little girl by a mother who should have protected her. The nurse looked at me and read my mind. She shook her head in revulsion while I took the shots I needed. I nodded in agreement. While I packed away my gear, the nurse put fresh bandages on the child's wounds and dressed her. She lifted her into her arms and walked to the door. I stood watching and said gently to her, 'Bye bye, sweetie,' as I waved the tops of my fingers towards her. The little girl lifted her head and looked at me over the nurse's shoulder and said in a barely audible voice, 'Bye bye'. They were the first words she'd spoken since her admittance to the hospital for her horrific burns. We had connected on some deep level. The experience was both heartbreaking and heartwarming at the same time. I've never forgotten that little girl. I hope she went on to recover, and find love and safety with caregivers who cherished and protected her from any further abuse or trauma.

* * *

'Survivors of rape and sexual assaults told me what happened to them, in all the gory detail,' I tell Sarah, my therapist.

'Obviously, I couldn't ignore what they were saying. I listened, and responded with compassion, despite the harrowing nature of what they were telling me. I not only witnessed and photographed their bruises, bites or stab wounds. They told me the specifics of what the rapist said to them, what he did to them and how they felt about it. I relived these crimes by hearing the survivors' stories. Day after day the tales of horror unfolded. Tales from women whose rapists had beaten them to the brink of death, tales of terrorised women who often second-guessed themselves, asking why didn't I do things differently? Why didn't I trust my instincts when I knew he was following me?

'Those details must have been hard for you to hear, over and over. It added another stressful dimension to your work that people don't often think about or talk about,' she says.

'Yes, it did,' I reply. 'And I recently discovered that rape survivors did not recount their victimisation to my male colleagues who photographed them. I can understand why. In most cases it was a male who raped the women I photographed, and a male photographer turned up to photograph their injuries. It's hardly surprising that female rape survivors chose not to share their stories with my male colleagues.'

'We call what you're describing *secondary traumatic stress*, or *vicarious trauma*,' Sarah continues. 'Or perhaps you've heard it called compassion fatigue?' she asks. 'With the high percentage of trauma survivors in your caseload, it's not surprising this might impact you and your colleagues,' she says.

'Back then, I'm not sure we even knew these terms. Although I could see the compassion fatigue in my colleagues, and sometimes in myself,' I reply.

'Tell me more about that,' she says, encouraging me to continue sharing.

'I read a great quote about this recently. I can't recall who said it, but it's so true. It went something like this: "The expectation that we can be immersed in suffering and loss daily, and not be touched by it, is as unrealistic as expecting to be able to walk through water without getting wet." And yet we were led to believe there was nothing abnormal about seeing, hearing, photographing or responding to the aftermath of so much brutal violence, tragedy and suffering day after day. The unwritten rules, within the police service, implied that what we witnessed should not impact or affect us in any way. Thinking back on it now, that's ridiculous, and wrong. What we needed to hear was that it was normal to be shocked and horrified by the grimness and brutality we witnessed and photographed. That it didn't mean we were weak or soft or any of those negative connotations that people ascribe to someone who shows emotion, especially men.'

'How do you think the compassion fatigue and response to vicarious trauma presented itself in you, and your colleagues?' she asks.

'Mmm. That's a tough one,' I reply. She waits patiently while I contemplate her question.

'I think it changes your world view,' I tell her. 'It stops you trusting people. You become sort of hypervigilant. Always scanning for danger, even in the most innocuous situations. Because you've seen horror, violence and danger against a backdrop of the most mundane living circumstances . . .' I stop talking for a moment to gather my thoughts and recall the memories I want to share.

'Please continue,' she says.

'During my years with the police service, and with the benefit of my university psychology studies, I could see that some of my photographer colleagues, and police detectives at scenes, had become emotionally numb, deeply cynical, or shut down and emotionally exhausted. Occasionally some were irritable or aggressive and barked orders at colleagues, or shouted at myself and forensic staff at scenes. I could see that the work had impacted them negatively, but they appeared to be unaware of this. Their exposure to death, violence, tragedy and the grimness of the work had changed them, but they didn't acknowledge those changes in themselves. There seemed to be a lack of self-awareness, and a lack of PTSD awareness.

'I recently read about a large study of UK police, which showed that one in five police officers and police staff were exhibiting signs of, or suffering from, post-traumatic stress disorder. More concerning is the fact that two thirds of those studied (17,000 police participants) were *unaware* they had PTSD or the signs of PTSD, so they continued to work despite their suffering and potential impairment. No doubt this may potentially hamper their ability to perform their police duties effectively or possibly lead to behavioural dysfunction while on or off duty. A quick scan of newspaper headlines in the past few years, regarding police misconduct, does make me wonder whether there may be some association between the two. It's something police management might examine more closely, and manage more effectively,' I say.

'Were you given any support by your management, to help you deal with these issues?' Sarah asks.

'Not really. I recall a visit to SO3 by a woman from occupational health. Only a single visit. I think she might have been a psychologist. Management told us to attend a group meeting one afternoon, and about twenty or thirty of us turned up, both photographers and administrative staff. Only photographers not working on division that day were able to attend, which was an oversight. The psychologist talked about PTSD and basically told us that we needed to look out for one another. That if we noticed anything unusual about a colleague's behaviour, if they'd started drinking more heavily, or if they were engaging in self-destructive or abusive behaviours, that we should talk to them, or bring it to our manager's attention. However, I got the impression that the photographers in attendance didn't take the meeting too seriously. An atmosphere of male bravado prevailed, with some joke-cracking, the usual stuff. None of the men admitted to feeling bad about a shocking scene they attended. The environment didn't lend itself to safely sharing, which trickled down from the management attitude. It was really a show-and-tell presentation, not an interactive one. None of my male colleagues wanted to lose face in front of other male colleagues. And yet they would talk quite openly to myself and to the other female photographers about the horrific jobs they'd attended and how they felt about them. I suppose because they felt we could empathise as we'd also witnessed such horrors.

'I don't think we benefitted much from one psychologist's visit. It was too little, too late. A few years ago, I heard that one of the senior managers at the photographic branch admitted in an interview to having unilaterally refused the offer of counselling for the photographers and SO3 staff. An ex-military man, and although a kind person, he bought into the notion of the *stiff upper lip* which influenced his decision-making. He admitted his error, and clearly, he lived to regret that poor choice, but it cost some of the photographic staff dearly in terms of their mental health.'

'How did that make you feel when you found this out,' Sarah asks.

'It made me angry to hear him say that. He had a duty of care to his photographers and he failed in that duty of care because of his poor judgement.'

Sarah nods her understanding, and I continued.

'Thinking back on it now, I don't know how I managed to stay so mentally well all these years, considering all I saw and photographed, combined with a lack of mental health support from SO3 management or a safe space to share the impact of trauma.'

'Please continue,' Sarah says, in a calm and encouraging tone of voice.

'It would have been helpful if someone from the MPS followed up with all the photographers, over the years, to find out if they needed any support after they retired, or left the job. But that never happened. Once you were out, the door slammed on you and that was that. There was, and is, no way to reach back into the MPS family to ask for support now, which is a grave oversight.'

Sarah nods her head as she listens.

'It's my understanding that things have changed for the better in the years since I left the MPS. SO3 management now *offer* photographers and forensic staff counselling and debriefing after bad incidents. But it's voluntary, not mandatory. So, in a still male-dominated environment, with few female photographers in the branch, I wonder whether the same *stiff upper lip* macho attitude prevails at management level, and consequently staff members continue to perceive counselling as only for the weak, repress their true emotions and feelings, and refuse to seek support to process the trauma they witness.'

12

Accidental and Suspicious Deaths

Acid Bath Man

'Fatal hydrofluoric acid burns,' came the cryptic reply from
the duty officer when he gave me my next assignment.

'What?!' I replied.

'Chemical burns. Like in chemical warfare,' he said.

'I wasn't expecting that,' I said. Horrific images ran
through my mind while he spoke.

'Nasty, by the sounds of it. So be extra careful,' he
said, and then proceeded to give me the address and
name of the OIC. When I arrived on scene, a large crowd
had gathered outside a cordoned-off ground-floor flat in
Crestwood. TV news vans and journalists from various TV
channels stood at the front of the crime scene tape. I knew
this was no ordinary scene, judging by the attendance of
the MPS Public Relations Officer, forensic professionals,
and the fire service hazardous materials (Hazmat) crew.
The OIC, Hazmat officer, lab sergeant, SOCO and forensic
pathologist stood together chatting inside the cordoned-
off area. I knew them all from working together at other
scenes, so we got right down to business.

'This is going to be a bloody nightmare of a scene to photograph and process,' said the forensic pathologist, in his booming voice. With a concerned look on his face, he directed his comments to me, the lab sergeant and the SOCO. 'I think the decedent has suffered chemical burns following exposure to hydrofluoric (HF) acid,' he continued. 'Although not a strong acid, HF acid is not only corrosive, but it penetrates deeply into the tissues. It can cause an irregular heartbeat which can prove fatal. I suspect that's what's happened here. A strong concentration of HF acid causes severe . . .' He continued to share his knowledge of HF acid, and the more I heard the less I liked it. By the time he reached the part about how HF acid could form a toxic cloud at room temperature, and exposure to it could lead to acid burns, severe pain and skin turning white and blistering, I thought to myself, I've heard enough. It sounded like a horror story. I had an urge to flee. But I trusted in the team of professionals managing this hazardous materials scene and the expertise of the forensic pathologist. I'd attended many scenes that were a danger to my safety, for a variety of reasons. I always put my own safety first at every scene. Having listened to all the experts, I knew if I followed their instructions to the letter, I'd remain safe and would shoot the photographs I needed without contaminating myself or dying, which was a real and terrifying possibility.

The forensic pathologist finished speaking and the Hazmat team leader began to share the dangers and issues regarding processing and photographing the scene and handling of the body for removal to the mortuary.

'Hazmat have vented the scene so it should be safe for you to enter now,' he reassured me. 'But hydrofluoric acid can burn through glass, ceramic, concrete and metal, so you'll have to make sure you, your clothing or equipment *do not touch* any of the potentially contaminated surfaces in the scene, otherwise you will get burnt,' he said. One of the biggest challenges that HF acid contamination caused was that it's a colourless liquid, which was visually indistinguishable from water. If it had been a coloured liquid, it would have made life a lot easier and less dangerous, because I could have seen the contaminated surfaces. I knew that the fire service Hazmat team had managed the inhalation risk, but the absorption risk by skin contact remained a threat.

I knew the decedent was in the bathroom. I set up my camera and tripod, loaded film and stepped into the hallway. I left my camera bag outside to avoid contaminating it. When I stood in the hall, contemplating the scene before me, I could see into the bathroom. It was a tiny, cramped space. I knew I'd have to work slowly and cautiously, so I didn't touch any surfaces with my crime scene suit, or gloves, or equipment. I could feel my heart pounding while I set up the first shot, looking into the bathroom. I could see the decedent in the bath. A gruesome sight, even for an experienced police photographer. But the danger to myself took priority. I could not let the sight of the victim's burns distract me, otherwise I could have ended up getting hurt.

The decedent was a middle-aged man. Facing towards the bathroom door and sitting in an upright position at the opposite end to the bath taps, he was in an almost full bath of water. Only the bath tray across the middle of the bath prevented his body from falling forward face down into the water. He was seated in what I could only describe as a bath of sludge: necrotic tissue from the burns had transformed into a kind of gooey paste and blended with the brownish decomposing liquids that had started to leak out of his orifices into the bath water. He was a large man, and his body, green and mottled, had bloated and discoloured from decomposition in the summer heat. Bodies could bloat to double their original size during decomposition, as this man had. So, I couldn't help thinking to myself that it was going to be a monumental and dangerous task to extricate him from the bathtub safely, and remove him to the mortuary for the forensic post-mortem that awaited me.

After taking the first shots from the threshold, I entered the bathroom slowly, with my tripod legs closed and my arms pinned by my sides. I turned in a tight circle to gauge the space and make sure none of my clothing or equipment touched any surfaces in the bathroom. In such a small space, it felt next to impossible not to brush against something, but I'd had plenty of practice at scenes. I felt like someone disarming a bomb. Holding my breath. I knew if I touched anything, I would get burnt and could die as a result, even with immediate emergency treatment. At the very least I'd be badly scarred by the burns. I could sense the gravity of the situation by the grave looks of the lab sergeant and pathologist who remained in contact with me, from outside the bathroom window. I started by taking some close-up shots of the victim's face. It looked congested and a purple bluish colour. The washer-woman skin on his hands and fingers had turned white, and in some places the acid had burned through layers of his skin, which I could see clearly while I focused my shots. The tips of all his fingers were white blisters, swollen and wrinkled, like small pickled onions on the top of five toothpicks. A white paste contaminated other parts of his arms and body. Skin blisters, large and small, that had a greenish hue, covered most of his body and face. I could not help feeling a sense of sadness at the thought of how painful and terrifying this man's lonely death must have been. Questions ran through my mind while I took his photographs. *Why didn't he run to his neighbours for help? Why didn't he ask someone to call an ambulance?* None of it made sense. He had filled the bath with water, probably in the hope of neutralising the hydrofluoric acid once it started to burn him, but he'd put the plug in the bath and sat in the bath of water, which didn't wash the acid off him, so it continued to burn him. I suspect he kept adding water to the bath in his desperation, because it was inches from overflowing.

Although not one of the strongest acids, HF acid is highly corrosive and causes severe burns that are extremely painful. Having seen up close what the acid had done to the man in the bath, my heart pounded at the thought of contaminating myself while I continued to take photographs.

While I worked, police officers went door to door to discover what they could about our decedent. We began to piece together the story and had a good idea of what had happened before we headed to Riverview Mortuary for the PM.

According to his neighbours, our decedent was a middle-aged man who lived alone and didn't have a job. Some said he seemed a little odd but kept himself to himself and didn't appear to be a bother to anyone. I got the impression from their statements that he may have had learning difficulties or suffered with poor mental health. People said that he'd often returned home with miscellaneous items, small items of furniture, pieces of wood and other things he'd recovered on his travels in the neighbourhood and decided to recycle and use in his flat. Some said they'd seen him mooching about on a nearby building site. Now the story started to make more sense.

Hydrofluoric acid is not the type of chemical the average person would encounter, unless they happened to be in the building trade or in other industries that use HF acid in their processes. Builders use it for glass etching, and metal cleaning. It's also used in electronics manufacturing and in some research laboratories. The building site story made the most sense in the case of our victim. It appeared that the decedent had been wandering about on the building site, most likely scavenging for items to bring home, or to sell. Somehow, he'd managed to contaminate himself with the HF acid and at the time hadn't noticed. *But wouldn't it burn him right away? How could he not notice he was burning?* I later learned, during the forensic post-mortem, that pain can start within the first hour, but sometimes it takes up to 24 hours before the pain of the burns begins.

The gruesome sight of that poor man's chemical burns was haunting and left a lasting impression on me. I've never forgotten him.

Grief at the Quarry

It was a summer day when I attended a fatal industrial accident in a sand quarry in the East End of London. It's not the kind of place that comes to mind immediately when you think of London. By the time I arrived at the scene, three fire engines and a team of thirteen firefighters, and police accident investigators were already on site.

On one side of the quarry stood a giant blue silo. It stood taller than two houses stacked on top of one another. The accident victim was a man in his early twenties who'd been driving a tipper truck on the site. His job was to drive his truck under the gravel silo, reach out of his cab window, pull a lever, fill the truck bed with gravel and take the load to another part of the quarry. There a worker loaded it onto trucks for distribution to customers. When I arrived at the quarry it was late on a glorious sunny morning. The quarry seemed strangely silent. The crew of men who'd been working alongside the victim hung about in a group. Restless and distressed-looking, they waited for the foreman to give them instructions. Their sadness and shock were palpable.

The man who died made a fatal error that sadly cost him his life. His job had become so repetitive, he'd lost focus. His colleagues who witnessed the accident said he'd dumped his load of gravel and stopped to have a smoke break. After which, he drove back across the quarry at high speed to collect his next load. Contrary to workplace rules, on that sweltering day, he had both cab doors of his vehicle open. He'd forgotten that he'd left the tipper still high in the air. The tipper hit the silo when he tried to drive under it and it turned the truck cab on its axle with great force. The impact flung the decedent sideways. Partially ejected through the open door, the force of the cab turning crushed his head between the low wall next to the silo and the door frame of his cab. He died instantly.

His colleagues heard the noise of the accident and ran to his aid. When they saw his head, crushed by the impact, they knew there was nothing they could do to save him. I'd photographed these horrific scenes often, but for the uninitiated, witnessing the catastrophic injuries and gory death of a colleague takes a toll. Photographing the decedent in such a confined area, with the truck wedged into the silo, and the overturned cab with the crushed decedent proved gruesome and challenging. When I'd finished taking photographs, it took thirteen firefighters to right the cab, extricate the victim's body from the cab of his truck, and wash down the gore from the site. When we'd finished our work, the quarry foreman invited us to have a cup of tea with the crew. Sensing their sadness and their need to show us their hospitality, the police accident investigators and I made our way back to the Portakabins to join the quarry workers. The foreman had bought fish and chips for everyone and they kindly offered to share their food with us. Quarry workers in dusty clothes and boots stood together. Others sat silently, eating. The two police accident investigators stood among the group of men, closer to the door. I was the only woman in the crowd of men, but that was nothing new. In the packed Portakabin, there was nowhere to sit. I accepted the offer of tea. Then silently, the workers budged up and made a small space for me on one of the wall-mounted benches. I squeezed into the tight space between two burly quarry workers. This was the first time I'd witnessed the sombre silence of a group of men in their collective grief. Nobody spoke. Nobody shed any tears. Although their sadness and distress hung heavy in the air in the tightly packed Portakabin. Something brought them together in their grief. This was the closest they could come to each other without comforting one another with a hug. Generously sharing food with us seemed to give them some small comfort. I ate fish and chips from chip paper, and welcomed a cup of tea in a chipped mug. Their kindness was touching and heartbreaking in equal measure. As a busy police photographer, I had to weigh up carefully when to remain at a scene once I'd finished my work, and when to politely refuse and be on my way. On this occasion, it was the right thing to do. Sharing food, and sitting in silence eating with this group of grieving men, it meant something to them. And to me.

Not Downton Abbey

The scene looked like a massacre had taken place. Blood covered the walls, furniture, doors, carpet and almost every surface of the small flat. Like someone had taken a paintbrush, dipped it in dark red paint and splashed it all about the place haphazardly. The duty officer sent me to the scene as a suspicious death. The amount of blood alarmed the first responding police officer who attended the call. He decided it was best to err on the side of caution and treat the case as a suspicious death until we confirmed otherwise. When I first saw the scene, I understood why he'd called for a photographer. It seemed like a gruesome murder had taken place. A blood beard had dripped down the decedent's chin and dried. Blood had splashed all down the front of his white vest, splashed on his white underpants, and even on his socks. He'd knocked the furniture over, probably in the throes of panic while he projectile vomited blood. So, it looked as though someone had ransacked the flat, which also raised suspicions.

Police officers conducting house-to-house enquiries started to gather information about the decedent while I worked. We discovered the dead man had been a heavy drinker. The pathologist suspected the decedent's long history of alcohol abuse had caused burst esophageal varices, which is often a sign of end-stage liver disease. The decedent had projectile vomited blood all over the flat. The critical loss of so much blood had caused mental confusion, and we suspected that's why he didn't go outside to shout for help from a neighbour. I had no idea how painful this condition was, but I felt the terror he must have experienced in the final moments prior to his death. It must have been so frightening to die this way, especially alone.

When I'd taken the photographs of the scene, and the decedent, the forensic pathologist arrived to examine the body. His preliminary assessment was that the cause of death was consistent with burst esophageal varices, and he'd know more when he opened the body. This was the only death of its kind I'd seen in my career. But not too long ago, I saw an episode of *Downton Abbey* and it gave me chills. In the middle of dinner, with a dozen guests at the table, Lord Grantham projectile vomited blood onto the white linen tablecloth, and all over his dinner companions. His dinner guests, splashed with blood, stared in horror while Lord Grantham flailed about and ultimately fell to the floor, bleeding profusely from his mouth. Seeing the spectacle played out on an international television show took me right back to that moment when I stood in the living room of the decedent's flat. Until I saw the results of alcoholic liver disease, and projectile variceal bleeding, for myself, I had no idea that such a horrific death was even possible. I rarely drink alcohol. Is it any wonder.

What a Deterrent

A late-night request to attend a suspicious death scene summoned me from my bed to a derelict flat on a run-down council estate in the East End of London. I often attended death scenes alone, with only a uniformed police officer stationed outside the scene, and the deceased for company. Prior to my arrival, a lab sergeant – a detective with specialist forensic training and years of investigative experience – had attended these scenes. In collaboration with a coroner's officer, and after doing their due diligence, the lab sergeant deemed the death not suspicious, or showing no evidence of foul play. This system meant that I spent a significant amount of time alone with dead bodies at scenes, but that never bothered me. The dead didn't scare me. The living scared me more. I spent time alone with murder victims and suspicious death victims and I talked to them as I worked. Each scene told me about their life. Whether they were rich or poor. If they shared a bed with a lover, a pet, or lived alone. What and who they loved, what they read, where they travelled, what they valued, the music they listened to, the type of sex they enjoyed, the clothes they wore and much more. Scenes surrendered the victim's most public and private moments to my camera lens. I had the rare privilege of entering a victim's private space, and although uninvited, I respected their homes and their possessions and the dignity of their dead body as I worked around them.

When I arrived on scene, it was the middle of the night. The boarded-up flat was pitch black inside. The two police officers at the scene accompanied me into the flat to show me where the body lay. They carried my CSI torch, as I had my hands full with my heavy camera bag and tripod. The flat was a mess. It was bitterly cold. Overturned furniture, and a floor littered with all sorts of debris made it a challenge to navigate a path to the body.

Once inside the open-plan living room, where the decedent lay, I set up my camera and tripod to take photographs of the deceased, focusing by the light from my torch held by one of the officers standing in the doorway. As I took out my flashguns from my camera bag, they said, 'We'll go back to the van to fetch you the Dragon light.' Before I had a chance to reply, they were gone. In the blackness I could barely see my hand in front of my face, as there was no ambient light coming into the boarded-up flat. Their laughter trailed off as they left me in the scene by myself with the mummified body. To take the necessary shots of the decedent, I'd positioned my tripod legs over his legs. I stood with one foot either side of his calves. I was alone in the darkness, standing awkwardly over the deceased. They'd walked off with my crime scene torch. I shouted after them, 'This is not funny. Come back here now,' but they'd gone. If I'd moved, I'd have fallen onto the deceased, or twisted an ankle and fallen onto the debris-littered floor. Neither seemed an appealing option. Being that close to a dead person didn't bother me, even in the dark. Falling on the decedent would have been undignified, unprofessional and disrespectful to the dead man lying on the floor.

At that time the police-issue torches didn't provide sufficient brightness to help when looking through a camera viewfinder in a pitch-black room. Police officers had access to a giant torch called a Dragon light. It looked like an oversized beige Thermos flask. So heavy, officers carried it in a sling over their shoulder. It gave off thousands of candlepower of light intensity, to help operationally while lighting rigs were en route. My crime scene torch, bright orange and the size of two house-bricks, had a powerful beam. I could light a large area with a pin-sharp white beam, or I could adjust the lens to a narrow beam of light. It would have done the trick had the officers not deliberately taken it out of the scene with them when they left.

I shouted after them, 'Yeah, not funny. Stop messing around. Come back here, now.'

My eyes adjusted to the darkness after a few minutes and shapes revealed themselves in the room. I talked with the dead man on the floor beneath me.

I continued to call out, but got no response. A busy on-call police photographer is not a person to trifle with, especially at a scene during the middle of the night. I knew other scenes would be waiting for me. Or I might even return to bed to catch a few hours of precious sleep between calls if I was lucky.

Eventually they returned with the Dragon light. They laughed and said, 'Was he well behaved while we were gone?'

'Ha, ha. No, he got up and asked me to dance,' I said. No doubt their aim was to leave me feeling nervous standing in the pitch darkness over a mummified dead body. What they didn't contemplate was that any police photographer who had worked on the streets of London for years saw so many dead bodies they didn't fear being close to the dead, even in complete darkness.

They switched on the Dragon light and it lit the entire room. The torch was bright enough to burn your eyelashes off. Once I'd focused on the shots I needed, they switched off the torch. I continued with the photography of the scene and one of the PCs relayed more background information to me while I shot the rest of the photographs.

A group of lads had broken into the flat by tearing off some plywood boards and smashing a window to climb inside. They were looking for items to steal and sell, to buy drugs. But instead, they found the mummified body of a man on the floor among the detritus and upturned furniture. In the darkness, it must have given them quite a scare. It was hard to tell from the scene whether the state of the flat was due to the deceased's actions prior to his death. Sometimes people flailed about, staggered around, and knocked over furniture, panicked in the throes of death. Or it may have been the burglars who'd overturned the furniture in their search for items to steal, or in their desperate panic to run out of the flat when, to their horror, they discovered the mummified man.

In people's minds, mummies evoke horror movies, gothic novels and ancient Egyptian curses. But this man's body was less shocking than others I'd photographed over the years. A naturally mummified body is rare. Finding one in a derelict flat in the East End of London even more unusual. A body mummifies spontaneously only under a limited number of environmental conditions that prevent it from decomposing in a more traditional way. It mummifies naturally when it's exposed to extreme cold, or in a dry atmosphere that rapidly dehydrates the body. The boarded-up flat had no heating or electricity.

When I knelt beside him to look closer at his body with my torch, I was fascinated and amazed at how well the spontaneous mummification process had preserved his face and body. His skin was a caramel toffee colour. It looked like oiled leather rather than skin. His body was intact, but shrivelled. His face looked peaceful, despite his empty eye sockets.

While I packed my camera gear to leave the scene, I laughed to myself at the thought of the shocked faces of the burglars who'd discovered the mummified man. Finding him had scared them so much, they ran screaming from the flat and called the police on their own burglary scene. No doubt the shock of that experience made them reconsider their burglary careers. What a deterrent.

Tragedy on the Thames

Thrashing around in the frigid brown water, I struggle to breathe. The force of the river sucks me into its murky depths. Panicked, I flail helplessly, arms reaching above my head, pleading. The brackish water stings my eyes and throat. I see daylight above me but I cannot reach the surface, no matter how hard I try. The weight of the water and the pull of the tide are strong. The river refuses to release me. My sobbing wakes me from the dark well of my buried grief. Gasping for air, my heart pounds in my chest, once again the drowning nightmare haunts me. Always the same nightmare. Every night for months after the disaster. And still, it comes from time to time, even after all these years.

When the phone rang, it took me a few seconds to wake up. I heard the duty officer's familiar voice telling me there'd been a boating accident on the River Thames. In my sleepy brain it sounded like a joke in bad taste. I couldn't fathom why people would be boating in the middle of the night. In my mind I had a vision of a small motorboat on the water. 'Are you serious?' I asked. None of it made sense in those first few seconds of his phone call on that August night. Once the veil of sleep had lifted, I opened my notebook to take down the address and details of where police needed me to attend. 'Go to Southwark Bridge and wait for further instructions,' Charles said.

'Officers are on scene. Keep me posted and let me know if you need any backup,' he added. I took a quick shower and gulped down a cup of sugary tea to wake myself up. At that point in time, I had no idea of the monumental and harrowing nature of the scene that awaited me.

Police had cordoned off Southwark Bridge by the time I arrived, about an hour after the accident, at around 2.45 a.m. The authorities had closed two of the arches of Southwark Bridge and the nearby Cannon Street bridge to boat traffic. I drove towards the gathering of police vehicles and officers in the middle of the bridge and introduced myself. They told me that a pleasure cruiser and a dredger had collided, and the smaller boat had sunk, almost under the bridge, not far from where we were standing. At that point police didn't know how many passengers had boarded the pleasure cruiser the *Marchioness* for the birthday celebration cruise down the river that left the wharf at around 1.15 a.m. From the middle of Southwark Bridge, I couldn't see any sign of a boat in the dark waters about 50 feet below us. But I knew the central channel of the Thames was deep enough for large ships to navigate, so I assumed the sunken vessel rested on the bottom of the river about 40 feet below the surface. With no immediate photographic tasks to undertake, I ended up as a spectator to the rescue operations on the river. Accustomed to getting to work right away at a crime scene or major incident, it felt voyeuristic and unseemly to stand and stare into the fast-moving waters of the Thames on that hot moonlit summer night. I knew there were fatalities. But at that stage, I didn't know how many lives had been lost.

I had not been on the bridge long when several helicopters arrived overhead. The MPS had scrambled their helicopters from the ASU base to work with officers from the Marine Policing Unit (MPU) Thames Division. India 99 lit up the river with the Nightsun, a thirty million candlepower searchlight which assisted police and other boats on the river searching for survivors in the water. Four MPS patrol boats assisted in the rescue, along with the *Hurlingham*, a sister of the *Marchioness*, whose skipper witnessed the accident. Other boats that witnessed the accident, or heard about it via their marine radios, threw lifebuoys into the water and rescued many people from the river. At that time there were no Royal National Lifeboat Institution (RNLI) boats stationed on the river, and few lifebuoys, because vandals had thrown them into the Thames so many times, for fun, that the authorities removed them from the riverbanks.

As the hours ticked by, I periodically updated the photographic duty officer when more information emerged, and I began to discover a sense of the mass fatalities. 'I'm going to need a team of photographers, and one or two videographers in the coming hours, and over the next few days,' I told him during our conversation at around 5 a.m. There was a stunned silence. 'Jesus Christ, what the hell happened,' he said. Not a man often lost for words, he quickly switched back into business mode. He trusted my judgement and agreed to round up a team of half a dozen photographers to start with. Most were not on call that weekend, as I was. We hoped we'd be able to reach enough of them, during the busiest bank holiday weekend of the year, to put together a team.

'Don't bother to wake anyone right now. Let them sleep until well after sunrise,' I said.

'Are you sure?' he asked.

'Yes, I'm sure. It'll be a long weekend of work, so we'll need them well rested and fed.'

From the moment I arrived on the bridge, I knew I wouldn't be going home for several days, as was often the case at major incidents. Perhaps it was the adrenaline that kept me energised to keep going non-stop at scenes like this. Cold, tired and hungry after spending half the night on Southwark Bridge we were all desperate for something to eat and drink. When dawn broke over London, a Red Cross food truck arrived on the bridge to offer us hot drinks and food. I'll never forget the kindness and generosity of the Red Cross volunteers. Always there to feed and support the emergency services. Never had a cup of tea and a sandwich felt so welcome.

'What's the scene like now?' Charles asked.

'Not much happening on the river right now, apart from the helicopters continuing to fly up and down, searching the foreshores. It'll be hours before salvage boats, divers and the body recovery teams arrive. It'll take time to position the heavy cranes and lifting equipment into place to raise the boat from the riverbed. Once that's done, the photography of the bodies in the hull, and the removal of the victims can begin,' I replied.

'Right oh, I'll ask the team to rendezvous with you on the bridge,' he said and he signed off.

The MPS had requested helicopter assistance from the RAF and the Coastguard helicopter. I immediately recognised the giant yellow coastguard helicopter flying overhead. It flew so low above us that I could feel the downdraft, and the water swirled below us from the strength of the rotor wash. Smaller boats struggled to stay in place because the rotor wash pushed them about. The loudness of the engines, the power from the downdraft and the blinding searchlights were a sensory overload. The two RAF helicopters and the coastguard helicopter flew up and down the river repeatedly, searching the water for survivors. Police recovered the first body from the river after dawn on the Sunday morning. At first light, the helicopters carried out a further search, again with no success. The RAF helicopter searched both banks of the river at low tide. By noon on Sunday, police decided that no further helicopter assistance was necessary.

The River Thames is a tidal river and was flowing fast, at about three knots on the night of the accident, so it didn't take long before people disgorged from the *Marchioness* found themselves much further up the river at Blackfriars Bridge and beyond. While I stood on the bridge looking into the dark waters of the Thames below, I shuddered to think how anyone could have survived the high tide that raced under the bridge below me. I had a sense of the terror of one minute being in a boat, having fun with friends and enjoying the festivities and the warm summer air, and the next minute ending up in the swirling brown waters of the Thames swimming for their lives in the cold water.

Not long after dawn, the first of my police photographer colleagues arrived on the bridge. I'd kept the duty officer updated from 3 a.m. and a colleague was a welcome sight after the night I'd had on the bridge. Although, at that time, nobody knew the scale of the loss of life, because there was no written record of the actual number of passengers on the *Marchioness*, I knew the work we'd need to undertake would take a team of photographers and at least one or two videographers. When more of my colleagues arrived, we ran through the photographic tasks that we'd need to complete, which included documenting the lift of the *Marchioness*, from the bridge, and from the water level, and aerial photographs of the scene and the vessels, and a lot more besides.

At 9 a.m. on that Sunday morning, police requested the assistance of Royal Navy divers who flew to London by helicopter from RN Culdrose. The dive team remained on standby. By about 10 a.m. the enormous salvage vessels the *Hookness* and the *Broadness* arrived on site and took their positions in the river below Southwark Bridge. Preparations began to raise the *Marchioness*. Divers located the wreck at about 11:20 a.m. and attached cables to its underside to lift it out of the water.

By the time the salvage ships took their positions on the river, I had been awake and on duty for more than ten hours. I was so tired I was working on autopilot. I was in a daze and exhausted. It was hard to process the scale of the deaths in that moment. But because I'd been first on scene I remained on site for the duration of the incident. After hours of waiting, the giant cables of the 200-ton *Hookness* salvage ship began to retract and slowly the *Marchioness* broke the water's surface. I could see the white, red and navy-blue hull of the pleasure cruiser slowly come into view. The collision had ripped the entire canopy off the *Marchioness*. Water poured out of the boat in a torrent while it hung and creaked on the enormous steel cables of the *Hookness*. Divers in red dry suits appeared at the surface and police helped them out of the water.

In the early morning hours of Sunday, word of the disaster had spread and I noticed a lot of boat traffic on the river. People arrived in all manner of large and small watercraft to gawk at the rescue operation. Many brought their children and their dogs, and were eating ice cream while they watched. I couldn't believe the ghoulish behaviour. It wasn't only a small group on the water, but also the riverbanks had begun to fill with people, three deep in places. Police asked the boaters to leave, because they were impairing the rescue operation and nobody wanted another boating accident while we were still dealing with a major incident. Police corralled spectators to one side of the riverbank, to try to control the crowd, and provide some privacy for the removal of the dead from on board the *Marchioness*. The crowd's behaviour was nothing different to the behaviour I'd experienced at crime scenes on land. Crowds will stand and stare. But in this situation, it felt wrong. It reminded me of how people attended public hangings back in the day, to entertain themselves. Workers on the *Hookness* salvage ship had taken off their t-shirts and were bare-chested, with big bellies hanging over their small shorts. Somehow the incongruity of that sight in such a solemn and sad situation felt disrespectful to the dead. Although it was a scorching summer day, it felt inappropriate that they would parade around half naked on a salvage vessel, during a body recovery operation, with half the world's press and TV cameras watching.

After taking photographs over six hours in the sweltering heat, while the salvage operation progressed, at around 6 p.m. on Sunday, after the *Marchioness* had drained, and the salvage crew pumped out the remaining water, recovery crew found the bodies of twenty-four party guests inside the hull of the boat. While it hung from the giant steel cables, all the bodies on board were photographed in situ, before specialist police body recovery crews and the lab sergeant removed them from the cruiser. Ultimately, twenty-four bodies ended up at Westminster Mortuary. I'd never seen Westminster Mortuary that crowded before. There were bodies everywhere, living and dead. It was a psychological overload like nothing I'd ever experienced. I knew our team of photographers would need to photograph every single body, for ID purposes, and their individual forensic post-mortems. It was an enormous and time-consuming undertaking for us all, not to mention heartbreaking and emotionally distressing.

Several of the bodies recovered from the boat showed signs of cadaveric spasm. Although a rare phenomenon, I'd seen it at scenes of violent deaths and other drownings. It's an instant rigidity of the body that occurs at the moment of death. But it's not rigor mortis. The cadaveric spasm preserves the last activity of the decedent. It's usually associated with a sudden, traumatic or violent death or strenuous muscular activity. A decedent may have their hand or hands tightly clenched holding a weapon, a gun, or a seatbelt etc. Sometimes a decedent's hands will be clenched to clothing, grass or foliage they grabbed for. Several of the victims had frozen in a cadaveric spasm where they were trying to remove their own clothing. Their hands clenched to the bottom hem of their clothing, as if to pull it over their heads, with their arms raised. It made for a heart-wrenching sight. Although it sounds odd, cadaveric spasm can provide useful information to forensic investigators regarding the manner of death. One young woman froze trying to remove a long knitted jumper, to be less constrained so she could swim free from the wreck.

I remember thinking how colourful they all looked in their summer party clothes, and how beautiful and handsome they were, even in death. Many were models and worked in show business and the entertainment industry.

After we'd worked in the mortuary for hours, myself and a colleague decided we'd better eat some long overdue food. We walked out of the back entrance of Westminster Mortuary into the bright, hot sunlight of a glorious summer day. It was a jarring contrast to the heart-breaking atmosphere inside the mortuary. A crowd had gathered at the gates. It finally dawned on me in my sleep-deprived state, that they must be the families and friends of the decedents. Police officers were on duty inside the gates. When they opened the gates to let us out, the crowd surged forward. We found ourselves in the middle of a distraught crowd of parents and friends, some crying, others shouting out names of dead friends and family, others asking questions, questions, questions. The two police officers did their best to hold back the crowd, who seemed to want answers from me and my colleague, because they'd seen us leave the mortuary. Overwhelmed, we pushed through the crowd. Suddenly I felt a hard tug on my sleeve. A woman, her face pained with grief and sadness, grabbed hold of my sleeve and shouted at me 'Have you got my baby in there?' It's a phrase that has stayed with me for all these years. I've never forgotten the suffering in that woman's voice. Many of the victims were the same age as me and the photographers who photographed the disaster. So, I could imagine that woman could have been my mother, searching for my body. I wished I could have told her the answer, but at that stage we didn't know the identities of the victims. Before I had a chance to reply, she vanished back into the crushing crowd. Her words and her desperate plea for answers have haunted me all these years. I'll never forget that phrase. I'll never forget the pain and the anguish in the face of that distraught mother.

SO3 photographers undertook an enormous amount of photographic work, both still and video, during the weekend of the disaster and in the weeks and months following the disaster. The photographs documented the wreckage, and parts of the boat discovered later. These forensic photographs provided marine accident investigators with clues to what happened to the vessel, independent of eyewitness accounts. Our team of photographers worked non-stop that weekend, with little sleep, or food. Ultimately, between us we photographed all 51 victims of the disaster. No single individual takes credit for the success of photographing and forensically processing such a major scene. It was a collaborative effort between police photographers, lab sergeants, uniformed officers, police forensic civilian experts, and many other investigators and experts. It took a team of photographers to document the disaster from beginning to end. We photographed all the bodies in situ, on the *Marchioness*. They were heartbreaking images, for so many reasons. We photographed the exterior and interior of the *Marchioness* when the salvage vessel moved it onto a sand bar at low tide on the north side of the river. A forensic team inspected the vessel from stem to stern, documenting and photographing all damage to the vessel. We photographed vessel debris recovered from the river and documented it in the same way we'd document a plane crash, piece by piece, item by item. Then we had to photograph the post-mortems of the twenty-four victims police recovered from inside the boat, plus the post-mortems of all the other bodies eventually recovered. Which made our post-mortem work even more grim and heartbreaking.

Not one of our management staff asked us how we felt having seen so much death and sadness that weekend. Nobody offered us counselling or even a debriefing. The Monday after the disaster weekend, I returned to work exhausted, business as usual. On to the next murder scene, and the next, and the next. Nobody seemed to grasp the magnitude of witnessing a major disaster with multiple loss of life and the psychological impact this has on the people involved. Looking back, I recognise I was in a state of shock after that weekend, but didn't realise at the time how deeply this incident had affected me. I know that big chunks of that incident vanished from my memory. Big gaps in time. But I kept going and eventually the nightmares subsided.

The lack of compassion or even a debriefing was an unconscionable oversight on the part of both the photographic branch and police management. Even a simple thank you from the SO3 or police management to the photographic team would have been much appreciated, but it never came.

It wasn't long after the disaster that a friend invited me to take a boat trip up the Thames in his barge. Although reluctant to go anywhere near the Thames, and terrified at the prospect of taking a trip on a boat, I said yes. I knew if I didn't try to overcome the fear of drowning, I would never manage to let it go. On the day we travelled up the Thames we hit the wake of a boat in front of us that sent us wobbling around in the water much to my horror. Dishes flew about, small items fell off the counters below deck and smashed to the ground, but we were all secure in our life jackets and managed to stay safely on board. Being tipped into the murky waters of the Thames was not a prospect I relished, so soon after experiencing the horror of the *Marchioness* disaster.

By the following summer I could still sense my fear of the water remained. I took an extended vacation and flew to Australia to try to shake off the psychological burden and perhaps at a subconscious level, to put some distance between myself and the Thames. When you work, and live, in London and you experience a major disaster with multiple fatalities, each time you pass that spot the memories flood back and you can do nothing to control them. The three months I spent in Australia gave me the distance I needed to heal. In hindsight it was a wise thing to do. While there, I decided to take a diving course to complete my PADI Open Water Diver qualification so I could dive on the Great Barrier Reef. After nightmares for months, I thought a diving course might be a way to make peace with the water, and overcome my fear of the water since the disaster. I explained the situation to the Dive Master, who was really understanding. He said he'd keep a close eye on me during the course, which he did. The first dive, in the 14-foot-deep training pool felt terrifying. Although I had a mask on and breathing regulator in my mouth, when it came time to descend, the terror of the water covering my mouth, then my nose and eyes made me panic. The first few attempts at submerging in the pool proved distressing and embarrassing, but with such a supportive dive master I relaxed and controlled my breathing enough to quell the panic I'd been feeling inside. Taking a diving course helped a lot in overcoming my fear of drowning. It may sound counterintuitive. You might be asking yourself why someone who witnessed the aftermath of a boating disaster and mass drowning of 51 people would want to go into the water for healing. But sometimes these things can have a cathartic effect and we don't always know how we've come to that place. It seemed right at the time, and in hindsight it was the right decision for me. We dived several times a day and did a couple of night dives in the pitch-black ocean. The diving course lasted a week. We sailed out to sea and lived on the dive ship. The colours of the Barrier Reef and the brightly coloured tropical fish soothed my soul. I've since read in archived newspaper articles that some of the survivors of the disaster took diving lessons to try to put their fear and trauma behind them. I have great respect for the water and the ocean and since taking that diving course I rarely suffer the drowning nightmares that lasted long after the disaster.

Many years later, I walked across one of the bridges over the Thames with another of the photographers who photographed the *Marchioness* disaster with me that weekend. Without saying a word, we instinctively stopped and looked down into the water. Silently the memories came flooding back. I turned to him and said 'You can still see their faces, can't you?' 'Yes,' he said, 'every single one of them.' I knew, because the memories of the victims flashed through my mind too as we looked down into the fast-flowing river.

Reflecting from a perspective of time and distance from the disaster, I think it would have been enormously healing to have attended some of the memorial services held over the years for the victims. I would have liked to have hugged the families of those who lost loved ones. I would have liked to mourn alongside them. To express my sadness, and grieve with them for their monumental losses. The closest I've come to paying my respects was to visit Southwark Cathedral, on my last trip to London, to see the *Marchioness* victims' memorial. It was the first time I'd seen the names and ages of the victims. They were nameless and ageless on the weekend of the disaster when we photographed them. On my visit to Southwark Cathedral, they were charging a fee to permit me to take a photograph of the memorial. It pained my heart. It didn't feel right. It wasn't about the money. But I put my camera away. I settled for touching the monument and reading each of the names engraved into the dark brown marble. Although sad, it felt good to come full circle, finally.

13

All Kinds of Everything

Raid on Illegal Drinking Den

'I spit on ya pussy bitch,' hissed the angry young woman as she was frogmarched towards me, her insolent glare steady with contempt. In that split second, it told me, you are the enemy.

Galiath, the towering flame-haired team leader, yanked the handcuffed woman off her feet when she spat at me.

'Now, now, that's not nice,' she said, tightening her grip on the back of the struggling prisoner's collar.

'Apologise to the nice photographer and let her take your picture.'

At six feet four inches tall, Galiath wasn't an easy woman to defy. A muscular wall of Kevlar body armour, in black flameproof overalls, a bulletproof helmet and black balaclava hid all but her eyes.

I had set up a makeshift photography station at the end of the cracked pathway that led from the front door of the shebeen. Galiath held the spitter still while I took a Polaroid of her. The prisoner made a loud hissing tooth-sucking sound directed at me, to show her contempt.

A jolt of anger shot through me at her crude insult. A long night's work in a stinking East London drug den and a chorus of abuse from dozens of prisoners had taken its toll. My flash of anger wasn't lost on Galiath. As she walked the spitter to the waiting police buses, she nodded her thanks to me. From behind her balaclava, her eyes were knowing and kind.

My work had begun at 3 a.m. at a disused building on an industrial estate about five miles from the target address. While I drove through the deserted estate, a wave of tiredness washed over me. I yawned when I stepped out into the cold night air. Even a shower at 2 a.m. hadn't lifted the fog of sleep from my brain. I climbed the wide staircase in leaps to shake off the tiredness. I stopped to catch my breath on the landing, and peered through the porthole windows in the swing doors. Muted male voices echoed in the disused office space. The 36-member SO19 firearms unit (think SWAT) team, dressed in black coveralls, stood together in small knots dotted around the perimeter of the room. Some chatted and laughed together. Some went over the entry plan. Others sat alone on the scuffed floor, with their backs against the wall, eyes closed and heads lowered in quiet contemplation. Heaps of black body armour, helmets and balaclavas lay next to each group. Black semi-automatic rifles stood in lines against the walls, like patient toy soldiers waiting to go into battle.

'Listen up everyone,' Galiath shouted when the briefing commenced. A hush fell across the room.

'We know from our surveillance intel that Parnell Perkins and Barrington 'The Butcher' will be at the den tonight. These two are nasty pieces of work. They'll shoot anyone who gets in their way.'

She handed out a batch of colour mugshots of the suspects to the team, and she continued speaking.

'They've a string of priors for drug trafficking and violence. We need them off the streets. Be safe out there. Let's go get 'em.'

At 5 a.m. on a cold Friday, I climbed on board a white cube van with Galiath and a dozen SO19 officers. I sat on one of the narrow benches that lined the wood-panelled walls. In a silent well-practised routine, the team, who moments before had been laughing together, donned their balaclavas and helmets. In an instant, the atmosphere changed. With only eyes visible, the effect was visceral and intimidating.

The van's roller shutter slammed down with a clang. Radio silence commenced as we drove away. Plunged into darkness, only the undulating breath sounds of the team broke the silence. The three-van convoy crept through the sleeping London streets. When we neared our destination, silent prayers filled the air. Ten minutes later, with headlights extinguished, the convoy came to a stop outside the target address.

Windows vibrated to the chest-thumping base of the reggae music. A sea of shadowy figures snaked silently towards the derelict house. It stood alone on an over-grown triangle of land; its seedy secrets hidden in plain sight. In seconds, the front door exploded off its hinges. A cloud of grey smoke rose into the air. Glass smashed and crunched under an army of boots when the SO19 team stormed in through windows and doors. Shouts of 'Armed police, down on the ground, armed police, down on the ground,' echoed through the house. Intimidated and confused, dozens of drink-and-drug-fuelled revellers soon formed a wall-to-wall carpet of humans, with hands cable-tied behind their backs.

I ran into the scene behind the SO19 team. My camera flashes exploded into the darkness. Ghostly faces loomed out of the blackness as if by magic. Stunned, surprised expressions frozen in each frame. Intense but familiar, the adrenaline rush hit. Time stretched and slowed as voices barked orders. Revellers screamed and swore, and music loud enough to crack the plaster blended in a chaotic muffled cacophony.

I stepped over dozens of bodies while the team cleared room after room. *How the hell did this many people manage to fit into such a tiny house?* I thought. I lurched from gap to gap between the spread-eagled bodies to avoid crushing limbs under my boots. The bodies I normally photographed didn't move, spit, or swear at me. Violent armed drug dealers and scantily clad angry crack addicts packed like sardines into a filthy drug den didn't make for an easy night's work.

K9 dogs did the first sweep of the scene. Slow and laborious, the team searched and seized weapons, cash and drugs. Bursts of light from my powerful flashgun marked the progress of the search when they lit up the dingy house, room after room.

The stream of prisoners came fast and furious to my outdoor makeshift photography studio. Face after face, insult after insult. They cursed, threatened and spat at me.

Polaroid after Polaroid, I ignored their teeth-sucking and vitriol. The photographs were as much for their protection as for ours. Documentary evidence of no injuries to their faces. I'd seen the value of this process before, when a cuffed prisoner brought into a police station by two officers, deliberately and violently smashed his head several times into a filing cabinet that abutted the doorway. I couldn't believe my eyes. It all happened so fast. After dozens of arrests and over a hundred and fifty mug shots later, the last of the prisoners boarded the waiting police buses and departed.

I went back into the scene to finish my work. Sweaty, skunky, alcohol-filled air hung in the rooms. I worked fast and tried not to breathe in the foul smell. Giant black concert speakers, and floors strewn with hundreds of beer cans and mangled cigarette butts were all that remained. The empty house was now a silent filthy shell.

Outside, a rumbling mob had gathered strength. Finishing off my last shots, I grabbed my camera gear and left the house. I took off my Kevlar vest, threw it into the back of my van with my camera gear, and slammed the doors shut. By now, dozens more gawkers had arrived. The atmosphere had grown tense. The agitated crowd hurled insults at me, and at the few remaining police on scene. Without a backward glance, I jumped into my van and locked the doors as the crowd closed in and surrounded the three-vehicle convoy. Fists banged on the roof of my van. Angry faces pressed up against the glass as I drove away.

* * *

I inevitably spent a lot of time working in places where criminals resided and plied their trade. And where they killed and injured those who got in their way. I spent time in filthy drug dens and at seedy scrap yards. One memorable scene that comes to mind was at a scrap yard, where the criminals had chained fierce, salivating Pitbulls to their caravan office at the entrance gates. The starved dogs barked ferociously, baring their teeth. They lunged at us. Their powerful muscular bodies speeding towards us while we hoped the chain was short enough that they did not reach us. With teeth snapping, they strained at the end of their chains trying to attack us. When we raided scrapyards, we took police dog handlers with us to remove these attack dogs so we could safely carry out our work. Not a job for the faint-hearted.

Once we'd eliminated the dangerous dogs' threat, the owners of the scrapyard treated us to something extra special. When officers searched the site office caravan, they came across several lunchboxes stacked up around the shelves, above the seating area, at one end of the caravan. I stood in the doorway while they searched. The caravan owner had collected human faeces in Tupperware containers, piled high on the shelves above the seating area. I felt sorry for the officers who opened the offending lunchboxes. We scrunched up our faces at the sight and vile smell of the disgusting collection. *Who would keep a faeces collection in lunchboxes?* The more scenes I attended over the years, the more I realised that there was no limit to how bizarre people could be.

Police raids and searches in homes or commercial premises are long and arduous tasks for all involved. Sometimes raids took four or five hours, depending on what officers were looking for. But unlike police searches in TV dramas, the searches I attended didn't leave the location turned upside down with stuff strewn about everywhere. Officers were considerate and careful in their searches and did their best not to disrupt the place more than necessary. At raids, I worked alongside the team from the moment the search began to the end of the search. I photographed evidence items in situ as the team discovered them. The usual finds were large wads of cash, all types of drugs, digital weighing scales, empty and full plastic drug baggies, marijuana plants, guns, knives, knuckle dusters, baseball bats, stolen credit cards and much more. In the process of searching, raid officers and I were often treated to unsavoury surprises like the human excrement collection. Not to mention the items we found stashed under upturned mattresses. *Who would keep a collection of used sanitary pads under their mattress?* The mind boggles.

Handcuffed prisoners remained on scene during most searches. They were not shy in expressing their anger about the raid, to myself and the police officers. At one scene, officers brought a male prisoner up to the tiny bedroom where I was taking photographs, of drug paraphernalia and cash, to ask him questions about the found items. He swore a blue streak at me, and suddenly pulled down the front of his jogging pants to show me his penis as he threatened to rape me. Officers removed him from the room before he had a chance to spit at me, which was a common practice for prisoners. A disgusting experience and a health risk if you're on the receiving end of it. They should have handcuffed him with his hands behind his back, for all our safety, but they were trying to be reasonable with him. No good deed goes unpunished.

Over the years I photographed many police raids, on drug dens, illegal drinking clubs, brothel raids, and raids on all manner of seedy places. I photographed S&M dungeons and places filled with all manner of sex toys and whips, chains and restraints, not unlike scenes from the red room in *Fifty Shades of Grey*.

Across London criminals used empty houses as *knocking shops* as police referred to them colloquially. Normally tipoffs came from disgruntled residents who noticed a steady stream of men visiting these properties day and night. Usually, the protocol was that we'd set up a photographic surveillance on the properties in question to gather evidence of the comings and goings of men at all hours. Pimps purchased or rented the houses and worked five, six or more girls or women who were expected to have sex with dozens of men over the course of a day. This took the girls and women off the dangerous street corners, but they were still slaves to their pimps and brothel owners. Once I'd shot enough surveillance photos as evidence that these properties were being used as brothels, police would raid the property with a photographer in tow. There's nothing quite like the experience of bursting through a door behind police officers on a brothel raid and surprising the occupants in flagrante delicto. Never a dull moment for a photographer on a police raid.

I photographed a lot of prostitutes over the years, dead and alive. I photographed the filthy scenes where their customers had kidnapped, robbed and assaulted them, or battered them within an inch of their life, usually on waste ground somewhere at the back of Crown Central Rail Terminal. This meant I had to drive around slowly, looking for gaps in the wooden construction fencing that enclosed the waste ground where the crimes took place. Naturally, a vehicle driving slowly in that red light area attracted attention, so I ended up receiving offers of sex as I searched for my crime scenes. I generally found that having a pleasant chat with the women and girls or Toms (as they were known on the streets), many not much older than myself, helped enormously. When I told them I was a police photographer and I was there to photograph the rape and assault scenes of one of their friends they realised I was on their side, so they were helpful. Having driven past the same streets so often, I started to recognise the faces of some of the girls and women, strolling in their miniskirts and torn tights, freezing in the cold as they smoked furiously waiting for their next client. Every time they climbed into a stranger's car might be the last time anyone saw them alive. The streets were treacherous for these women and girls.

As a young woman, this seedy underbelly of London was quite an eye opener for me. Pimps coerced girls and women into prostitution, addicted them to drugs and then exploited them mercilessly. Innocence and financial desperation often led them into forced prostitution. But it was the pimps and the people running the operations that were making an enormous amount of money. The unfortunate girls and women involved were coerced or threatened into having sex with dozens of men every day, seven days a week, all year round.

I remember photographing the injuries on a fourteen-year-old girl. She had been a child exploited in forced prostitution for two years, when a vigilant female police officer arrested her for a petty theft offence. When the officer interviewed her at the police station, she noticed that bruises and abrasions covered the girl's arms and legs. Through careful and gentle questioning, she discovered the girl had run away from home in the north of England at twelve years of age, and took a train down to London, as so many runaways do. At the train station in London a man intercepted her and promised her a warm bed for the night and food. Naively she accepted his offer. This is a common scenario, with both boys and girls being preyed upon at bus stations and train stations across London, and in other major cities in the UK. Fortunately, plain clothes police patrol the stations and watch CCTV to avert such tragedies.

This girl's captor wasted no time addicting her to hard drugs, which kept her compliant and spaced out. His coercion, and her need for a steady supply of drugs to feed her addiction kept her from leaving her pimp. Pimps kept these girls and boys dependent on them, so they kept earning money for the pimp day and night. When the story unfolded during the questioning of this girl, she realised that her interaction with the police officer was her opportunity to safely escape from a life on the streets. A life of violence, forced prostitution, drug addiction and early death.

I photographed her bruises and documented all the injuries on her body. By the time I had taken photographs, she seemed less fearful and terrified than when the officer had first introduced her to me when I arrived at the police station. She was looking forward to taking a bus up north to stay with an aunt who had promised to shelter and care for her. That police woman saved the young girl from a life of misery, pain, violence and possibly being killed on the streets of London. There were no funds available to pay for a ticket for the girl, so the police officer bought the girl's bus ticket out of her own money. The officer's compassion and kindness towards this vulnerable fourteen-year-old victim touched my heart. I had seen many of these private kind gestures from various police officers over the years, but they never made the newspapers.

When I said goodbye to the girl, I could see the hope in her eyes. Kindness shown to her by that police officer gave her a second chance at a normal life. I often wonder what happened to that beautiful young girl.

Not all my photographic assignments were grim and horrifying. I fortunately did have an opportunity to see how the other half lived when I photographed embassies, VIP residences and other potential high-risk target locations. Two of those most memorable occasions come to mind.

Royalty and Diplomatic Protection

The ambassador's residence stood within a gated, high-walled compound. An imposing three-storey house, in one of London's most exclusive neighbourhoods gave no indication of its high-profile residents. A butler opened the door and escorted me to a beautifully appointed room at the rear of the residence. Expensive Persian rugs adorned the polished wood floors and complemented the exotic and sumptuous earthy orange-themed décor. Giant windows bathed the room in a soft natural light. The ambassador's wife, an elegant beauty, sat in a plush beige armchair at the far end of the room. On the wall behind her, her portrait gazed down upon us. 'Good morning. Lovely to meet you,' she said as she rose to shake my hand. 'You must have coffee with me before you start your work,' she added, summoning the butler when I agreed. I had no concerns about drinking coffee at this scene. There were no chipped mugs or unsavoury tea cups in sight.

A graceful and charming conversationalist, the ambassador's wife soon put me at ease. We had a pleasant chat over coffee, then it was time to start work, photographing the entire residence for contingency-planning purposes.

Police put contingency plans in place in anticipation of an emergency arising; a siege, a kidnapping, bomb threat, hijacking or a hostage situation. Photographs (both terrestrial and aerial) of high-profile and VIP target locations assist police crisis management teams, and special forces, in the management of their response to an incident.

Photographs confirm the layout of the premises, entrances and exits. They are continually updated, so the images are current and consistent with the blueprints of the building in question. Police use the photographs with operational units to train for and respond to these incidents, and along with other intel, form a base from which to manage the response.

Special Escort Group and Tea with a Princess

During my rotation on the public relations team, I accompanied one of the experienced PR photographers on an assignment. At one of the events I attended with him, I met HRH Diana, the Princess of Wales and her two young sons.

Our task that day was to photograph the princess while she attended an event to thank the officers of the MPS Special Escort Group who were part of The Royalty and Diplomatic Protection Group. They were the armed motorbike outriders in high-viz yellow jackets that drove ahead of and behind the princess's car to keep her safe while she undertook her royal engagements in London. Their job was to move her vehicle through traffic quickly and safely. The event took place at the HQ of the Motorbike Division, at a hangar in West London. We drove in and parked at the far side of the hangar, close to the steps that led to the offices on the floor above. The event was private, so no press photographers or public were in attendance. While we stood by our vehicle, unloaded our gear, and talked through the photographic plan for the event, we heard the police radios crackle into life. The princess was on her way. Her convoy was two minutes out. Every royal visit is timed right down to the minute for safety reasons, and nobody knows the route the VIP convoy will take apart from the first motorbike officer that leads the convoy across London. This changes for every convoy. This keeps the VIP safe, because the route taken cannot leak out ahead of time to anyone who might consider kidnapping or targeting the VIP. By the time we finished gathering our equipment and got ourselves into position for photography of the receiving line, the shutters rolled up and we could see the police convoy. I could feel the excitement as the cars turned into the road and headed for the hangar. Knowing the Princess of Wales and the two heirs to the throne were in the vehicles heading towards us was a thrilling experience. I'd seen the princess in the newspapers and heard about her charity projects. So, finally having an opportunity to see her in person was a great honour and privilege. When the princess's car drove into the hangar and the shutters closed, it didn't take long before she stepped out of the car. She walked over to the receiving line of police officers. She looked radiant and was much taller in real life than I'd expected her to be. She wore a navy blazer and a floral summer dress.

Although I was an experienced police photographer, I hadn't undertaken any public relations work, so my job that day was to watch and learn. I'd carry the gear bag, load and reload film fast, and hand the cameras back and forth to my colleague who took the photographs of the princess and the princes. He was under a lot of pressure to ensure everything went smoothly so we got the photographs we needed. When you're a PR photographer at an event, you make yourself as invisible as possible to the person you're photographing. You're not considered a guest at the event in the official sense, although you're able to enjoy the atmosphere and the experience. But we were there to take photographs and we needed to focus on the work. While the princess greeted officers in the receiving line, I remember thinking the smell of all the different aftershaves the police officers wore was enough to make my eyes water. I felt for the princess. When I looked around, I realised that apart from the princess, I was the only other female in this gathering. When the princess began shaking hands, she suddenly stopped and said, 'Oh, I don't need this.' With great delight she ran back to her vehicle, opened the door and threw her clutch purse into the back seat. She smiled broadly and seemed relaxed when she returned to the receiving line.

She knew she was safe from the prying lenses of press photographers. Considering what she'd been going through in her private life at the time and the paparazzi tormenters she endured daily, she was gracious, cooperative and patient while we set up various shots with herself and the princes. Apart from the receiving-line photographs, we took some fun photographs of Diana with the boys on the police motorbikes.

The princess had an equerry with her who monitored the time and made sure everything ran smoothly. Timing an event down to the last second is imperative for safety reasons and to keep the princess on schedule to ensure she reached every event on time. The princes looked relaxed and happy being with their mother. They were lively and ran around. The moment they saw the police motorbikes, they wanted to climb up on them. Motorbikes and little boys, you can imagine the excitement. A crowd of officers gathered as they showed the princes their shiny motorbikes. Both princes received scaled-down police memorabilia, police jumpers, police bike helmets. They put them on right away and were thrilled. Every now and then Diana would remind them of their manners and make sure they were saying please and thank you. They were such natural and unforced interactions between a loving mum and her two sons.

When we'd finished taking photographs Diana went to sign the guest book nearby, and asked if somebody could help the boys down off the bikes. That was my job. I ended up lifting Prince William and Prince Harry down from the motorbikes. It was a unique experience. Next on the agenda were the speeches and then refreshments for the guests of honour. By then we were off duty from a photographic perspective. We stood and had tea and biscuits and waited for the speeches to begin. While I was standing near the food table, that groaned with biscuits and cakes and all sorts of tempting goodies, Prince Harry rushed forward and attempted to help himself to a handful of biscuits from the plate within his reach. Princess Diana, standing next to me, stepped forward and gently took his hand away from the plate. She whispered to him that he had to wait his turn, and that he should ask if it was Ok for him to have a biscuit. He did as she told him. To hear the princess speaking with her sons in such a loving and caring way was wonderful to witness. Her humanity, kindness and love for her young sons shone for all to see, although I did see a sadness in her eyes.

I had seen the princess in many hundreds of photographs over the years, but I'd never seen her in person. To stand next to the most famous and most photographed woman in the world was a unique and unforgettable experience. Tall and elegant, with bright blue sparkling eyes, she lit up the room. She seemed a little shy and slightly embarrassed with all the attention from the large group of male police officers. Perhaps that was why she stood next to me, because we were the only two women in the room. Soon the speeches began. The princess offered her thanks to the gathered crowd for keeping her safe on her travels.

The princess stayed at the event for about an hour. As people dispersed, we came down the stairs behind her as she walked back to her car with her bodyguard. He put the princes into the car and Diana climbed in beside them. We loaded our gear into our vehicle nearby but couldn't help noticing they were leaving, so we turned to watch. Suddenly the door of the princess's vehicle flew open and she jumped out and ran back towards me. She stretched out her hand to me, smiled broadly and said 'I'm so sorry we were not introduced. Thank you for taking the photographs. It's a pleasure to meet you.' She then shook hands with my colleague and thanked him also. She hurried back to her car and they left. Her kind gesture spoke volumes about her warmth and compassion.

The fact that she had noticed myself and my colleague were the only two people in the large gathering who had not been introduced to her showed how much she cared about *everyone*. She went out of her way to come back to talk to us. To shake our hands. To make sure we knew we were seen. What a kind-hearted human being she was. It's a memory I will always treasure.

14

Fatal Accidents

Black Rats and Tales from the Road

Flashing blue lights clicked rhythmically atop the police car's roof. Mangled vehicles sat in the pool of darkness at the bottom of the hill. Police cars, parked diagonally, blocked both ends of the road. The crumpled wreckage came into focus through my camera viewfinder as I shone my torch into the darkness. The sweet smell of blood mixed with fuel vapors filled my nostrils. I could taste the air as I photographed the carnage. In the dark tree-lined valley, the accident investigation team and I worked like a well-oiled machine.

Then, through the silence, the sound of a throaty engine rumbled and then roared as a vehicle hurtled towards us. I could hear it but couldn't see it, yet. The engine revs grew louder as the vehicle crested the hill. The symphony of sounds echoed off the rows of darkened houses in the stillness of the night air.

I had a bad feeling. *How can he not see us, I thought, lit up in our bright yellow and silver high-viz jackets, standing in the road, blue lights flashing?*

'He's not going to stop!' I shouted to the accident investigator.

I grabbed my camera gear and leapt to the safety of a driveway.

'Oh yes he is,' came the reply from the traffic officer as he stepped out into the centre of the road, raised his hand, and waited.

The driver of the vehicle slammed on the brakes and his car screeched to a halt, coming to rest inches from the traffic officer, who never flinched. I'd never seen anything quite like it. I had visions of needing to call an ambulance and another traffic unit to investigate the second fatal accident scene within a scene. Fortunately, we all went home safe that night. But not before the traffic officer had given the offending motorist a loud dressing-down, and a handful of fines for speeding and dangerous driving.

Fatal motor vehicle accidents are not always what they seem. What at first might appear to be a drunk driver careening off the road, could turn out to be a vehicular homicide (or suicide) upon closer inspection. MPS photographers photographed every fatal motor vehicle accident for this reason. Trained accident investigators, usually uniformed police officers with specialist forensic investigation skills, attended and investigated every fatal accident as a potential homicide to determine how the accident happened and to establish the cause of the accident, and who was at fault. The process is painstaking and time-consuming, taking measurements of yaw and skid marks, and noting damage to the vehicles, and the victims, the weather conditions, the condition of the road surface, the lighting and so forth. It's even more challenging in bad weather, at night, or when miles and miles of traffic is backed up and drivers shout abuse at the investigation team. The photographs of fatal accidents assist the investigators in writing their reports and can aid in accident reconstruction. The photographs are an integral part of the investigation and we shot them as a precautionary measure in case the evidence, vehicle inspection, and/or autopsy subsequently proved that the accident was not simply an accident but was a vehicular homicide or a suicide staged to look like an accident.

On a rainy night in Hackney, I drove to meet officers at the scene of a fatal road traffic accident. Rain lashed down on us while we worked at the scene. Although Pentax cameras were extremely robust and not generally bothered by the rain or extremes of temperature, on this night the rain won the battle. In the middle of documenting the scene on a busy roadway, my camera failed. I grabbed my backup camera but that also failed after a short time. The rain soaked the second camera despite my best efforts to protect it. I was embarrassed to find myself in the middle of a fatal accident scene with two cameras that no longer worked and traffic backed up in all directions. In a busy city like London, it doesn't take long before you have a miles-long traffic jam on your hands. And a lot of angry, horn honking drivers letting you know how they feel about it. Not to mention the torrential rain that soaked us all through and through. I had a sudden brainwave about how I could sort out the camera situation. I asked the officers on scene to call for a car from the nearest police station. An area car arrived pronto and drove me, with my two wet cameras, back to the station on blue lights and sirens. It didn't take long to reach the police station. I ran to the women's toilets with my wet cameras. I sat on the tiled floor and disassembled both cameras and dried them piece by piece, under the hand dryer. I put the cameras back together, did a check to listen to the sound of the shutter to make sure they were both working and back I went to the scene, as fast as they could drive me there safely. I finished the fatal accident photographs and we all went on our way. Quick thinking in a crisis is a skill every police photographer must have in their toolkit.

Motorbike Mayhem

The duty officer sent me to the scene of a motorbike fatality in the East End of London. By the time I arrived, a crowd had gathered and stood huddled together in the warm summer sunshine. From beyond the crime scene tape, they watched with rapt attention as police cordoned off the scene and briefed me on what had occurred. It was unusual for me to arrive at a scene to find a body covered. On this occasion the OIC felt the public nature of the scene required that they cover the body, so the full horror of what lay beneath the body sheet was not on public display for all and sundry. I advised the officer to warn the crowd to leave and let us get on with our work and respect the privacy of the deceased man. The first warning resulted in some of the gathered crowd dissipating and retreating to a respectful distance, or going back to their homes. However, despite several warnings to turn away, that the scene was gory, several bystanders decided to remain and continued to stare in anticipation of us uncovering the body. Obviously, there was no forensic value to me in photographing a dead body lying in the road covered with a white plastic sheet. After one final warning the police officer assisting me removed the sheet from the body. The full horror of this motorbike crash was on display for all to see, despite our best efforts to disperse the crowd.

The man who died had been riding a trail bike along a stretch of road for several hours prior to the crash. The witness statements from those who remained on scene told us that the victim had been driving up and down the road with his four-year-old toddler on the seat in front of him. For some reason he thought this would be a thrilling experience for his daughter. Fortunately, he handed her back to her mother so she was not on the bike with him when he collided at high speed with a lamp post. The impact of hitting the lamp post caused horrific fatal injuries. Parts of his flesh and bones lay strewn around the road, and mangled into the motorbike's metal frame. It was a horrifying sight and proved too much for some of the bystanders. One lady almost fainted, so her friends walked her home. Others gasped in horror when we removed the plastic sheet from the decedent. At many fatal motor vehicle accidents, the ambulance service had removed the victims prior to my arrival. Naturally they did everything they could to save people's lives while they raced through the streets to the emergency room on blues and twos. But in some cases, victims were still at the scene, often mangled into the wreckage, or at times thrown into a field or nearby obstacles like signposts. None of it was pleasant to witness or photograph.

I photographed the scene as quickly and efficiently as possible, so undertakers could remove the man's body from public view. While it might seem callous to leave a body on public display at a crime scene, sometimes it's necessary so no forensic evidence is lost and the scene is methodically inspected and documented before the deceased is removed.

At the time I remember feeling angry with the crowd, that they should be so disrespectful to the decedent. But in hindsight I understand the psychology of why people gawk at these gory scenes. They wonder what happened and fear it could happen to them. It's as if they feel they need to see this horror for themselves to understand and perhaps blame the victim, to make themselves feel safe. I could almost hear the thoughts running through their heads at the scene, 'Well I wouldn't be so stupid as to drive a motorbike up and down the street at high speed like that, so this will never happen to me.' It's a way of justifying to themselves that this awful situation couldn't happen to them because they wouldn't have done anything that crazy. It's a way of distancing themselves from their own mortality.

* * *

Arriving Before the Ambulance

I remember going to photograph the scene of a fatal accident one night in East London. When I arrived at the crash, the investigator walked through the scene with me to share what had happened so I could tell the story of the accident in a logical sequence. While I'd attended hundreds of fatal motor vehicle accidents and knew the procedures by heart, speaking with the crash investigators and working closely with them to meet their needs was a big part of my job. At a fatal crash scene, items from vehicles, and the victims' body parts are strewn everywhere. My job was to make sure I missed nothing, and that I photographed every detail of the crash site in a way that would show the jury what the scene looked like when the accident happened.

Four or five teenagers had occupied the vehicle, and both speed and alcohol had been factors in the crash. Ambulances had removed the victims from the scene before I arrived. But I didn't hold out much hope for several of them, as their teeth and gums and other pieces of flesh that should have still been attached to them were strewn around the crash site. As I was there to photograph a fatal motor vehicle accident, I knew that at least one or more of the victims had died on the way to hospital. As I was wrapping up my last few shots, and anticipating returning home to bed for a well-deserved rest – it had been a busy weekend – a call came over the radio to the crash investigators that there was another scene of a possible fatal accident a couple of miles from where we stood. The accident investigator shouted over to me 'Finish your shots, pack your gear, you're coming with us.' I threw my gear in the van and ran over for details. There were two police vehicles with me that night. The lead investigator told me simply to drive behind him, keep pace, and not let any vehicles into the space between us. The second traffic car at the scene would follow closely behind me, both with lights and sirens. We started off slowly and soon the pace picked up, cars moved out of our way as if by magic. Fortunately, the roads were quiet that night. It was an exhilarating experience driving mere feet from the bumper of the police vehicle in front of me. Not to mention having a police vehicle driving close behind me. It didn't take long for us to travel the couple of miles to the second accident scene. Not surprisingly, we were the first to arrive. As we jumped out of our vehicles and ran towards the smoking vehicle, we heard screaming and groaning.

A vehicle with two male passengers had sped down a hill, lost control at the base of the hill, and hit an enormous plane tree. The vehicle folded almost in half like a V shape. The engine block went up the tree and the back of the car folded up behind it. When the accident investigator pulled open the driver's door the smell of alcohol nearly knocked us over. The driver was a drunk young man who screamed at us in an angry tirade of swear words. The investigator assessed the driver's injuries and left me with him while he went to talk to the passenger. When I knelt to comfort the injured man, I noticed his thigh bones sticking through his jeans. The force of the crash had smashed his femur and driven both ends of it through the material. His lower legs and feet were trapped in the wreckage. We did our best to comfort him and offer immediate first aid until the ambulance arrived, which seems like an eternity when you're waiting with a screaming injured casualty. I realised the other passenger had walked away from the crash and was pacing in an agitated manner nearby, smoking furiously and shaking. The second officer was speaking with him to find out what happened and to assess his need for medical attention. It wasn't long before I heard sirens in the distance. The doctor arrived in a fast car with a flashing green light. He was alone, and thankfully he arrived way before the ambulance, which was reassuring for the man trapped in the wreckage, no doubt. The doctor climbed into the seat behind the driver to assess his injuries. He spoke calmly to the intoxicated man who responded by swearing and screaming. He must have called that poor doctor every name under the sun, and that was even before the doctor started to do anything to him. This was a new experience for me, the screaming, the swearing and the sight of the broken bones and blood pouring out of his legs, and other parts of his body. The gore didn't bother me. It was more distressing to have a person you were trying to help abuse you. Most of the people at my crime scenes didn't talk back or swear at me. It gave me valuable insight into what the traffic officers and paramedics had to contend with when they turned up to these accidents. The accident investigators took it in their stride, and calmly suggested to the young man that perhaps if he hadn't had eight pints of beer and climbed behind the wheel, he might not be in such a dreadful situation. It's hard to feel compassion for drunk drivers when you've seen and photographed the carnage their selfishness causes and the pain and misery it inflicts on others. So often the drunk driver walks away from a crash site unscathed, but the innocent party they hit is not so lucky and they lose their life.

15

Whirly Bird

India 99

'Don't worry, we won't drop out of the sky like a stone,' James said, as India 99, the Bell 222 police helicopter, climbed higher into a clear blue sky.

'When we reach 3,000 feet, I'll disengage the rotors from the engines, and we'll start to descend rapidly. If I drop the collective fast enough, we won't hit the ground,' he continued, somewhat amused, as I listened in horror from my seat in the rear of the aircraft.

'And you couldn't have picked another day to do this, preferably when I'm not on board?' I replied.

'We're required to conduct safety drills on a set schedule. It's good for you to experience an autorotation drill. It'll be fun, you'll see,' he said. I didn't believe him. An 8,000lb helicopter, with three crew, and 200 gallons of kerosene on board, falling out of the sky at hundreds of feet per minute, was not my idea of fun.

When we reached the appropriate altitude, James held the aircraft in a hover for a moment and looked back at me. 'Brace yourself. Here we go,' he said, giving me a thumbs up. When James disengaged the engines from the main rotor, we began to drop out of the sky at a terrifying speed. I knew James only had a matter of seconds to lower the collective (a lever used to adjust the pitch of the main rotor blades) to prevent the rotors from slowing down too much. During an autorotation, the main rotor blades turn solely by the upward airflow through the blades, unlike in powered flight when airflow pushes downwards through the blades. If the main rotors had stalled, the situation would have been unrecoverable. The two-foot-wide steel blades would have flapped about uncontrollably, and sliced through the fuselage, or cut off the tail cone or rotor, and we'd have crashed to our deaths. With the comforting hum of the twin engines now hushed at idle power, I watched the ground rush up to meet us. My stomach leapt as we fell towards the earth. After what seemed like an eternity, James reengaged the main rotor system to the engines and we jolted back into powered flight. The comforting slap, slap, slap of the powered rotor blades cutting through the air came as a huge relief. I released the breath I'd been holding. Although I don't recommend autorotation drills, once used to them, they aren't quite as terrifying, especially when a former military pilot, who flew combat missions, flies the aircraft. But I never forgot it, and while I never learned to love falling out of the sky, I loved flying.

Flying over London at 144 miles an hour is a privilege few experience. Hooked from my first flight with the ASU, I loved the sensation of being above the hustle and bustle of the crowded city. Being able to see for miles in any direction was an incredible feast for the senses. Stretched out below us, a carpet of long skinny gardens with fences, fences, fences. Everything fenced off in London. *Stay Out* the fences tell others. Gardens lovingly tended and groomed to celebrity perfection, adjoining gardens overrun and wild with despair. Laundry hung from criss-crossed washing lines strung out from house to fence post, square shadows cast in lines like a shadow puppet show for clothes. Ivy-covered buildings looked cozy in their snug overcoats of lush green. Orange cranes grouped together like crosses on the landscape. Green cranes like aliens on the Thames waterfront. Patches on the flat rooftops where the rain had worn a dark patch. Grey satellite dishes all facing south, in silent worship of the satellites passing over England.

While most Londoners will have heard a police helicopter flying overhead, or circling above their neighbourhood, and some complain about the noise keeping them awake at night, many may not be aware of the critical role the helicopter plays in crime fighting and crime prevention. The helicopter *does not* circle overhead unless the crew is actively searching for a suspect or a missing person on the ground, or when assisting ground units. The helicopter crew may be searching for a dangerous armed suspect, gone to ground in a residential neighbourhood, or a lost dementia patient who risks freezing to death if they're not found fast enough. Aerial photography is another reason the helicopter orbits, with the aircraft tipped to the left, from where the photographer shoots their images.

* * *

It's not easy to make a helicopter pilot air sick, but I almost managed it on one occasion – not intentionally of course. I needed to photograph a building in the heart of central London. The densely packed roads and lanes at the back of Oxford Street presented a challenge to photograph from the air. Reading a map book on your lap while the aircraft circles, and reconciling the page with the moving map on the ground below is a unique challenge. For this assignment, the pilot needed to position us at an angle that turned the helicopter almost on its left side for the tight orbits above the tiny winding streets below. Because the pilot sat on the right side of the aircraft, and I took photographs from the left side, it made for a sickening experience for the whole crew, but especially for the pilot, who could not see the scene I was looking at below. So, my comms instructions to him went something like 'Left, left, left, tight left, keep coming around,' as I shot the images of the target. Turning so sharply at this angle meant that myself, the pilot and the observer were almost parallel to the ground, and straining against our seatbelts. But the pilot fared the worst as he was effectively flying blind. He had only my instructions to guide him as he hung out of his seatbelt at a sickening angle. As for me, I was looking down directly to the ground 1,000 feet below through an open window, which felt more like looking through a hole in the floor of the helicopter, not the door. After a few tight orbits, I heard the pilot say 'I'm going to vomit if we don't turn out of this orbit soon.' 'Just one more turn and we're done,' I said, too busy to think of vomiting. It was a physiological and cognitive overload; the noise and vibration of the helicopter; the

severe angle of the turns; the constant chatter from six
radio frequencies; the cold wind whipping around in the
cabin; and a moving map of the ground as we orbited,
while I had to keep the target building in sight and in
focus as we turned. I worked quickly to shoot my scene
photographs. We all breathed a sigh of relief when we
turned out of the orbit, and allowed our stomachs to
settle down after the feeling of nausea this type of flying
inevitably caused. Speed and efficiency were imperative
when I shot aerial photographs. I had to photograph the
scene right the first time, and work fast, and give the
pilot precise instructions as we orbited, to secure the
photographs of the target. The aerial images needed to
be of the highest quality to ensure they were admissible
in court.

From up in the air, it was easy to forget the *other*
London that I knew so well. The London filled with
murder and mayhem, grimness, death and misery. I felt
free of all that when I was in the air. London from
a helicopter is a treasure map of colour and curiosi-
ties. Everything is different from the air. Red buses like
Dinky toy cars. Perfect patterns mown into the lawns in
parks and gardens, that you would not notice from the
ground. Paths worn bare as people criss-cross the park
on the grass. All the different shades of green of the
rounded treetop canopy. Railway tracks, red and rusty
like a child's train set. Archways under the rail tracks.
See what's beyond the walls. Red cars stand out in the
London sunshine. The Thames, the colour of builders'
tea brewed a little too long. Historic buildings are gift
wrapped in white plastic, like a giant present. Boats in

St Catherine's Dock, sparkling their wealth at us, as they bob and creak on their moorings in the marina. Sandy-coloured blocks of low-rise housing too closely packed for comfort, and yet the yawning gaps of wasteland with not a soul in sight, hidden behind hoardings that warn 'Keep out'. The rhythm of the shadows falling across the rooftops of London. Long chimney pot shadows. Forbidden alleyways. Badly patched rooftops. Playing fields devoid of life, and tennis court nets sagging as they wait in ghostly silence for the children's return. Some businesses have painted large signs and telephone numbers on their rooftops. Who will call? A message from God or the passengers of jets leaving London who are high above the clouds faster than you could dial the phone number. Seeing the Thames at low tide – beaches in the city, the foreshore exposed on both sides of the river. If you know the tide times it's possible to walk along the foreshore, but first check with the Port of London Authority to find out which areas you're permitted to walk along and when. If you're lucky you might even see a mudlark searching for ancient and modern treasures washed up by the river's tides.

The ASU's three aircraft can reach any location within the M25 in about twelve minutes from a cold start. While the aircraft is spooling up, the pilot plots the course into the onboard GPS and contacts air traffic control and the MPS controller. By the time it takes to spool up (for the rotors to reach full speed), about three minutes, and with all the start-up checklist completed, the helicopter lifts off, travelling backwards and upwards from the pad, and turning full circle at the end of this procedure.

Leaving the pad in a reverse takeoff puts maximum pressure on the twin engines, and if anything is going to fail, it's likely to fail at that moment. The reverse takeoff provides the pilot with the safest and quickest return to the pad for a safe landing. Once we'd backed away from the helipad with no issues, we turned and flew nose down across the fields. The nose down aspect helped us pick up speed on our way from Lippitts Hill into the city. It's not the most comfortable position to be in, either as a pilot or as a passenger, because all I could see were the green fields and hedges flashing past below us through the front windows of the aircraft, as we hung forward in our seat belts. Once the nose came up again, my stomach settled, and I enjoyed a panoramic view of the city stretched out before us.

The Bell 222 could carry two crew and between five to eight passengers depending on the seating configuration. With a row of seats removed from the middle of the aircraft, it gave me plenty of room for photographic gear and to move around the cabin. This seating configuration allowed me the space to kneel or crouch on the floor of the aircraft by the open window to take photographs. The removeable window, attached with butterfly clips to the aircraft, was secured by thin wire cables. It fitted into a pocket slot in the base of the door to prevent it from accidentally detaching from the aircraft, or blowing back into the cabin and causing injury or worse.

The noise level inside a helicopter cabin is loud enough to damage your hearing, so ear protection is crucial. We carried spare headsets in the aircraft for those who flew with us on occasion. The pilot, the police observer and

I each had our own custom-fitted, white flying helmets with dual visors, both clear and brown tinted – think *Top Gun* – that incorporated a built-in comms system we plugged into the ports above our seats. Without wearing headphones or a helmet with integrated comms, it's impossible to hear the pilot or the police observer who are mere feet away in the cabin. The noise level inside the aircraft, from the twin engines and the rotors is in the range of about 80 to 90 decibels. By comparison, a lawnmower is about 90 decibels, and an average vacuum cleaner around 75 decibels. We generally flew over the city at about 1,500 feet which reduced the decibel levels. Occasionally we needed to fly lower which meant an increase in the decibel levels. When a job required me to photograph a location covertly, I had to factor in the noise level of the aircraft and limit the number of orbits around the target. For covert operations I planned the assignment in detail. Once I spotted the target on the horizon, I knew I had one orbit, maybe two at most, to shoot the photographs, without alerting the criminals to our presence overhead.

It's hard to describe how loud it is inside a large twin engine helicopter. And how much louder it got when I opened the door or window to take photographs. Even on warm days, at 1,500 feet up, the howling wind is still cold enough to take your breath away as it bursts into the cabin and whips around the inside of the aircraft like a mini tornado. I wore lambskin gloves, like the pilot, for flying photographic assignments, because fingers freeze when holding a camera out of the aircraft window. Even on assignments that took only one or two orbits, my hands froze in that short time. The kid gloves were soft enough to feel the camera controls, and provided enough of a barrier to keep my hands warm enough to function once I opened the aircraft window or door.

The MPS, as the second largest police service in the world, founded the Air Support Unit (ASU) in the 1980s and were one of the few police services to have an ASU in operation 24/7/365. Aerial crime scene photography was *not* an option for most police services in England at that time. Having the helicopter resource at our disposal provided the MPS photographers with an opportunity to recommend to the SIO when aerial photographs would be of benefit to an investigation, coupled with terrestrial photographs and video. Because I flew weekly with the ASU, the helicopter and aerial photography option was never far from my mind, with respect to its value for detectives. When I worked at the Mucking Tip body recovery scene and we uncovered the dismembered body parts of the victim, I knew an aerial perspective and aerial photographs would be crucial to the investigating team and for jury members when the case came to trial. Because the scene was enormous (it was Europe's second largest landfill) it would have been too convoluted to describe in words alone in a statement for court. Terrestrial photographs would not have adequately conveyed the vast scale of the location, and the exact positions where we recovered each body part and their relation to one another due to the undulating and challenging terrain. Shooting 120 medium format film also permitted us to enlarge images for court to poster size or larger, while retaining detail and providing the highest quality evidentiary photographs.

Aerial photographs are a valuable resource for detectives investigating serious crimes such as murder, rape, terrorist attacks, disasters, sieges and more. They provide detectives with a different perspective of the scene. Although preferable, it wasn't always possible to take aerial photographs at the time of the incident. Gusting winds or a low cloud base sometimes grounded the helicopters, but once weather permitted, I shot the photographs as soon as possible after the fact. My photographs gave investigating officers an opportunity to see several critical locations in one large photograph, to complement a series of photographs taken from ground level. Aerial photographs froze the scene as it was at the time of the murder. They showed the tree canopy cover, the direction of parked vehicles on the roads around the scene, the proximity of the attack to the victim's or the perpetrator's home, or the route the victim walked prior to their assault/rape/murder. If the victim walked past a temporary structure, such as a workmen's Portakabin, and this was a critical component at the scene, construction crews might move or demolish it before a criminal trial. Council workers may prune or chop down shrubbery or trees and clear dense undergrowth or tree canopy that hid the perpetrator while they lay in wait for a victim. Many critical components of a crime scene may be gone by the time a case comes to trial. The aerial photographs provide a permanent record of the scene, for use at trial or years later by cold case detectives reconstructing a crime scene. It's more cost effective to take aerial photographs of a multi-location crime scene than it is to bring jury members to multiple scenes. Police also use aerial photographs to plan major police operations, such as policing events at Wembley Stadium, the second largest sports stadium in Europe, shepherding thousands of football supporters to and from the venue, safely. They also use the photographs to brief teams planning raids on locations where police suspect criminal activities are taking place. Crime scene aerial photography plays an important role in many different types of major crimes, such as murder, kidnapping, sieges, disasters, terrorism and bombings, to name a few.

Rotors Running Pickup – Don't Lose Your Head

If the crew needed to pick me up at a murder scene, I parked my van at the nearest playing field, park, or flat open green space. I changed into my fireproof (not female-friendly) flight suit, boots and flying helmet, while I waited for the helicopter to arrive. With few exceptions, notwithstanding some FAA restrictions, the MPS helicopters could land almost anywhere, if safe to do so, unlike commercial helicopters. They rarely shut off the engines during a pickup, as we'd have to wait for three minutes to spool up again. We could not risk that delay when the MPS controller might call the helicopter to a chase or other urgent call.

All my pickups by the crew were 'hot' pickups, which means the rotors kept running at full speed. A dangerous situation if you're not flight safety trained. 'While the rotors are in motion, always wait for the thumbs up signal from the pilot before you approach the helicopter. And never approach the helicopter from the rear, when the rotors are in motion, or it might cost you your head,' Sgt Tony Evans calmly explained during my flight safety training with the Air Support Unit (ASU). I nodded my understanding, as the gory image of a decapitation scene flashed through my mind. His words of warning came back to me whenever we did a hot pickup. I never took for granted how dangerous these landings/pickups were, but having flown with them regularly, I knew the type of location that presented the fewest hazards to the helicopter, the crew and members of the public. The pickup location needed to be flat, with no overhanging cables or trees too close. It needed to be a location free from debris, otherwise the downwash from the aircraft would fling loose gravel about during landing, which could damage the helicopter or people and vehicles nearby. The dust kicked up by the downwash from the rotors could cause a dangerous mini dust storm. Also, the downdraft could rip off signage and suck it up into the rotors, or injure members of the public in the vicinity.

I sat in the back of the aircraft, beside the window directly over the stub wing, on the left side of the helicopter, and used the middle window for aerial photography on the Bell 222. When we were close to the target location, I unbuckled myself and strapped my body harness to a tether attachment point on the floor of the aircraft. Once securely harnessed, I let the pilot know and he reduced our airspeed, so it was safe for me to remove the window. One mistake, like removing the window before the aircraft had reduced speed sufficiently would have been enough to blow out all the windows of the aircraft, and kill us all, as James told me during one of our flights together. We all had to be on our 'A game' when flying. Safety is of paramount importance. We all worked closely as a team. One mistake by any of us could cause the deaths of all of us on board, not to mention collateral damage to those on the ground, in the event of a crash. The flying skills of the MPS civilian pilots impressed me enormously and yet they rarely received accolades for their work. It's not until you fly assignments with these talented pilots that you appreciate their incredible flying skills. There's so much going on in the aircraft, on the ground with police in pursuit of suspects, not to mention air traffic control and at least six channels of chatter in the comms headsets. It's mindboggling.

Heart Pickup from Heathrow

One day the ASU controller tasked us to fly to Heathrow Airport to collect a heart for transplant. Landing at one of the world's busiest airports proved quite a hair-raising experience. With special permission, we hovered near the apron at the end of the runways, as we watched the jets landing and taking off every 45 seconds. Their landing lights blazing like jewels glittering in a grey-blue sky stacked high into the air on the approach to Heathrow. Once landed, the police observer ran to collect the heart and hurried back to the helicopter. I'll never forget that moment when he opened the door to hand me the cooler that contained the heart. There's no feeling quite like this. I held the cooler, emblazoned with red writing, 'HUMAN ORGANS FOR TRANSPLANT', on my lap for the flight. Such a precious cargo. I didn't want to risk it toppling over during the flight and bruising the heart. While we flew across London at top speed, I thought about how sad it was that I held a human being's heart in my hands, and that meant a family somewhere were grieving the loss of their loved one. And conversely knowing a heart was on the way must have brought enormous joy to the family whose loved one would receive it, to save their life.

We flew the heart to one of London's older hospitals south of the river. With no helipad, we had to land on a small triangle of grass at the rear of the hospital. Drooping power lines and trees surrounded us. We circled the landing site first, to give us a 360 degree view of any obstacles or dangers to the aircraft. Once the pilot deemed it a suitable landing spot, we were all on high alert as we descended onto the impossibly small patch of grass. Fortunately, our pilot that day had spent years flying large transport helicopters and Chinooks out to the oil rigs off the coast of Scotland, and prior to that he'd been a military helicopter pilot. That assignment certainly tested his skills and our teamwork.

We were all aware that to be viable, the heart needed to reach the recipient within about four hours of removal from the donor. London traffic jams could have prevented it reaching the recipient fast enough. The donated organ had travelled from outside the UK, so the clock was ticking. We knew we were in a race against time to fly the heart across London to the waiting transplant team. I still remember the group of doctors and medical staff at the back doors of the hospital, dressed in scrubs, their white coats flapping in the powerful rotor wash from the Bell 222. They looked hopeful and relieved as the observer took the cooler from me and delivered it safely into their hands. There was no better feeling in the world than seeing their faces.

He Didn't Look Up

I had to abandon my work mid-assignment, on occasions. A high-speed chase unfolding on the ground took priority over photographic assignments. I was in the middle of photographing a rape scene location with the window open when we were assigned to search for an armed robbery suspect who'd gone to ground. He'd managed to lose the police units in pursuit. When we arrived overhead, each of us scanned the ground below for the suspect. Ground units described him as a male, wearing a white t-shirt, a green jacket and blue jeans. We orbited, searching the terrain, but saw no sign of him. Then, I noticed a nearby railway station platform crowded with commuters shielding their eyes against the strong sunlight, looking up at the noisy helicopter above them.

I knew from previous chases that a target will add or remove items of clothing to disguise themselves from police in pursuit. As the chase progressed, our suspect had taken off his green jacket and thrown it into bushes on the chase route. The Bell 222 helicopter was a beast of a loud aircraft, you couldn't possibly ignore from the ground. It's not a sight people experience often, a helicopter flying directly above them at a thousand feet or less. Naturally people stare up at the noisy aircraft. Others turn in circles watching the helicopter as it orbits, in a typical search pattern. As we orbited, I spotted a man standing on the train platform. He fitted the description of the suspect. Although we circled numerous times, he never looked up at the helicopter circling above him. This made me suspicious. I pointed him out to the police observer.

'Well spotted,' he said. 'That's our guy.' We continued to circle overhead and informed the ground units that we'd spotted the armed robbery suspect standing on the railway platform with the other commuters. He had a sawn-off shotgun in his backpack that he'd used in the robbery. The ground units closed in and took him safely into custody. They positively identified him as the armed robber from the nearby bank robbery. I proudly claimed this as my first *aerial collar (arrest)* in my police career.

During photographic assignments, the ASU or MPS controller might request our presence at a police chase unfolding in another part of London. We could fly from one side of London to the other in about twelve minutes. It didn't matter where we were, we answered the call. When not taking photographs, I reverted to my role as a crew member; another set of eyes to observe chases on the ground, and to watch out for any obstacles or dangers to the helicopter, such as cables, aircraft flying too close, high-rise buildings, antennas and radio towers etc.

One memorable chase involved a man driving a car at high speed through the densely populated streets of South London. When patrol officers stopped his vehicle, he decided to flee before they had a chance to speak with him. A chase ensued. Because a police chase, with several police vehicles, is a dangerous and costly affair, the MPS controller requests helicopter assistance. Once India 99 arrives overhead, it allows the ground units to drop back. If the adrenaline-fuelled driver of the car thinks police are no longer pursuing him, he's more likely to slow down, or abandon his vehicle and take off on foot. The helicopter takes over the chase and directs the ground units to where the suspect vehicle is heading. Ground units, anticipating the vehicle's arrival, block its path with a rolling roadblock (on motorways), or these days throw out a spike belt to puncture the vehicle's tyres, if it's safe to do so.

Fleeing drivers take off from the police for various reasons, although sometimes the reasons are not good ones. Instead of stopping and taking the consequences for one offence, they add a slew of charges to their criminal record. Not a wise move.

When we arrived on scene, the chase had been underway for ten minutes. The ground units tried to keep the car in sight. Several units had joined the chase. The ground unit that stopped the vehicle had run the plates through the PNC (Police National Computer) to identify the registered owner. Often stolen vehicles were involved in chases. The pursued driver drove like a maniac. What he failed to understand is that from the air it's easy to see speeding vehicles from miles away, because they are going so much faster than the rest of the traffic, so they stand out. It's also easy to spot road racers, speeding motorbikes and drivers crossing double white lines.

When our fleeing driver came to an obstacle, he mounted the kerb, although pedestrians were walking along the busy streets. We recorded the chase footage on video and the observer's voice calling the chase, as evidence for court. The car kept going, hitting parked cars and other obstacles in its path. It mounted the pavement numerous times. It sent obstacles flying as it smashed through them. It reversed out of a dead end street at high speed. It drove into a crowded marketplace and sent stalls and fruit flying, wrecking half of the market as it crashed through the short stretch of road. It looked like a scene from a movie car chase. If I hadn't seen it with my own eyes, I probably wouldn't have believed it. The fleeing car bounced off cars as the panicked driver oversteered. The onboard instruments were clocking his speed on the ground, which was imprinted on the video shot for court. It ripped off bumpers and wing mirrors of cars parked on both sides of the road. Debris littered the road and the footpaths in its wake. It wasn't long before he'd shredded the tyres and they went flying off and he was driving on rims, and sparks flew.

When a driver is that frantic his adrenaline is pumping and he'll do almost anything to escape. The fear of police pursuit and capture seemed to make him oblivious to the danger he inflicted on innocent bystanders, not to mention the danger to his own life, as he drove with reckless abandon. In a final desperate move, our driver ended up in another dead end street. Trapped, he had no choice but to surrender and was taken into custody. This story serves as a reminder that, no matter how fast you drive, you can't outrun the police helicopter.

Bottoms Up at Belmarsh

Not all aerial assignments were such heart-stopping, high stakes as high-speed chases. On one memorable occasion, I was assigned to photograph a maximum-security prison at Belmarsh. A 'Category A' men's prison in Thamesmead, South East London, it opened in 1991. It housed 900 of the most dangerous convicts in the United Kingdom including gang members, convicted terrorists and multiple murderers who'd killed three or more people. Prior to the assignment, the ASU requested special permission for us to fly over the prison's tightly controlled air space. We didn't want to alarm the prison authorities by flying over the prison without giving them prior notice.

On the day I photographed the prison, hundreds of prisoners were out in the exercise areas of the sprawling prison complex. The noise of the Bell 222 soon attracted their attention. With the same orange, red and white striped livery as the MPS police cars, it wasn't hard to identify us as a police helicopter. While we circled above the low-rise sand-coloured buildings of the rectangular shaped compound, the prisoners put on quite a show.

They pulled down their trousers and track suit bottoms and en masse, bent over and treated us to the sight of their pale white bottoms. A few decided to show us their genitalia. Others gave us a double dose of the middle finger or the reverse victory salute. Some gave us the forearm jerk to express their contempt, an obscene gesture that translates to 'Fuck you' in many cultures.

I laughed loudly as I looked through my camera viewfinder to see dozens of pasty white bottoms mooning us in the sunlight. It gave the pilot and observer quite a chuckle too. It's not a sight that would shock a police photographer. I'd seen more human anatomy, dead and alive, in my photography career than most people see in a lifetime. *Come on lads, you'll have to do better than that* I thought as I finished my last shots and packed away my gear.

It wasn't only the prison exhibitionists at Belmarsh who gave us an eyeful of naked flesh. The naked and partially naked sunworshippers on London's rooftops should perhaps be more aware that they are visible to police helicopters – the eyes in the sky. So, to all those in London who sunbathe topless or naked on the rooftops of grand Georgian mansions, or blocks of flats, know this – I got a front row seat to the show, and so did my crewmates. Pasty white bodies, in stark contrast to the grey rooftops, have a way of attracting attention. I could see people clearly on the roofs, or on the ground, from 1,500 feet, without any special equipment. The summer weather brought naked Londoners on to their rooftops in droves, to escape the heat of the city and enjoy some undisturbed sunbathing. But what people may not know is that police are duty bound to investigate reports of indecent exposure, or outraging public decency. With a police officer on board the aircraft, and the technology to pinpoint an address accurately, it's entirely possible that a person sunbathing naked or semi-naked could be arrested for breaking the law. Please keep this in mind the next time you plan to go naked sunbathing on your rooftop.

16

London Under Attack

Blue flashing lights filled my rear-view mirror. Shit, that's all I need, I thought to myself. I kept going. Driving at speed through London's empty streets, I was the only other vehicle on that stretch of road at 2 a.m. on a cold November morning. As they gained on me, their bright white head-lights, flashing left and right, were blinding. I pressed harder on the accelerator. They whooped the siren as they pulled up behind me, inches from my rear bumper. But I didn't stop. Flashing lights bathed the cab of my unmarked police van in an eerie midnight blue. The sirens whooped again. I checked my rear-view mirror, but they'd gone. Now they were alongside me. Pacing me. Less than two feet apart, wing mirror to wing mirror, we drove down the empty one-way street. They lowered their window and shouted at me to stop. I opened my window to speak with them.

'What the hell are you playing at? Pull over,' shouted the female officer.

Suddenly she recognised me and began to laugh. 'Oh, for fuck's sake, it's you,' she said.

Heather, the driver of the police area car, was an officer I knew well from my work in the Stoke Newington district, a high crime area that regularly availed itself of my photographic services.

'I'm in a hurry to a scene,' I shouted back at her as we hurtled on, pacing one other.

'Well in that case, let's get you there safely,' she replied, over the roar of the engines. She manoeuvred her police car out in front of my van. With a blue light escort, I drove close behind them to the police cordon about two miles away. There they left me, but not before giving me a warning not to let them catch me driving like that again in their district.

Although the police officer at the cordon had witnessed my police escort stop within inches of the crime scene tape, he raised his hand, palm towards me to indicate I should stop. I slowed down, stuck my police ID out the window and shouted to him that I was the police photographer for his scene. Despite this, he walked over to speak with me. Usually, officers at the cordon were expecting me, and after a glance at my ID would lift the crime scene tape to let me drive through. Frustrated at yet another delay, I stepped out of my vehicle to explain that officers on scene were waiting for me.

'You can't go any further,' he said, his tone panicked.

'It's my job. They're waiting for me,' I explained, as patiently as I could. 'They can't lift the cordon until I photograph the scene.'

And still he insisted. 'I've instructions not to let anybody through. It's not safe.'

'But that doesn't include me,' I reassured him. 'If I don't do my job, we'll all be here until sunrise. Then there will be chaos, with all these streets closed off and homes evacuated and people trying to go to work, and back home.'

Reluctantly he allowed me through the police cordon. I jumped back in my van and raced through the last mile of silent streets to reach the scene where officers were waiting for me.

'What took you so long?' the gruff anti-terrorist officer asked when I stepped out of my vehicle.

'You wouldn't believe me if I told you,' I replied. We left it at that. Apart from myself, there were only two other officers present. The silence was eerie. The usual hum of traffic had vanished. It was as if London held her breath.

With cursory introductions out of the way, and anxious to photograph the scene, I asked, 'So, what have you got for me?'

'Follow me. I'll show you, but be careful where you step,' the bomb disposal officer cautioned, pointing towards the ground ahead of us where some detonators lay. 'They'll blow your leg clean off if you step on them,' he told me. We stepped over several silver cylinders with wire tails, no larger than a cigarette, that lay in our path. Parked by the side of the road, the dark blue heavy-duty Volvo truck stood with both cab doors open, evidence of its occupants' hasty escape. Behind the driver's cab, a small ladder leaned against the open side-entrance doorway that led into the rear cargo area of the truck. From ground level I could see a white substance, covered in plastic wrap that filled half the doorway. Planks of wood disguised the cargo load. The bomb disposal expert climbed into the back of the truck.

I handed him my tripod and camera bag and climbed in behind him. The floor was artificially high from the large cargo, so our heads almost touched the roof of the lorry. We walked to the back of the truck and spoke for a few minutes while we surveyed the detritus on the floor in front of us and discussed what he'd like to have shown in my photographs. Waste materials and boxes were strewn about on the floor of the truck.

'So, which one's the bomb?' I asked him, nodding towards the littered floor as he began to climb down the ladder and let me get on with my work.

'You're standing on it,' he said calmly. 'All three tons of it.'

As the largest Irish Republican Army (IRA) bomb at that time, there were enough explosives packed into that blue lorry, underneath me, to have destroyed a large swath of London and kill thousands of people. Had two vigilant uniformed police officers not stopped the suspicious-looking furniture lorry at 1 a.m. that morning, and intercepted the enormous bomb before it reached its intended target of the Lord Mayor's Show, which regularly drew crowds of up to half a million people, the three tons of explosives would have caused carnage, misery and destruction beyond comprehension. Those brave police officers were not carrying guns, and yet gave chase to the armed occupants. Police charged one man with attempted murder of a police officer and conspiracy to cause explosions. The defendant pleaded not guilty to both charges. A court sentenced him to twenty-five years in prison.

A year after the Stoke Newington bomb incident, I found myself once again at another bomb scene. But this time I saw up close the catastrophic devastation that a one-ton bomb could inflict on the streets of London.

I stood alone in the eerie silence of a devastated City of London street, outside the Hong Kong and Shanghai Bank, Bishopsgate, on a bright Saturday morning, staring in disbelief at the mind-numbing devastation from the massive bomb explosion. Damaged and collapsed buildings lay in ruins. The blast left nothing untouched. The skin of buildings, peeled back from the blast, revealed their skeletons. The density of rubble, twisted metal, wood, bricks, mangled aluminium and steel was beyond comprehension; two million square feet of devastated office space surrounded me. My boots crunched on a jade-green sea of five hundred tons of glass blown out of the surrounding tower blocks by the enormous explosion, as I walked through the empty streets. London, like a war zone. The bomb crater, an enormous gaping hole punched through the fabric of the roadway revealed the secrets of the earth below. Metal pipes bent in half like straws, and fractured sewer lines lay strewn among the clay and wreckage. Water spurted high into the air, jets firing out in all directions, hissing and impatient to escape. An incongruous rainbow-coloured water fountain roared down in a torrent onto the silent debris-strewn streets.

The scale and severity of the damage was incomprehensible. The force of the explosion had blown apart desks and filing cabinets in offices high above me in the surrounding tower blocks. While I picked my way through the knee-high debris, thousands of sheets of paper fluttered to the ground from above like a silent ticker-tape parade. But this was no celebration. Alarms rang, urgent and desperate in the ghostly silence, persistent in their unanswered calls for help. Vertical blinds billowed from the gaping windowless holes in the office towers around me, their white tentacles reaching out on the wind into the shadowy canyons, like fingers on dozens of hands pleading for help.

As I walked through the ghostly streets, formulating my plan for scene photographs, enormous smoky brown panes of glass crashed to the ground around me, whistling in the wind as they fell and smashing with such force, they sounded like bomb explosions. The square white gaps in the towers looked like giant missing teeth. All the while, debris fell from the surrounding buildings as the wind gusted and items continued to disgorge from the gaping floors of the offices above.

The massive Bishopsgate bomb sent a mushroom cloud up into the sky. The bomb caused extensive damage to buildings within a half mile radius. We found pieces of the Iveco truck over half a mile away from the blast site. The blast destroyed St Ethelburga's medieval church and severely damaged a second church, along with the Nat West Tower and Liverpool Street station. The IRA bombers had specifically targeted the financial heart of the City of London, displacing thousands of city traders and financial services workers. But they hadn't accounted for the resolve shown by the displaced companies and workers, who were back at the scene of devastation on the Monday morning after the blast. All dressed in suits and ties, ready for a day's trading. Photographs of the crowds of city workers, and their show of defiance to the terrorists were splashed across every newspaper. They set up in makeshift offices and found nooks and crannies in which to work. They would not let a bomb defeat them.

It all began when one of the national newspapers received a coded warning by the IRA at 10 a.m. on a Saturday morning in April. The Bishopsgate bomb exploded on the anniversary of the Easter Rising (The Easter Rebellion) of Irish republicans against British rule in Ireland. It was a powerful explosion that killed a British photojournalist and injured 44 others during a period of heightened IRA terrorist attacks on the city of London. It was a one-ton bomb made of fertiliser and diesel, and created a blast with the same forces as 1,200kg of TNT. Terrorists had hidden it in the back of a stolen Iveco tipper truck parked outside the Hong Kong and Shanghai Bank. They gave two telephone warnings, but unfortunately the police were still evacuating the area at the time of the explosion. That same day, two other small devices exploded in hijacked minicabs at Manor House Tube station, and at St Pancras. Fortunately, there were no injuries from those two explosions.

I worked at the Bishopsgate scene for the entire weekend, along with two other photographers I'd called for backup. Specialist officers had to comb through every inch of the scene to recover bomb components to recon-struct the device. But besides this arduous and time-consuming task, police brought shredders to the scene to safely dispose of the hundreds of thousands of confidential financial documents that had rained down on us for the entire weekend from the blown-out windows of the office towers above us.

We photographed every tiny sliver of the bomb components and the vehicle that contained the bomb. It's a
fascinating but painstaking process, and team members
require the utmost patience and attention to detail. At
that time officers used large sieve-like devices, similar to
what you might see in a garden when someone wants to
remove stones from their soil, only with a finer mesh.

As the day progressed, we heard that a photojournalist
had gone to the scene but nobody had heard from him
for hours. He'd been due to attend a family gathering
and when he didn't show, his family alerted the police.
Later that day we searched for his body and ultimately
discovered him inside one of the buildings not far from
the blast site. He'd gone into one of the foyers to take
shelter. The building we found him in had suffered
damage but was not destroyed. It was most likely the
shock waves and force of the blast that had killed him.
He was sitting on the ground with his back to the wall.
I couldn't tell his age, and never knew what he looked
like because of the heavy layer of dust and debris that
covered him completely. When I searched the newspaper
archives for articles about the Bishopsgate bomb while I
wrote this book, I suddenly came face to face with a large
colour photograph of him. His young face frozen forever
in time. His bright blue eyes lively and full of promise.
Seeing his face for the first time took my breath away.
Tears ran down my face because this was the first time
that I'd *really* seen him, even though I'd photographed
him all those years ago at the bombing scene.

During this period of heightened terrorist activity,
bomb threats and bombings were a frequent occurrence.

It rattled everyone's nerves. For our own safety, we checked under our police vehicles for explosive devices. People were on alert and the bombings seemed never-ending. It was exhausting. In 1992 alone, there were more than thirty bombing incidents in London, which kept our team of photographers busy. The Bishopsgate bomb was the last major attack in Britain before the IRA's 1994 ceasefire.

The scene of devastation was overwhelming. I knew it would be an enormous challenge to photograph from the sheer scale of the devastation that surrounded me. A favourite tactic of the IRA was to plant secondary devices that would kill, maim or injure first responders. All our SO3 photographers approached each bomb scene with great caution. The idea that the scene was boobytrapped added an extra layer of enormous stress, at an already high stress scene.

Police photographer colleagues and I had photographed the bomb attacks on mainland Britain over decades, but in the late 1980s and 1990s the IRA bombing campaign had become deadlier, with IRA bomb makers constructing ever-more sophisticated devices that unleashed greater destruction and loss of life. Early in my career I attended the bomb scene at the Royal Marines Music School in Deal, Kent (South East England), which killed eleven people, mostly soldiers, and wounded twenty-two. The Deal bombing was my first introduction to the horror and carnage of a bomb scene; the destruction, sadness and pain that multiple murders brought to the friends and families of those killed and injured. Over the years, the bombings continued at a relentless pace. There were

IRA mortar attacks on Downing Street that came close to killing the sitting Prime Minister and key cabinet ministers, and the London bombings continued through the 1990s. A huge car bomb exploded outside the Baltic Exchange, in the heart of London's financial district, a year before the Bishopsgate bomb. That bomb killed three people and injured 90 others. Rockets were a new IRA tactic, and the IRA fired twelve mortar rounds at Heathrow Airport, in three separate attacks. I photographed several of those scenes from the ASU helicopter. The IRA targeted Heathrow to cause maximum disruption and economic hardship. It was quite a challenge to photograph the damage the mortars inflicted on the apron, while the airport continued to operate and planes landed every few seconds. The mortar attacks on Heathrow were the last IRA attacks in Britain before the ceasefire, which lasted until the massive 1996 Docklands bombing that ended the ceasefire.

17

Living with the Dead

'What do you think the darkness takes from you?' Sarah asks, when my eyes fill with tears.

'I think that over time it can take a heavy toll,' I reply. 'The constant exposure to the worst that humanity has to offer can transform you. It has a cumulative effect. Witnessing what one human being can do to another human being, and how little respect they have for the value of life, either their own, or the lives of others, can permanently change you. Only ever seeing cruelty, spite, viciousness, horror and violence can make you bitter, cynical, angry and unfeeling, and trusting of no one.'

'Tell me more about that,' Sarah asks gently.

'Although being a police photographer is an enormously rewarding job; truly a job like no other. And a job that I loved. It can be physically and mentally taxing in the extreme. And you must know when it's time to leave, to save your sanity.'

Sarah sits quietly while I gather my thoughts.

'I knew the exposure to the deeds of so many evil people had started to seep into my being. Over the years I began to feel that I could trust no one. Everyone I met

I eyed with suspicion. You shut down. You shut off emotionally. I saw it all around me. I never wanted to end up permanently damaged, or severed from my tender emotions. Although resilient and mentally strong, I had always been sensitive, tender and emotional, from the time I was a child. My mum often tells me the story of when I was six years old and playing in the front garden of our home. I saw a woman pushing a pram walk by with a young child. She'd been crying. She looked frightened and dishevelled. One of her stockings was torn and the other had fallen around her ankle. But she strode on with purpose, nonetheless. I ran into the house and told my mum. We must help that woman; her stockings are torn and she looks so sad. My mum is one of the kindest, most loving women you could ever meet. She ran out of the house with me to see if we could help, but by that time the woman had vanished. Mum said I always noticed when someone was sad or in need of help. That desire to help is still as strong as it was in that six-year-old girl. I try to find ways to help others, as often as I can, even in some small way. I try to be kind. Because there is not enough kindness in the world. I've often thought that if there were more kindness, perhaps there'd be less cruelty and violence. People need to be much kinder to each other. My police work taught me that.'

I loved my job at Scotland Yard and I never wanted to leave. I'd flown with the Air Support Unit for two and a half years, but my new assignment transferred me back to scenes of crime duty full time. The thought of going back out on to the mean streets proved unbearable. I didn't want to end up as a hard, cynical, untrusting person for the rest of my life. I'd seen it happen to other photographers and police colleagues. I knew I could not allow that to happen to me. In hindsight, I should have told someone how I felt, but they never asked and I never told them. I had no exit interview to speak of. They never asked if there was anything wrong. They never tried to persuade me to stay. They never asked if I needed counselling. Or if I just needed a change to a different department, with a lower stress level. I'd seen it happen to others over the years. All that unique experience and valuable forensic photography skills allowed to walk out the door, unchallenged. Sad as I was to leave, I believe I made the right choice – for my sanity and for my life.

'Do you think you've regained a sense of safety and serenity since you left your police photography work behind?' Sarah asks.

'Yes, I do. Moving away from London helped me to live a more peaceful life, where I feel safe and serene, most of the time. Living in a low crime area where people are good to one another has helped me to recover my compassion and value my humanity. And two years of therapy, and writing my book, has proved cathartic and enormously healing,' I reply, as I smile at Sarah.

While you're still in *the job*, you have the support of your colleagues, who've had similar experiences – the kind of experiences that most people outside the job can barely imagine. I think it's much harder to cope when you leave. The memories don't go away, but who do you talk to? You're on your own. Although, thankfully, I have found my tribe again on social media, which has been a comfort, especially over the past few years as I wrote my book.

But I've heard of too many police officers going to pieces or taking their own lives once they leave the job. Photographers and police officers are not afforded the time or the support to process the horrors they experience. They go from job to job and by the time they retire, after decades, they have a mountain of unprocessed trauma that haunts them. Once they slow down and have time to ruminate, that's when they need support. That's when the nightmares start. But once you're out, you're out. And it can be a lonely place. It doesn't have to be that way. If it were a psychology experiment, none of us would have been allowed to leave without a debriefing, or at the very least some follow up to see how we were doing and if we needed any help. Forensic photographers and other forensic staff have witnessed daily horrors, often for decades or entire careers lasting forty years. The police service has a duty of care to its employees and that duty of care should not end when the individual leaves the police service. It reminds me of the saying you sometimes see in fine china shops, 'You break it. You pay for it.'

When a male supervisor told photographer Berenice Abbott that 'nice girls' don't go to the Bowery, she replied, 'Buddy, I'm not a nice girl. I'm a photographer . . . I go anywhere.'

Back in the mid 1980s, it was a radical act for me, as a young woman, to dare to enter the male-dominated fields of professional photography and the police service. Day after day I coped with the thinly veiled condescension, sexism and misogynistic behaviour of *some* of my white, middle-aged male colleagues and *some* police officers who felt I hadn't earned a place at *their table* and that police photography was not a suitable job for a woman. Thankfully, my younger colleagues were not of the *old boys' club* mindset and welcomed, rather than tolerated, the presence of female photographers in the branch. But to be accepted as an equal, I had to be a better photographer than my male colleagues, which added additional pressure to an already high-stress job. As one of only six women photographers in a group of 86 photographers, there was no blueprint for success. There was no *how to* manual to survive the microaggressions and the condescending faux endearments directed at me because I happened to be female. Outnumbered by male colleagues at every crime scene – not a single female detective or SIO worked on *any* of the murders documented in this book – I had to learn to cope on the fly, as each unique situation arose to challenge me, over and over.

Nothing can prepare you for the sights, the smells and sounds you'll experience as a police photographer. Crime scene photography is not just a visual experience. It's an immersive experience. It's visceral and emotional. At homicide and suspicious death scenes I saw and smelled the victim's blood. I tasted it at the back of my throat when I swallowed. I felt the coldness of their dead bodies. Through my latex gloves, I felt their brain matter splattered against warm concrete. I felt the sun-baked flesh of a young woman ripped apart from the impact of a train, as I collected pieces of her body on a sweltering summer day. I heard the wails of grieving mothers that tore through my heart, and their pleading questions that seared into my brain. For most people these experiences are beyond comprehension. Beyond their worst nightmares. For the police photographer they are transformative. They seep into your core. They become a permanent part of the fabric of your being. Once you've crossed that line, there's no going back. You must learn to live with the dead.

Revisiting the past, without professional psychological support, can be a dangerous and even deadly undertaking. My personal journey back into the darkness has not been without pain, discomfort, nightmares and sleepless nights. Writing this book unsettled me and dislodged *my dead people* from that dark place where they reside. But during the sessions with my therapist, I came to realise that too few people who witness horrific events during their working lives are given, or take, the opportunity to process and work through all they have seen.

Writing this book has helped me to process the trauma I witnessed. Although it has been a long, hard road, I'm glad I took the journey. As I recalled and wrote each scene, I finally began to revisit the feelings and emotions that had lain dormant or hidden away for so many years. In the still male-dominated world of policing, the instinct is to minimise, avoid or bury the pain and those feelings. But I've discovered that processing the feelings, painful and distressing as it might be, leads to catharsis and healing.

Over the years I've accepted the fact that, in some of the cases I worked on, there was no resolution and the perpetrator remains at large. Despite the high clearance rate of Scotland Yard's excellent murder squad detectives, I knew police might not arrest a suspect for decades after a crime was committed. But I knew they would retrieve and analyse my crime scene photographs and use them in court, even if the case came to trial years later. I've never lost hope that one day they will solve all my murder cases. Knowing that my photographs may help to solve a murder decades after I'm dead and gone is a legacy I'm proud to leave behind. I hope that the families of the victims I photographed find some small comfort in knowing that a kind, loving, compassionate woman was with their precious loved ones soon after their death. I will carry them with me always. They are not forgotten.

There's a TV crime show called *Cold Case* that I watched as I wrote this book. A team go into the archives and review unsolved cold case murders. They are working for the victim, although the victim has long since gone. At the end of each show when they solve the case, the victim appears to the detectives and they see the victim smiling, and then disappear. Those few seconds on screen really touched me. I thought it so appropriate. Everyone who works to solve a murder would be so fortunate to see the smiling victim just one more time, letting the detectives and police photographers know they have received justice.

Multiple rounds of deep cuts to police budgets have resulted in the loss of numerous MPS specialist operations units, the forced layoffs of specialist staff, hiring freezes, cutbacks on training and equipment have all taken a toll. Scotland Yard's SO3 Photographic Branch closure was one such major loss at the end of 2015. The purpose-built state of the art forensic photography facility was sold and bulldozed to make way for an apartment complex.

Changes in camera technology and the ubiquity of digital cameras has put the specialist forensic photographer in jeopardy, and has impacted the number of expert photographers employed by police services throughout the United Kingdom and around the world. Police officers, with minimal photographic training, are now regularly provided with cameras to use at terrestrial crime scenes and for aerial photography assignments. Anyone with a smart phone now audaciously describes themselves as a photographer. But just because someone is given a camera, it does not make them a professional photographer. No more than giving someone a flight suit makes them a qualified pilot. I know who I'd prefer to photograph a loved one's murder scene. Sadly, the era of the specialist forensic expert photographer has almost ended.

As I cycled around the lake near my home on a sunny day last summer, I noticed a middle-aged woman lying on a bench. She seemed to have a collection of bulging plastic bags with her. And the way she was lying asleep instinctively gave me cause for concern. I cycled by her the first time, but something about her demeanour troubled me. When I cycled back to where she lay, I stopped and went over to investigate. I bent down gently and asked if she was Ok or if she needed help. She opened her eyes and sat up, a little startled by my intrusion, but nonetheless smiling. Once I realised she was Ok and didn't require an ambulance or support of any kind, I turned to leave, but she patted the bench beside her. I sat down next to her for a chat. She told me all about her current situation – she was between homes and couch surfing, hence the bags. I listened and we talked like we were old friends.

After about 20 minutes of lively conversation, I stood up to leave and finish my bike ride, as the day had grown considerably hotter. Before I left, she asked me, 'Why did you stop to ask if I needed help?' I thought for a moment and then replied, 'It was something about the way you were lying there with all your bags that worried me.'

I don't know why, but I found myself telling her that I used to be a police photographer, and I had seen a lot of sadness and pain and witnessed situations where people *hadn't* stopped to ask if someone needed help. And perhaps if they *had* – if someone had taken the time to ask – a life could have been saved.

The woman listened intently as I spoke, her hands shielding her eyes against the hot sun as she looked up at me from the bench. Then she stood up and asked if she could hug me. I opened my arms and walked towards her and hugged her tightly. She held on to me like her life depended on it. When she finally let go, she stood back and thanked me. Then she said something that amused me. She looked at me and said, 'But you seem so normal and happy and full of life.' I laughed, put on my bicycle helmet and waved her goodbye.

Appendix
Books and Research Reports

Enough: The Violence Against Women and How to End It
by Harriet Johnson (William Collins, 2022)

Fix the System, Not the Women by Laura Bates (Simon & Schuster, 2022)

Honour: Achieving Justice for Banaz Mahmod by Caroline Goode (Oneworld Publications, 2020)

In Control: Dangerous Relationships and How They End in Murder by Jane Monckton-Smith (Bloomsbury Publishing, 2022)

Invisible Women: Exposing Data Bias in A World Designed for Men by Caroline Criado Perez (Vintage; 1st edition, 2020)

The Macho Paradox: Why Some Men Hurt Women and How All Men Can Help by Jackson Katz (Sourcebooks, 2006)

Men Who Hate Women: From Incels to Pickup Artists, the Truth about Extreme Misogyny and How it Affects Us All by Laura Bates (Sourcebooks, 2021)

No Safe Place: Murdered by our Father by Bekhal Mahmod (Ad Lib Publishers Ltd, 2022)

No Visible Bruises: What We Don't Know About Domestic Violence Can Kill Us by Rachel Louise Snyder (Bloomsbury Publishing, 2019)

See What You Made Me Do: Power, Control and Domestic Abuse by Jess Hill (C Hurst & Co Publishers Ltd, 2020)

Shamed: The Honour Killing That Shocked Britain – by the Sister Who Fought for Justice by Sarbjit Kaur Athwal (Virgin Books, 2013)

Why Does He Do That? Inside the Minds of Angry and Controlling Men by Lundy Bancroft (Berkley Publishing Group, 2003)

Working Stiff: Two Years, 262 Bodies, and the Making of a Medical Examiner by Dr Judy Melinek and T.J. Mitchell (Scribner, 2014)

Writing As a Way of Healing: How Telling Our Stories Transforms Our Lives by Louise DeSalvo (Beacon Press, 2000)

'Gender-related killings of women and girls: Improving data to improve responses to femicide/feminicide', UN Women/UNODC research report, 2022

Acknowledgements

Writing *The Darkroom* has been a profound journey of self-discovery, catharsis and healing. Putting my words on paper provided an unexpected sense of release and transformation. In many ways, this book became a therapeutic tool, a source of strength and a testament to the transformative power of storytelling. In the act of revisiting the past, I discovered that not only did I heal old wounds, but I have found solace in sharing these stories. I hope I have created a space for others to connect with their own stories of resilience, hope and healing.

Writing a book is a collaborative effort, and I am grateful to the incredible team of people at Orion and Seven Dials who made this book possible. Your unwavering commitment to excellence and your dedication to bringing my book into the world has been an inspiration. I am deeply indebted to the many individuals who contributed their expertise and support to make my book a reality.

To my literary agent Jessica Papin whose wisdom and encouragement have been a guiding light on this long journey to publication. Thank you for your unparalleled excellence, your support and your unfailing belief in my book. Your unique blend of professionalism, kindness and warmth is exceptional. I'm incredibly fortunate to have you as my agent. I look forward to many more exciting chapters ahead.

To my dedicated editors at Orion, Jamie Coleman, commissioning editor, and George Brooker, editor. Thank you both for your skillful editing and thoughtful feedback as we worked through the revisions and polished every page. I couldn't have asked for a better duo to guide me through this process.

A heartfelt thank you to Meryl Evans for being the legal compass that steered me safely through uncharted waters and ensured my book navigated the complex legal landscape unscathed so it could shine without legal impediments.

Special thanks to Project Editor Jo Roberts-Miller. Your willingness to go above and beyond the call of duty, and your dedication to ensuring the seamless journey of my book from a raw manuscript to its final printed form is truly commendable. Your commitment to quality and attention to detail have been crucial in making this project a success.

To all those, although unnamed, who played a part in bringing this book to fruition, your contributions have been immeasurable. I am deeply grateful to each and every one of you.

Last, but not least, a heartfelt thank you goes out to you, my readers. As an author, there's nothing more gratifying than knowing that my words have resonated with you. Your support and feedback are invaluable.

Your continued interest and enthusiasm for this challenging subject matter is a constant source of motivation for me to keep writing. Thank you for being a part of this wonderful journey with me.

About the Author

A.J. Hewitt is a professionally trained photographer who spent almost a decade as a forensic photographer with New Scotland Yard. In her debut non-fiction book *The Darkroom: Case Files of a Scotland Yard Forensic Photographer*, she lifts the veil on a world shrouded in secrecy, until now. She takes readers on an enlightening journey into darkness, murder and mayhem.

Hewitt attended Art and Design College to study photography, art and design. She then pursued a Bachelor of Arts degree (double major), graduating with distinction. Insatiably curious and a lifelong learner, she is in the final stage of completing a psychology degree. She is a voracious reader, an open water scuba diver and has travelled widely, with her cameras, on four continents. A storyteller at heart, whether through her camera lens or with a pencil and paper, she's a born raconteur who enjoys turning even the most mundane experiences into hilariously entertaining stories.

Having spent tens of thousands of hours photographing crime scenes, and attending court as an expert witness, she brings a unique insider's perspective to her writing.

She envisions turning her vast lived experience of homicides, forensics and crime scene investigation into more books and a screenplay.

Her philosophy in life is simple, be kind and laugh often.

Connect with AJ on Instagram @scotlandyardcsi and Twitter/X @ScotlandYardCSI.